Growing Your Family Tree

About the Author

Cherry Gilchrist is the author of nearly thirty books, whose subjects range from alchemy to Russian folk lore and personal relationships. She is also a writing tutor, and her particular interest in life stories led to the publication of *Your Life, Your Story: Writing Your Life Story for Family and Friends* (Piatkus 2010). *Growing Your Family Tree* springs out of her quest to research her own family history, which began out of curiosity and quickly developed into a passion. Cherry also enjoys travelling, and often teaches and lectures on cruise ships. She and her husband, artist Robert Lee-Wade, live near Stroud in Gloucestershire.

Growing Your Family Tree

CHERRY GILCHRIST

piatkus

PIATKUS

First published in Great Britain in 2011 by Piatkus

Copyright © 2011 by Cherry Gilchrist

The moral right of the author has been asserted.

A CIP catalogue record for this book
is available from the British Library.

ISBN 978-0-7499-5370-6

Typeset in Swift by M Rules
Printed and bound in Great Britain by
MPG Books, Bodmin, Cornwall

Papers used by Piatkus are from well-managed forests
and other responsible sources.

MIX
Paper from
responsible sources
FSC
www.fsc.org   FSC® C104740

Piatkus
An imprint of
Little, Brown Book Group
100 Victoria Embankment
London EC4Y 0DY

An Hachette UK Company
www.hachette.co.uk

www.piatkus.co.uk

I have written this book in memory of my parents, Kathleen Owen and Ormonde Phillips, who were so interested in family history themselves, and who would be astonished if they knew that I was now following in their footsteps! I'd also like to pay tribute here to my ancestors in the Owen, Walker, Masey, Brown and Lee families on my mother's side. I have learned so much from researching their lives – about love, tenacity and courage in particular.

I would like to dedicate this book to my granddaughters, Eva and Martha, who light the way forward.

Acknowledgements

I would like to offer warm thanks to all those who took part in my survey about the nature of the family history experience. More than sixty family historians patiently answered questions about their research (see p. xiv), added in extra stories and family records and were incredibly generous both with their time and in sharing their thoughts and feelings about a pursuit which plainly means a great deal to them. Their responses have been essential to the making of this book, and I'm deeply grateful to everyone listed here:

Geraldine Ames, Maureen Amey, Lorna Armstrong, Ann Ashcroft, Lizzy Attree, Angela Blaydon, Maggi Blythin, Sue Brookes, Keith Cracknell, Barbara Croom, Ken Davies, Susan Daynes, Christopher Draycott, Irene Sandra Duff, Tam Llewellyn Edwards, Sandra Evans, Alison Ferry, Vicky Furness, Joan Gardner, Ruth Gilbertson, William Oates Goldthorp, Robert Griffith, Charles Halifax, Bernard Hall, Joy Hamer, Brenda Harry, Elizabeth Hatt, Mick Henry, Kate Holloway, Naomi Jarvis, Ron Lampard, Jim Lepp, Sheila Macgregor, Sheila Miller, Norma Mills, Rob Milson, Dorothy Priestly, Jeanette Randall, Miriam Roberts, David Smith, Anthony Sant, Pat Saunders, Michael Saxby, Sheila Saxton, Karen Shortland, Fran Sinclair, Teresa Slaughter, Evelyn Sumner, David Swidenbank, Virginia Sylvester, Josie Taylor, Patricia Theodoru, Elaine Turpin, Ian Vickers, Elizabeth Waine, Steve Ward, Margaret Ware, Lorna Warren, Janet Webster, Geoff Wilkinson, Valerie Wright, Ken Zinyk.

Survey Citations

For the sake of stylistic consistency and ease of reading, I have used forenames only in the text when quoting from the survey, and have added an extra initial (or sometimes two) to indicate the surname where there is a duplication of first names.

Please note that a few of the respondents chose to use a pseudonym when their words were quoted in the text, but were happy to have their real names included in the Acknowledgements. One lady of modest disposition preferred to remain completely anonymous – my thanks go to her as well!

Contents

Introduction

What makes us who we are? How much does our ancestry shape our identity, and how relevant is this to us anyway? After all, most of us are keen to assert our individuality and independence. In the earlier stages of life especially, we may struggle to be different from our parents, and to show that we have broken free of old values and restrictions. We want to prove that we are creative, autonomous beings. But alongside this there may also be a sense that part of the picture is missing. And as time passes, this grows as we welcome a new generation and mourn the loss of parents and older relatives. If not sooner, then later we begin to wonder how the whole pattern fits together. Where have we come from? Do some of the traits that we see in our children stretch back through previous generations? Maybe our own passions, ambitions, talents and quests are a much greater part of the family heritage than we realised.

Researching your family history can be an eye-opener in this respect. It results in much more than names and dates, for it can give a sense of the whole life of the family, as it has been lived by your ancestors and is now currently being enacted by you and your living relatives. It's a tapestry with many threads woven through it, and one which each of us is still weaving today.

The jump from seeing ourselves purely as individuals to being part of a long process can come as something of a shock. In contemporary society, most of us put a premium on that unique individuality and some people may feel no connection to the past, and precious little to other family members alive today. In other societies, though, the emphasis is the opposite, and it is the life of the family, including the ancestors, which is paramount. For instance, in Chinese culture, the presence of ancestors is invoked during rituals; they form an important part of spiritual practice, and reverence for them is considered to be the most sacred of human feelings. In this way, a person receives his or her sense of validity from their connection with their ancestors, and expects to benefit from the kind of life force generated by a family composed both of living relatives and past ancestors. In this way too, a family is felt to have an identity that is stronger than the individuals who compose it, and the ancestors from its past are believed to contribute to the welfare of the living, often as wise guides and protective guardians.

Exploring your family history can restore a dimension that is largely overlooked in today's world. We are indeed individuals, with a greater or lesser degree of choice to shape our lives, but we are also part of a long procession of men and women who enter and leave the theatre of life, and whose actions count for something beyond their own life span.

Researching family history is potent; you may find that it changes your attitude to relatives you've known, and that those who you have never personally known become a part of your life once you learn their stories. By understanding them, you may start to understand yourself better, even if this means relinquishing something of personal self-importance and realising that your own moment of acting in the pageant is just a tiny part of what has gone before, and what will process towards the future.

Judy, an American cousin, who I discovered through my family research, puts it this way:

> This is such an amazing journey we're taking to find our ancestors. To begin with so little and to come so far. I truly believe they are watching over us and helping us in any way they can. To be found is not to be forgotten. And the more we learn the more we come to know these people and to love them. If there is an afterlife, and we will one day meet them there, what a joyous reunion that will be.

Growing Your Family Tree

Growth is the theme at the heart of this book. There are three ways in which this growth comes about through working on your family history. The most obvious way is that your family tree will grow; as a consequence of research, you'll discover more family members to record on it, along with the dates and details of their lives.

It's also likely that you will quite literally 'grow your family'. When I began researching my own family history, I had hardly any living relatives left in my family. Now I have found at least thirty new cousins, many of them third cousins, a relationship where we share a great-great-grandparent. Emails, meetings, and friendships have resulted. It has been enriching for me personally, and I hope it will reinstate something of the extended family for my children and grandchildren too – something which has been so nearly lost in this contemporary world. So family history is not just about the past, but is also about enlivening and growing your family for today and the future.

Then there is growth for you yourself. I've mentioned how your personal perspective can be changed by family history, and this can generate a whole reappraisal of your place in the family, in history and, indeed, in the world itself. Looking at the past can change the present. It may also inspire you with new creativity, leading to fresh projects and artistic pursuits. It can deepen your knowledge and appreciation of history too. And you may take on a new role within the family network, as a chronicler, story-teller or wise sage versed in family lore.

What Does This Book Offer?

This book aims to equip you for the journey that you take in researching your family history, and suggests various avenues to explore which will help to give you a more rounded experience along the way. It is of value both to beginners and to more experienced family historians in this way. Along with this (especially for newcomers) goes the need for technique and method to help you find information about your ancestors, or any other individuals you wish to research, so this is specifically included in Chapters Four and Five. Even if you are already compiling your family tree, it's worth reading these chapters, since they also include some great tips from other experienced researchers. The book also provides a substantial Resources section (see p. 248) with references to recommended books, manuals, websites and software.

The experiences of other family historians

To provide a unique resource for this book, I conducted a survey about the experience of family history, and had over sixty replies, which contained wonderful stories, research tips and reflections on the nature of doing family research. Quotes from these are used to enliven and illustrate themes throughout the book. You can also find a transcript of the questions asked in Chapter One, and an acknowledgement of the individuals who contributed at the front of this book. (Please note that a few names have been changed in the attributions for quotes, to protect individual privacy where requested.)

Activities in this book

Along the way, you'll find suggestions for various exercises and activities that you can carry out to enhance your knowledge and experience of family history. These are designed to be rewarding whatever stage you're at, whether you're a complete novice or an experienced researcher. Please feel free to adapt them to your own circumstances.

The book at a glance

One of the chief features of this book is that it explores this process of growth experienced through researching family history, relating it to personal experience and the effect that the research may have on you. The themes below will all be tempered and, I hope, enhanced by this. They are listed according to the stage at which they appear in the book, rather than in order of importance:

- Different ways of defining a family lineage
- Planning your search, and the practicalities of setting up a family history project
- Gathering stories, papers, mementos and memories from existing sources and relatives
- Exploring the nature of the ancestors in different cultures
- Basic research methods for investigating your family history and gathering material
- Ways of organising your research and data
- Communicating with other researchers and getting help from different sources
- Expanding the family network and discovering 'new' relatives
- Building up portraits of individual ancestors
- Visiting sites, homes and landscapes associated with your ancestors
- Creating a personal heritage archive of your family mementos and heirlooms
- Discovering the stories within your lineage
- Discerning the threads that run through the generations, and the wisdom distilled within the family
- Sketching out the lives of individuals named in other contexts, e.g. a sampler, a will or a house deed
- Connecting to your ancestors, and making a place for them in your life
- Writing up your family history
- Undertaking creative projects inspired by family history
- Story-telling: passing on family lore to the next generation

I hope you will feel as excited by the journey ahead as I do whenever I type a name into a family history website to search for an ancestor or plan a visit to a small town that my forebears came from. It's a journey that's full of discoveries, surprises and maybe new friendships too.

This book honours the value of your quest and suggests many and varied ways to help you get the fullest experience of exploring your family history.

Figuring out Family Relationships

It can be confusing getting used to all the different family relationships spanning several generations. In this book, I refer to 'great' and
2 x great, 3 x great and so on in connection with grandparents and
aunts and uncles. My 3 x great-grandmother is therefore my great-
great-great-grandmother. It's a convenient and contemporary form,
using the relevant number with an 'x' sign, but you may come across
other variations. Remember that each increase in number, or each
extra 'great', signifies a generation further back. Aunts and uncles can
also trip up the unwary, as their 'greats' are out of sync with your
grandparents: your grandmother's sister is your 'great-aunt', but your
great-grandmother's brother is your 2 x great-uncle.

Finding out more distant relationships, especially the degrees of
cousinship, can be even more perplexing. I use a diagram to help me,
and since I've got used to the system, and understand the principles,
it's become reasonably easy for me to check out any new relative who
I discover. The key is to check back to the direct-line (or 'common')
ancestor whom you share, and work forward again from there.

Common Ancestor	Child	Grandchild	Great Grandchild	Great Great Grandchild	Great Great Great Grandchild
Child	Sibling	Niece or Nephew	Grand Niece or Nephew	Great Grand Niece or Nephew	Great Great Grand Niece or Nephew
Grandchild	Niece or Nephew	First Cousin	First Cousin Once Removed	First Cousin Twice Removed	First Cousin Three Times Removed
Great Grandchild	Grand Niece or Nephew	First Cousin Once Removed	Second Cousin	Second Cousin Once Removed	Second Cousin Twice Removed
Great Great Grandchild	Great Grand Niece or Nephew	First Cousin Twice Removed	Second Cousin Once Removed	Third Cousin	Third Cousin Once Removed
Great Great Great Grandchild	Great Great Grand Niece or Nephew	First Cousin Three Times Removed	Second Cousin Twice Removed	Third Cousin Once Removed	Fourth Cousin

This table shows how you can calculate the relationship of one person to another in your family tree. I'll take two examples from my own tree to show how it works:

Debra and I are both directly descended from Revd Edward Owen; he is our 2 x great-grandfather (written on the table as 'great-great-grandfather'). So we are both great-great-grandchildren of Edward. We can now use the 'Common Ancestor' square, at the top left of the table, to represent Edward, and then select the horizontal top row to represent me, and the vertical row Debra (it doesn't matter which way round these go). Now we look along each of these rows to find 'great-great-grandchild'; note these two positions, then travel down from the top row, and along from the vertical row, to see where these two lines meet up. They join at 'Third Cousin', so Debra and I are third cousins.

Jane, however, was my mother's first cousin, so our closest direct-line ancestor is my great-grandfather David Richards Owen, who was actually Jane's grandfather. Once again, taking the Common Ancestor square and travelling across for me, and down for Jane, we reach 'great-grandchild' for me in connection with David Owen, and 'grandchild' for Jane. See where these lines meet up, and we arrive at 'First Cousin once removed.' This is our relationship to each other.

In general, 'pure' cousins (second, third, fourth cousins, etc.) have the same relationship to a common ancestor, just as Debra and I are both 2 x great-granddaughters of Revd Edward Owen, and are, therefore, third cousins. We belong to the same generation, irrespective of our ages. Cousins 'removed' have a difference of generation; Jane belongs to one earlier generation than I do in terms of the family tree, so we have a 'once-removed' cousin relationship. The 'removed' then increases in number for each generation, to 'twice-removed', 'three-times-removed' and so on.

Note: Some diagrams use the term 'grand' and 'great grand' in connection with niece and nephew; this is often used instead of 'great' and 'great great' or '2 x great' in connection with aunts, uncles, nieces and nephews. This helps to avoid the anomaly of great-grandparent and great-uncle or –aunt being from different generations. In these terms, my great-aunt would be my grand-aunt. You are also likely to find this used in Family Tree software as well.

CHAPTER ONE

Setting Out On the Journey

I'm sitting in the Powys record office, researching my Welsh ancestry, when a couple walk in, wanting to investigate the husband's family history.

There's no room, officially, since all the visitors' seats are booked for the day, but the archivist offers to help them for ten minutes, just to get them started.

'I want to find where my grandmother spent the last years of her life.' The man, probably in his late sixties, is able to provide a couple of pointers to the date and place.

The kindly archivist opens up the 1901 census for Wales on the computer. 'No problem. Look, here she is, with her sister at Rhyader. They're living in an inn – it seems that the sister is the landlady.'

'What?' exclaims the startled grandson. 'But we were a teetotal family!'

The archivist doesn't comment. It's not the first time she's seen someone faced with entirely unexpected and possibly unwelcome information.

'Let's look ten years earlier, in 1891,' she suggests. 'Yes, here she is again – running her own pub this time.'

'I can't believe it,' says the man. 'My father wouldn't even let me have a drink till I went to university!'

He's obviously shocked. This brief spell of research has completely overthrown the picture he has of his family background, and my guess is that it will never be the same again. And he doesn't quite know yet whether he's thrilled or horrified by the discovery that his ancestors were not all on the path of temperance, as he'd been led to believe.

I can't help being amused for personal reasons as I eavesdrop on this exchange, since my own 3 x great-grandfather, who I'm researching in the same archives, died in a pub in Rhyader. A little earlier than this man's grandmother, though, so she can't have actually pulled his last pint!

My own visit to the archives proceeds peacefully enough, but for this man, a brief foray into his family history has been an encounter with dynamite. It will radically change his outlook on his ancestry, and perhaps affect his sense of his own identity too, even at this stage in life.

A Quest for Identity

Family history is full of surprises. But, in fact, it is rarely dull, and is likely to bring us a range of powerful experiences, discoveries that can be exciting, unsettling, joyful, heart-warming, saddening, reassuring or astounding, depending on their nature. It becomes a deeply personal pursuit, even though it involves ancestors whom you may never previously have heard of. Their lives and stories can become intensely important to you, and as you get to know them, they become a part of your own identity, and of how you understand your family background. Researching your ancestry is also a way of expanding your sense of family beyond the span of your immediate lifetime, and a way of seeing its place in history. And this historical perspective links you, as an individual, directly to the events and culture of the past. History is lifted out of the pages of dusty books and is within your grasp.

Interest in family history is growing rapidly today, and this goes hand in hand with a shift in our general perspective on history over the last twenty years or so. We now ascribe greater value to social history, in terms of how people lived, where they worked and what they ate and wore. Things have moved on from the days when a school history lesson was mostly about kings, battles and trade treaties. Oral-history projects abound, recording memories of 'living history' or a vanishing way of life, and we now recognise that people from humble backgrounds can have meaningful stories to tell.

So it's not surprising that family history, or genealogy as it is more formally known, can find a place in this context. It's a way for us to acquire our own slice of history, and to discover the stories and dramas within it. As Kate, one of the respondents to the survey I conducted, said: 'I enjoy reading family sagas and researching a family tree is a bit like creating your own saga, albeit backwards.' I can vouch for that; it's thrilling to see how families migrated, married and made or lost fortunes over the course of even a couple of hundred years. We are participants in these storylines, and they form a heritage which we can reclaim when we start investigating our ancestry.

A growing desire to know and own our roots may also stem from the increased social mobility and more frequent break-up of families in modern society. Over the last hundred years or so there have also been great waves of displacement, as families have been dispersed by work shortages, political upheaval or war. There are probably few of us whose families haven't been affected in this way somewhere along the line, so looking into family history offers a way to learn how and why this happened, and where our families originated.

Kindling an Interest in Family History

Where does your own interest in family history come from? What brought you to it in the first place? While it's true that family history has become more popular in general, this doesn't go all the way to explaining how we come to take up the quest as individuals. A moment of reflection on this interest, along with illuminating insights from survey respondents, may help to uncover the deeper sources from which it springs.

The unexpected flame

A passion for family history isn't always an obvious development in our lives, and may, in fact, happen right out of the blue. Many of us who are now keen family historians never intended to go down that route. As Olivia says in her reply to the survey:

> I had no interest whatsoever in my family's origins until I was asked to accompany a genealogy-obsessed friend to the record office one day in the '80s and to my surprise I too caught the bug – big time! ... As my own parents were diffi-cult people, I felt that any relations I might have could possibly be the same, so I approached family research with a detached view, purely for the thrill of the chase.

Like Olivia, I love 'the lure of the chase', and the detective work that other participants in the survey also claim as one of the main attrac-tions. But this wasn't always the case. Earlier, I had sworn that I would never take up my father's passion for family history. However, I had a sneaking interest in certain stories he had discovered, which tickled my imagination. There was the thirteen-year-old heiress who ran away to France with her lover, an Indian princess who married into the family and a magistrate shot dead in his garden by IRA rebels. I couldn't help relishing these tales. But I also sensed the decline of this Anglo-Irish lineage, whose glory days were past, and whose descend-ants had trickled almost to a halt. I didn't particularly want to lay claim more closely to that kinship.

My mother's side, however, which had hardly been researched at all, seemed sturdier, and had its own share of intriguing, if humbler, family members: the great-uncle who had emigrated to Canada, and who had sent me – a pony-mad little girl – pictures of the Calgary Stampede each year, my grandmother who had started off in service at one of the stately homes of England and my great-grandfather of Welsh descent, who whisked his new bride off to America and returned some fifteen years later with a large family in tow. His wife came from a butter-making family in the West Country; what was the story there?

I wondered. Then there was the lure of the other maternal great-grand-mother's maiden name, Lee: could it be Romany? I speculated. I had always fancied gypsy blood. (See Appendix I, p. 244.)

But mostly I stifled my interest, yawned politely when my father gave me yet another transcript of the family tree and decided to follow my own path, without consulting my ancestors for approval. Time passed, as it does. I had children of my own, who grew up, and a marriage which broke down. My parents died, and with that came the shock that I was in the generational lead, with no one above me in the pecking order, and that it was my turn next to become an ancestor. This ancestry, whose influence I had resisted, began to seem more appealing, and I also experienced a new and rather scary freedom, to find who and what I was in this respect.

In 2004, I signed up for a one-day course on how to research family history on the internet. Within an hour, I was looking at a 1901 census return for my maternal grandfather's family. I had known my grandfather well as a child, when he had already retired as a Baptist minister, but here was a whole different window on his life. In the census, he was a teenager, working as a grocer's assistant and living with a host of siblings, most of whom I'd had no knowledge of, and in the care of parents whose names I didn't even know: my great-grandparents, David and Mary Owen who, as I was later to find out, had returned from America and settled in Northamptonshire. I felt I was gazing into the household itself, as though looking at a doll's house with the front opened up, and seeing all the characters occupied with their various tasks inside. The past had, in some mysterious way, become the present for me.

That was how it started.

Time of life

It's not uncommon for the family history bug to bite in mid-life or later. Very few of the family historians who responded to my survey could date their involvement back to childhood. A couple of those who did had been boys who liked the idea of the smart uniforms and derring-do that their ancestors could offer.

'I suspect that the interest was sparked by my great-grandfather's photograph which showed him standing proud in his drum major's uniform while he served in the Leicestershire regiment,' Ian recalls.

Chris was a little older, already in his early teens when he glanced through a book on coats of arms in a reference library. 'There was a reference to a Richard de Draicott, baron and Bertram de Draicott who "took up the cross" in the last crusade in 1270. I wondered, somewhat fancifully, if these ancient Draicotts could be my ancestors.' They were indeed, but it took Chris another thirty years to prove it.

For most, though, interest only came after they had reached a certain point in life, sometimes triggered by the death of a parent, 'intimations of mortality', or personal bereavement, which in the case of Lorna A., made her 'look for distractions'.

External triggers

Sometimes the nudge to take up family history comes from the circumstances we find ourselves in; although the main desire to research has to come from within, it can certainly be triggered by events.

TAKING ON THE TASK FOR OTHERS

The search may present itself in the form of a solemn duty. In 1969, Angela became appointed as the ancestral historian of the family, when she made a deathbed promise to her grandfather:

My paternal grandfather would recite an oral family history at every opportunity. He was staying with us not long before his death in April 1969 ... I was in my early twenties at the time. He was obviously very serious and told me he wanted to talk to me. He talked about the family's past generations and told me how sorry he was that he didn't know any of the history prior to his grandfather. At this point he asked me to promise him that at some time in my life I would research the family history. He emphasised that he didn't expect me to do it there and then, but just so that he knew that when he died someone in the family would take on the responsibility. Well, of course, I promised him, knowing that at the time he was ninety years old, besides which he badgered me until I did promise! I knew it wouldn't happen for some years, but in 1980 I embarked on the research.

HELPING OUT

Some have found their way into family history as a result of helping others. Valerie agreed to help her sister out with family research on the internet simply because she had the time and her sister didn't. 'I started to search for family history information sites. From that moment on I was hooked!' And when Charles's wife was asked to trace some death records in connection with her work as a medical secretary, she and her husband realised that a stint in Somerset House in London (where such records were kept at the time) could also be an opportunity to look at their own family trees.

Miriam dates her interest back to a school project twenty-eight years ago when her son brought a family tree home to complete. Elizabeth H. too experienced something similar:

> Wanting to keep in touch with my grandson, whom I didn't see very often, I sent him an old photo of my dad's van (he had an electrical engineering business). My grandson was interested in cars, etc. and wanted to go to Holloway Road – the address on the van. This led me to write, perhaps about once a week, a brief history of the family. Later on I wrote my memoirs.

SERENDIPITOUS CIRCUMSTANCES

Some of the triggers for starting family history are less predictable, and may stem from entirely unexpected circumstances. Two survey informants happened to meet someone with the same unusual surname as theirs. In Josie's case, when her father found that he was working with a colleague with the same surname, further investigation on her part eventually proved their connection. 'I introduced members of a large branch of the family to each other. Reunions followed,' she recalls.

Ron was attending a medical conference and noticed another Lampard on the list of delegates. His wife, who was accompanying him, started to scan all the faces in the room for any family resemblance. 'Within seconds she identified him accurately with a conviction that would have had the police sergeant in charge of an identity parade drool with delight.' Although the two Lampards couldn't instantly establish their link, 'he did confirm my grandfather's remark that we all came up the Dover Road as Huguenots'.

What some might call coincidence, others would call synchronicity – in other words, a meaningful combination of circumstances which don't necessarily happen by chance, and which can have an extraordinary effect, or unexpected result. The incidence of synchronicity certainly seems to play a significant role in the quest to find one's ancestry, and we'll hear of other striking examples as the book progresses.

Three Motivations

We've seen that the reasons people begin working on family history are varied, but also that there are common factors to be found among them; now these common elements can be distilled further, into three prime causes which underlie the quest and provide ongoing energy and inspiration to continue with it. I'll define them here as:

- what you have
- what you've lost
- what you hope to find.

They may sound simple, but I suggest that they are fundamental to our involvement with family history. They tie in too with a very ancient concept of 'three-ness' at work in every event or action. These have sometimes been defined in spiritual or philosophical terms as a sacred trinity, or as fundamental energies that can be named as the active, receptive and unifying forces. So if we take these in terms of researching family history, they are all present; even if one is predominant, the other two will feature in some way, and together they fuel our progress. We can also consciously draw on the one or two that are less obvious to rev up a flagging search or explore in a new way.

As I define them here, you may want to check out what they mean to you, and to jot down your thoughts about them. Your personal notebook is a good place to write (see p. 11); reading your notes over at a later stage may act as a touchstone to encourage you.

What you have

What is your family heritage? You can consider this both in terms of material items, such as mementos and letters, and the less tangible elements, such as stories passed down through the family. Think about your family characteristics and outlook too, which form part of your heritage. What you have available already is a wonderful starting point, which triggers new questions and a desire to complete the stories already sketched out.

THE FAMILY LEGACY

As the older generation dies, the traces that they leave behind may trigger the curiosity of those who inherit their possessions, which can include old records, portraits, photographs and hand-drawn family trees. The legacy can be one of memories and stories too, which may have come your way at a very early age. In Evelyn's childhood there was no radio or television in the household, and her parents would entertain the family by talking about their lives when they were younger, and showing her their albums of photos and postcards. Anthony too traces his interest back to early years, when he had to live with his grandmother during the Second World War, and was thus 'instilled with the history of her Lincolnshire family'. For both, the stories they were fed in childhood eventually acted as the trigger to start their

Keeping Track of Your Experiences

As you begin your journey into family history, you may find it helpful to think about the circumstances which have brought you to this point. Why do you want to delve into the past? What has given you a nudge? This is not only the story of your family, but is the unfolding of your own story too; your quest to find your ancestry is a part of your life story. The journey involves you personally, and may affect your outlook and your future choices in life.

So although your main focus is on recording the data and stories you discover, take some time too to record your own experience along the way. Keep a 'travel journal' if you like. To start off with, you might like to look at the questions from the family history survey that I conducted (opposite), and answer them for yourself, as a way of summarising where you are at present. If you are completely new to family history, they won't all be relevant yet, but you could answer at least the first one, perhaps also questions 14 and 15, and come back to the others later on.

Keep a personal notebook

Researching family history can be a vivid and exciting experience. Keep a record of your journey, and note down your impressions at the time. This will help to crystallise the experience, as well as giving you material which could prove useful later on. If you write up your family history, for instance, you might want to include a first-hand account of meeting your new-found third cousin from Australia, and sharing family photos with her. You can also include reflections on family stories, any relevant dreams, and ideas for creative work related to your discoveries, such as painting or poetry. As a writing tutor as well as an author, I am keen on persuading people to make notes and records of their experiences, so I'll use the same tactic for family history. Start your notebook now!

The personal notebook is probably best kept separate from the notebooks you use to record factual data from the records you search and list lines of enquiry that you'd like to pursue (see p. 101).

SURVEY QUESTIONNAIRE

1. What made you interested in family history?
2. How long have you been researching it?
3. Have any interesting stories or discoveries emerged?
4. Are there any themes running through the generations?
5. Is there anything you wish you hadn't discovered, and why?
6. How do you approach your research (e.g. internet, archives, family papers)?
7. Have you any good search tips?
8. Have you found new living relatives this way, and have you met any of them?
9. Have you ever made any serious mistakes in your tree, which you've had to undo, and if so, how did this affect your research?
10. Do you feel that family history has put you more in touch with your ancestors? Do they seem in some sense 'alive' for you?
11. Do you feel that you have learned anything from your ancestors or from their lives?
12. Has family history changed your sense of your own identity?
13. Are you planning to write up your family history, or pass it on in some way?
14. What do the rest of your family think about your research?
15. Have you any further reflections on the nature of family history and what it means to you and others?

research. As Ken D. sums it up: 'Every family has a story – many stories, in fact. I wanted to know about ours. How they lived, struggled, coped with family tragedies. I was lucky; both parents kept letters which are priceless to me.'

The legacy may also be the proud recalling of an illustrious ancestor: Joseph Priestley, Joshua Reynolds, an archbishop, and the Dukes of Orleans were all mentioned in the survey, plus, not surprisingly, families said to have come over to England with William the Conqueror. Notorious ancestors also have a peculiar fascination; Bernard's interest was triggered by a colourful character in the family:

> It was my great-great-grandfather, the Revd Augustus Joseph Tancred, DD, said to have been born in Cork in 1802, a member of the first Cape Parliament, who fired my imagination, not least when I discovered from a reliable source that he was reputed to have eloped with a nun.

(We will hear more of the Revd Tancred's colourful story later.)

In Chapter Three, we'll be considering how to gather in family memories and mementos, and how to assess whatever you can from existing sources. For now, however, you might like to think over in a general way what you have to hand, and to ponder what this means to you, and how it might inspire your quest further.

What you've lost

Many of us come to family history with an acute sense of what we've lost, especially the tales of an older generation, and the chance to ask parents and relatives about their memories. Loss by definition can be sad, but it also prompts us to make new discoveries.

Even if loss is not your main motivation for working on family history, take a look at your own circumstances and find out where any residual sense of loss may lie; there is bound to be a little pocket of it buried somewhere.

REGRETS AND LONGINGS

Alison admits to her own sense of loss as a motivator in her search:

> As a child, I often asked my father about his family and received vague answers. We lived in the Far East, and I only saw my grandparents when we were back in the UK on leave which occurred every three years. They told me stories of their early lives in Japan and Italy and I remember a few of them but, of course, I now wish I had taken more notice and written everything down ... When my father passed away in 1988, I decided to find out more about his family tree. By then, we were living in Australia and all the records were in England; this presented a challenge. However, I looked upon this as a new hobby, bought some family history magazines, joined the local Family History Society and slowly learned the ropes.

Here is Irene's tale:

> I suppose I was interested in my family tree from being a teenager, when I became aware that my mother owned hand-written details about preceding generations of her family ... It was only after she had died that I became seriously interested – in fact, only in the last four to five years – and, of course, with hindsight, I wish I had started earlier, if only to please my mother, although it would have been quite an arduous task before the aid of modern technology.

Both Irene and Alison were able to turn their losses to good account, redeeming them with positive discoveries. There is certainly great sadness embodied in the knowledge that relatives from the older generation have passed away, and can never tell you their stories again. But there can also be incredible joy and exhilaration in discovering far more than they ever told you, or could have told you, and in revealing a panoply of ancestors who may bring you new pleasure and pride.

THE MISSING PARENT

A significant sense of loss may be felt by those who have little or no information about their families. Lizzy relates: 'My father died when I was a baby and we have never been clear about who his father was or where he came from.' And Janet recounts: 'My interest in family history stems from my birth. I was illegitimate and I really wanted to find out where my father was born and how his family would fit into what I knew of him.'

It's also quite common to know much about one side of the family, and virtually nothing about the other; sensing this gap can eventually turn from idle curiosity to a burning longing to discover everything about these relatives. As mentioned earlier, it was the lack of genealogy on my mother's side that propelled me to find out more about her origins; my father's side had been thoroughly worked over, and didn't hold my interest in the same way.

ADOPTION AND GROWING UP WITHOUT PARENTS

There is also the special challenge facing those who are adopted, or who have been brought up by guardians or in care. The route to discovering birth parents has to be taken through official channels, usually on reaching adulthood, if that information hasn't been passed on already. But once there is enough to go on, the path of family history will hopefully lie open to adoptees and parentless children too, even if the evidence is more slender, and questions about a missing parent still remain.

What you hope to find

Jot down all the things you hope to find or achieve, if you don't immediately have one main aim. These could range from very specific wishes – 'I'd love to know what happened to Uncle Walter in the war', for instance – to broader desires, such as wanting to feel a part of history. They might also stem from a particular family story; I wanted to trace an ancestor who had purportedly fought at the Battle of Waterloo, and a runaway heiress who married into the family for love.

In both cases, as I shall recount later, I did trace the stories and found out the truth, even though this didn't conform exactly to the tale that had been handed down!

Don't make this a research plan, as we'll come on to that later, but just a general wish list of what you'd like to discover. Keep it light, and don't worry if you end up with a somewhat fragmented list. It will be worth taking a look at it further down the line too, and checking if it evolves at all as you work on your family history project.

Tying the three together

After you've identified the three motivating factors, consider their balance as a whole. Which is predominant for you? Is your heritage the driving force that you want to use as a springboard to discovery? Is it an aching loss that you want to make good in some way? Or is it primarily something that you hope to find, spiced perhaps with a keen curiosity to track down stories and missing relatives?

Although these divisions may not be completely fixed, they are helpful to reflect on, and can help to show what colours your search, and what your aims are based on. Review them every now and then, and find out if the balance has changed at all.

The Journey Ahead

The television programme *Who Do You Think You Are?*, which is shown in the UK and the USA revealing the ancestry of various celebrities, has given many people the incentive to start researching their own family history. Even the title has passed into popular culture as a widely used catchphrase. As each new series begins, archivists brace themselves for an increased wave of visitors to their record offices from people who want to discover amazing facts about their own ancestors. Surely they too fought with Cromwell, sailed on the *Mayflower*, founded a major department store or flew aerobatic stunts? Finding all this out looks rather easy on television, and the attraction lies not just in the facts that are unearthed, but often in the intensely emotional stories that emerge and which affect the subjects whose past is being investigated. An actress weeps, first for shame as her criminal family past is uncovered, and then with profound emotion as she discovers a saintly parish priest from earlier years, who gave his life in the service of the poor. A hard-line presenter, who has reduced leading politicians to quivering wrecks, crumbles when he learns that a great-grandmother died of exhaustion, working as a cleaner to scrub other people's floors. We see the turn of fortune's wheel, as families rise and fall in the social scale and are swept up in world-shaking events. A colourful pageant of history is created, in which each family plays a part, and to which each individual makes a unique contribution.

Would we too like to be given the kind of opportunity that these celebrities enjoy, and have this pageant laid out before us? I, for one, would rather take this journey of adventure for myself. I want to follow the clues that arouse my curiosity, and tease out leads that may bring me face to face with startling stories from the past – gems that I can uncover and marvel at. The process of revelation is more intense when you experience it at first hand, and there is nothing like the sense of satisfaction that your own research brings. Once you've experienced it, I doubt that you would want to trade it in for ready-made genealogy.

The process of discovery

Whatever your first step on the path of family history, you are sure to make discoveries that you never expected, and tread a different route from that which you imagined. It is a magical process, and I believe that once you set out on this quest, in good faith and with a good heart, all kinds of magical events happen. Landscapes yield up their mysteries, helpers appear at the right moment and amazing stories emerge from dusty archives. It's not entirely a primrose path; there are setbacks and frustrations, and even your own feelings may swing between wild enthusiasm and reluctance to go one step further. It's like the quest in a fairy tale where the hero or heroine is tested and challenged, suffers reversals of fortune and stumbles across tantalising puzzles before finally reaching the goal.

We'll come across some of these tales and experiences throughout the book, but for now, here is how the journey started for David Sm. It's a quiet story in its own way, without dramatic events, but it encapsulates the sense of following a trail and the happy coincidences that can allow this to happen.

> On a visit to see relatives in Yorkshire, I decided to stop and look around the churchyard where I knew my grandparents were buried. Quite a number of the graves were overgrown and, as the graveyard was quite big, I knew I had little chance of finding the grave. I had earlier got talking to a man who was driving a small mowing machine. He now stopped work to talk to another man. When I explained to this other man what I was doing, I found out he was the vicar in 'mufti'. He asked me to come to the vicarage in thirty minutes.

When David arrived at the vicarage, the minister asked him various details about his grandparents and was able to give him exact dates of their death and burial. He also pointed him towards the Huddersfield Library, where full records were kept. David immediately travelled there, managed to locate these and was directed also to the local register office where he traced and obtained his grandparents' death certificates. That was the end of one trip, but the start of a much longer one. It was an experience he says, that 'set me on my family history journey'.

Planning the Journey

It's now time to plan your own journey. If you are starting from scratch, it's an exciting moment as you choose the route that you wish to explore. If you have already come some way along the road, I suggest that you regard this as a staging post, a place at which you can review your aims and renew your interest.

Every personal journey into family history is an individual experience, never identical to any other. That's what makes the research process fascinating in its own right. It's also why the old conventional aim of assembling a hierarchy of genealogical names and dates is not enough for most of us. We may look diligently for these, and they can form the backbone of family history research, but it's the experience of discovering our ancestors, and finding out about them as real people, that makes all the difference and, as it were, puts flesh on the bones.

Your aims and journey plan

Take a little time now to figure out your plans for the journey by considering the implications for your own search. I suggest that you make notes on the following nine questions, keeping in mind your response to the three 'motivations' that were explored earlier (see pp. 8–15). Answer the questions simply from what you know and remember at present, even if your ideas are hazy, without feeling that you have to research them in any way. This will help to identify the intentions at the heart of your search, before they become overlaid with all the new information that your investigations will yield. Don't be concerned if they are not crystal clear, and you can expect them to change somewhat as your research progresses.

Your answers may be very brief, and some of them may be in the form of further questions, but do jot all of them down. Keep them safe, and look at them from time to time. They will act as a kind of compass for your research, and may help to get you back on track if you become overwhelmed by the amount of information that you acquire en route.

1. WHICH ANCESTORS WOULD YOU LIKE TO RESEARCH?
Would you prefer to follow your father's or your mother's side? Even if you plan to follow both in the end, it will be much easier, and probably more rewarding, if you take up just one to start with. In the next chapter, we'll look further into the implications of this choice – both personal and cultural – but at present, just consult your own immediate wishes in this respect.

2. WHICH INDIVIDUALS WOULD YOU LIKE TO FOCUS ON?

You can also pick out certain individuals who you'd like to know much better. Perhaps Great-Aunt Alice was a suffragette, or you've heard that one of your forebears made a fortune through the railways? Investigating the life stories of two or three specific and interesting ancestors can be very rewarding. Ideally, select ones within the branch of the family that you'll be researching to start with. You can, of course, investigate them independently of any family line but it's easier to dovetail it into the part of your family tree that you'll be focusing on.

3. HOW FAR BACK DO YOU WANT TO GO?

It's tempting to pursue your ancestry back into the remote mists of time, but in order to keep your research realistic, you may need to tailor your aspirations. If you're interested in covering several different branches of the family eventually, then it's better not to be too ambitious in terms of how far back you go. If, on the other hand, you are content to stay with one family name or line, then it's feasible to try to get back three, four or five hundred years, at least. Bear in mind, though, that, in most cases, it takes more effort to trace ancestors back prior to the late eighteenth century, because there were fewer records available then. I myself am happy with reaching back into the eighteenth century, since I now have a spread of family lines I'm researching, and I can discover their characteristics and stories better if I keep within this time span. I also feel that I can get to know ancestors who have lived in the last two hundred and fifty years as individuals, and that it might be more difficult to connect to those from earlier times. Altogether, it's a matter of personal preference, as well as developing an understanding of what the task involves.

4. ARE THERE ANY STORIES YOU'D LIKE TO TRACK DOWN?

Many, if not most, families have stories in circulation about the deeds of earlier relatives or ancestors. These make great material for research, and experience shows that there is usually a nugget of truth within them. Often, once the layers of legend have been stripped away, and the real story exposed and filled out with the facts, the truth can prove even more fascinating.

To illustrate this, I'll return to the story of my ancestor who had reputedly enlisted in the Horse Guards and fought at the Battle of Waterloo, at which, we were told, he was wounded, and survived by lying in the open air until he could be rescued. The family legend contrasted this with the fate of another soldier in the battle – a famous boxer who was also wounded, but who crept into a dunghill to keep warm. He caught an infection and died. I enquired into this when I began my research, and eventually found that the ancestor in question was my 3 x great-grandfather Edward Owens, a shoemaker from Wales, and the one who died at a ripe old age in a pub in Rhyader (see Appendix I, p. 244). He did indeed fight in the Napoleonic Wars, but not at Waterloo, however, and not as a Horse Guard. Instead, he was a foot soldier at the Battle of Corunna. Despite his less exalted status, his regiment did fight at the heart of the battlefield, and he also served in Ireland, the Netherlands and Sicily during his thirteen years of military service. Edward was later awarded a Peninsular Medal with a Corunna Bar, and had the honour of becoming a Chelsea Pensioner. Over time, his story has emerged more fully (I'll recount some of the details in succeeding chapters), and, from the seeds of a family legend, an exciting real-life narrative has been constructed through patient research.

So the task suggested here is to make a note of any stories handed down in the family that you'd like to investigate, however fanciful or far-fetched they may seem. There could be more truth in them than you realise.

5. WHO ARE YOU DOING THIS FOR?

This might seem an unnecessary question. But you may encounter arid and frustrating times while doing family history research, so that knowing who you are doing it for can help you to keep going. Ideally, you'll want to do it for yourself at least. It's difficult to keep searching over a prolonged period for information in which you're not personally interested, so it's better to ensure that you have a healthy curiosity of your own right from the outset. This, of course, may grow or decline as time goes on, but personal commitment is important. Having said that, I have come across a few successful husband-and-wife teams, where one does the research for the other.

Who else are you doing it for? Perhaps you want to put together a family tree for children, nephews and nieces, or grandchildren? This is a common motivation, and even if the lucky recipients-to-be don't show any interest as yet, they may in time appreciate the heritage that you are creating for them. Sometimes, too, we do it for those who have passed away; I have a keen sense of filling in the gaps that my mother always wanted to know about her ancestry, and although she's no longer here to share my discoveries, in some ways I feel that it makes reparation for missed opportunities to listen to her memories in her final years.

So who would you like to share your research with, who may benefit from it and whose memory might you honour by creating a family tree?

6. WHO WILL HELP YOU?

Is there anyone out there who can help out with research or, at the very least, act as a sounding board for your latest gems of information? This isn't essential, but it's certainly a bonus if you have a research pal or two. A partner may often be willing to let you bounce ideas off them and spill out your excitement at the newest discoveries. (My husband is very patient in this respect, although I can now read the subtle signs which indicate that he might have had enough for the time being.) Brothers and sisters may or may not be as interested as you, so you are fortunate if there's one who shares the involvement.

As you grow your family tree, you are likely to grow your family as well, and cousins who you make contact with can be excellent sources of support and further information; you may be able to pool your finds with them. So if you don't have any immediate helpers or family history buddies, look out for kindred spirits along the way. In Chapter Five, we'll also consider other professionals or individuals who may be able to help with specific aspects of research, but for the moment, I suggest thinking about people already in your life who might share the journey or at least be interested in hearing about your quest.

7. WHAT TYPES OF RESEARCH AND ACTIVITIES WILL YOU DO?

Right from the start, I advocate planning your research around a variety of approaches. This keeps your interest fresh. The main data sources and research tactics are discussed in Chapters Four and Five, and further information is given about other activities in later chapters. Much will depend upon your individual circumstances, but here's a preview of the key approaches for you to consider:

- Research family records on the internet.
- Visit county record offices and other archives and libraries.
- Read family history magazines. (They are invaluable for keeping up to date with the latest resources available.)
- Go to family history fairs to browse material (books, charts, software, historic material) and to chat to stallholders and other visitors.
- Join a family history society. Most offer talks and seminars, plus a journal and facilities for members to help each other with research.
- Visit museums with an emphasis on social or military history connected with your family.
- Explore areas where your ancestors lived.
- Talk to members of your immediate family, both the older generation and your contemporaries, to glean their knowledge and memories.
- Try to discover 'new' relatives and forge connections with them. Online sites such as Genes Reunited are usually the best way to find new cousins.
- Consider meeting up with newly found relatives.

Write down some ideas for activities you'd like to follow up along these lines, and any more that come to mind. Allow yourself a generous timescale of two or three years so that you don't feel pressured to take them all on at once.

8. ARE YOU READY FOR CHANGE AND DISCOVERY?

Doing your family history can cause major changes in your perspective. It will almost certainly change the way you feel about your ancestors, and even about relatives you've known personally. I've found that this is beneficial; those who I thought of as elderly and old-fashioned have now acquired a youth and a past. I understand their stories better, and the kind of lives they led. It's refreshed my view of them.

But there could be upsets in store too: if an ancestor turns up who has done something awful – examples of incest, cruelty and murder do appear on family trees, as various survey respondents confirm. Perhaps you might discover that a relative isn't exactly who you thought he or she was, or is not even a blood relative at all. So ask yourself if you are prepared to change your views of your family, and accept what might come along.

There is also the very real chance that you may get so absorbed in your ancestry that you think about it all day, and dream about it all night. (I remember taking a trip through a Scottish glen with a friend who relived his ancestors' battles there in tedious detail as we drove. He looked as if he was in a trance, and I thought he was crazy. That was before I became interested in my own family history, but I've kept it in mind, as a warning not to forsake the present for the past.) If so, you will probably emerge from this phase again quite naturally, but it's something to watch out for.

Norma is aware of this potential problem: 'I think I am in danger of becoming too involved, and it is important every so often to have a break and leave the research for a while. Otherwise, it seems to take over most of my thoughts.' She has a good solution for keeping this in check though: 'Whenever I watch period dramas on TV now, I imagine my ancestors in place of the actors.'

With all this in mind, it may be worth making a resolution at the outset to keep your research in an appropriate proportion to the rest of your life.

9. HOW MUCH TIME AND MONEY DO YOU WISH TO SPEND?

Researching can take up a lot of time, so for some, it can only be a project for retirement. However, with careful forethought and time management, it's possible for most of us to fit in some family history research along with a job, family commitments and other interests. Even two hours a week will pay enormous dividends, and this can be enhanced by factoring in a number of complete days in the year when you'll visit record offices, family localities and so on. Just three or four days will be valuable in this respect, and probably bring you a great deal of pleasure too.

It's easy to get absorbed in your research, and spend far more time online than you'd intended, for instance, so you may want to set a limit on the sessions, and tear yourself away ruthlessly when time's up. It can be draining, sitting in front of the computer screen, and you may find that you get only diminishing returns once mental energy starts to decline. Decide what length of session may work best for you in general, probably somewhere between half an hour and three hours.

Family history for many is a journey that lasts for years. 'Genealogy is a bit like gardening – never completed,' as Lorna A. points out. But those ancestors aren't going anywhere, as another respondent remarked, so the pace can be slow if need be. Of those people who answered my survey, most had been researching for over three years, and some for more than twenty. So if you think you might be in it for the longer term, it's a good idea to expect to take breaks now and then. This is something to bear in mind, rather than necessarily plan out, since often you can't be sure just when you'll feel saturated and want to turn your attention to other things, or when personal circumstances may make it difficult to continue for a while.

Money does come into family history. If you use the internet, you will almost certainly want to take out a subscription to a genealogy website to access its records collection. Buying birth, marriage and death certificates involves fees, and you are likely to purchase software, plus a few books and family history magazines. Then there are visits to record offices and other places connected with your family history. According to a recent study, most family historians spend several hundred pounds a year on their interest. Taking everything into account, including travel, I reckon that many of us are spending between £500 and £1000 a year. So if you are on a very limited budget, be aware of this when you start. And even if money isn't so restricted, it's worth keeping an eye on spending.

Here are some considerations to help you plan your time and budget:

- How long might you spend on your family history project altogether? Six months? Two years? Note down your answer – but don't expect to stick to it!
- Now think in terms of your ongoing research schedule, which is easier to plan for. Figure out roughly how much time you can afford to spend on researching your family history each week or month.
- Decide how long you'll usually spend online at any one time. Be prepared to time your sessions, and try to sign off within your time limit, to avoid mental burnout.
- Be ready and willing to take breaks in your research from time to time, which may last months or even years. Allow family history to rest gently, when needs be. Make a note of periods of time when you think you'll possibly give it a rest, e.g. for a couple of months in the summer, during intensive work projects or in the run-up to Christmas.
- What is your budget for family history in annual terms? How much are you prepared to invest in website subscriptions, in travel and other expenses? Allow something for unexpected spending, for a task or trip that really intrigues you. Write down your figures and keep them to hand.

Now it's time to consider the place of the ancestors in your life, and questions of family lineage, which will also help to prepare your search and establish a connection with your family past, before beginning the search itself. In the next chapter, we'll look at how ancestors fit both into different cultures and our personal experience, and how we can represent lineage and ancestry with symbols and charts which link us more clearly and closely to them.

CHAPTER TWO

On the Trail of the Ancestors

A s you move backwards in time into family history, you begin to penetrate a new world, one inhabited by your ancestors. These are your forebears; they are people who you have never met, but something urges you none the less to trace, name and know them.

In the 'old days' of genealogy, names and dates were considered paramount. Proof of lineage, a few deeds of bravery, a rogue ancestor or two and good women who bore strong sons were the stock-in-trade of family history. At least, this is how genealogy often came, and why I and many others initially resisted going down that path. I am not disrespecting the work of family historians, my father among them, who sought records so patiently before the days of the internet, and who completed family trees with such diligence. But the desire to discover family history is surely part of something bigger, linking us to a universal human interest in ancestry, which includes acknowledging these ancestors, and feeling their presence in our lives. This passion may well have been there underneath the surface in traditional genealogy, but was outwardly constrained by a convention that placed bare facts above all else.

The Welsh Voices

My own initial experience of encountering my ancestors was far from conventional, but it was astonishingly vivid, and heralded certain events and discoveries which followed shortly afterwards.

It happened one summer night, a few years ago. I had been working on my Welsh line of ancestry, trying to figure out the branch of the tree which I could now trace back to my 3 x great-grandfather, Edward Owens of Abbeycwmhir, the soldier who fought in the Napoleonic Wars (see Appendix I, p. 244).

All that night, my sleep was disturbed by what seemed like a babble of voices. I heard people chattering insistently, and I knew that they were my Welsh ancestors. I could not make out what they were saying, but I had the distinct impression that they wanted to be 'found' again, and that they wanted their story to be told. Edward's own insistence came through, and I inferred that his special wish was for his prowess as a soldier in the Napoleonic Wars to be remembered and, perhaps, for his medal to be found again.

This might seem like fantasy. However, it made a profound impression on me, and within a couple of months extraordinary things started to happen. A seemingly random hit on a website for a Welsh chapel led me to finding two separate lots of new cousins, also direct descendants of Edward Owens, and still living in the same region as my ancestors in mid-Wales. I had previously thought that everyone had moved away from the area. When I met up with Harold, my third cousin, he shook my hand, looked deep into my eyes, and said, 'You're the first member of the family to come back for a hundred years.' It was a powerful connection to make.

I was swept into a whirlwind of activity on that first expedition. With these two families, I looked at photos of my ancestors that I had never seen before, heard anecdotes about their lives, including those relating to a 2 x great-aunt who was a midwife and a herbalist, and was shown the local places associated with them. I also saw pieces of furniture actually made by our joint 2 x great-grandfather Edward, son of Edward Owens the soldier. He'd turned his hand to cabinet-making as the small stipend he received as a Baptist minister couldn't support his family. Beautifully made, of polished oak, the cupboard and two tables that my ancestor had created took my breath away as I touched them.

After this, research went like greased lightning in the Powys Archives, and I was also able to trace the existence of Edward senior's medal up until its last publicly recorded sale in the 1970s. The speed at which all this unrolled was incredible. I felt that I had unlocked a door to the past, and that it was the wish itself of the ancestors to be known and acknowledged by their descendants that fuelled my search.

Ancestors in Other Cultures

In modern Western culture, it may seem odd to assert that the ancestors can make their presence felt, but in many other cultures it is a natural assumption. Ancestor veneration is, or has been, important in practically any society that we might care to study. African, South American and Aboriginal Australian cultures all have strong beliefs in the significance of the ancestors, and practise customs which acknowledge the part they play in family life. They are variously thought, for instance, to guide their descendants, govern the local landscape and assist in divining the future. In shamanic practice, still found in countries such as Mongolia and Siberia, magician healers enter a trance and depart on a journey to the spirit realms to encounter the ancestors of the villagers, who will then give them counsel for the wellbeing of the community.

Ancestors in such cultures may be seen as deities, spirits or souls of the departed – there is no one definition, and often the boundaries are hazy – but their existence at some level is taken as a given. On the whole, they are not deified in the sense of worship, and therefore scholars nowadays prefer to use the term 'ancestor veneration', as this reflects more accurately the broad sweep of customs associated with the ancestors.

When my husband and I visited Bali early in 2010, by great good fortune we hired a taxi driver who was keen to show us some of these customs. He drove us to a temple built into the rocky hillside, known as Goa Lawah. It is a popular venue for funeral ceremonies, and renowned for its colony of sacred bats, which reside in a cave at the back of the temple. Situated at a place where sea and land meet (symbolising the border between the present life and the afterlife, our driver told us), the temple acts as the mediator for the soul that must take its journey from one to the other. The body is first cremated, and then the ashes are placed in a coconut shell and taken down to the shore close by, where they are thrown into the ocean. A line or rope, with up to 2500 ceremonial coins tied to it, is cast into the waters as well, and the mourners cry out for the dead person to return to them as they draw it back to shore again. Two times more the line is cast and the call goes up for the deceased to come home.

After twelve days have passed, the family members return to the same spot, and collect some kind of object (our driver was vague on this point – perhaps a stone from the shore, or something left over from the ceremony) which they carry reverently back to their home. This object is then placed in the domestic shrine, where it is believed to embody the spirit of the relative, now an honoured ancestor. From this time on, this ancestor will watch over the family, and protect and bless its members.

It might seem as though Western society is far removed from such practices, but we too have our graveyards, where flowers are renewed, and relatives go to remember their loved ones. On Remembrance Sunday in Britain, we honour the dead of the two world wars, and in Russia, practically every newly married couple has a photo taken in front of the local war memorial, where the eternal flame burns to commemorate the fallen soldiers. There are traces of interaction with the departed too, in Western customs, such as the feast of Samhain or Halloween in Irish tradition, when food and drink was and perhaps still is left out for the dead. We mark roadside casualties with shrines of flowers and symbolic objects. In Russian Orthodoxy, the first forty days after the death of a person are thought to be a journey during which the soul suffers various trials and temptations before reaching a more blessed state; at the end of these forty days, families may hold a 'remembering feast' to honour the departed and the arrival of the soul in heaven.

I won't dwell too long on funeral customs here, although I will take up the theme of the nature of the ancestors and the human soul again in Chapter Eight. Family history itself does not deal directly with the transition between life and death, except to record the facts of the date of death and the funeral. On that point, though, many of us find that the receiving of the death certificate for an ancestor is a solemn affair, as was the case with my Great-Aunt Sophia, whose story I will relate in the next chapter. And my visit to the local registry to record my father's death in 1997 made a deep impression on me – a sombre ritual in which the dignity and restraint of the officiating registrar emphasised how my father's name was being entered in the Book of Life for the last time.

I've also heard anecdotes about ancestors being 'brought back' into the family again after research has rediscovered and reinstated them, especially if they had been excluded from the tree because of some stigma such as illegitimacy; modern rituals for this can include tracing the grave, and laying a wreath there, or 'including' them in a family gathering.

The main question here though is whether ancestors are in some sense 'alive' to us, and in my survey, the majority of respondents affirmed that indeed they were. This will probably mean different things to different people, but it's certainly a strong component in our experience, in one form or another. We request their presence in our lives, and in one way that is not so far removed from the Balinese ritual which I witnessed.

Another experience of my own had slipped out of my mind entirely, but while gathering together material for this book, I came across a forgotten entry in a notebook that I had written several years ago in Moscow: 'Woke up at 5 a.m. after seven hours solid sleep – with an impression of my relatives and ancestors at my right shoulder, flowing out of it in a wavy shape like a kind of stream. A warm and light quality to it.' At that time, I wasn't prone to thinking about my ancestors, but I had just returned to Moscow from Siberia, where I had visited a shaman and had a healing session with him. As already mentioned, shamanism and the cult of ancestors are firmly bound together, and it seems that this powerful experience may have awoken the connection between my individual life and that of my forebears.[1] It was probably no coincidence that shortly after this encounter, I decided to start researching my own family history, even though I hadn't made a conscious connection between this and the shamanic consultation in my mind.

I've described several of my own experiences here because I think it's important to acknowledge them. From talking to others, and reading their comments in the survey, it seems I'm not alone in this, even though our present-day culture provides little scope for affirming the presence and influence of the ancestors. We can approach family history like genealogists, or ancestor veneration like anthropologists, but unless we bring the personal factor into either of these contexts, they may remain dry and unconnected to our lives today.

As Awo Fa'lokun Fatunmbi says, writing from the point of view of the Ifa religion, associated with the Yoruba people of Africa: 'Communication with your own ancestors is a birthright … You cannot know who you are if you cannot call the names of your ancestors going back seven generations. Remembering names is more than reciting a genealogy, it is preserving the history of a family lineage and the memory of those good deeds that allowed the family to survive.'[2]

The Circle of the Ancestors

At this point, I would like to introduce you to an interesting and unusual way to invoke your ancestors. I first heard about it at a concert celebrating the life of the nineteenth-century poet John Clare, who was himself firmly attached to his roots and ancestral landscape. During the performance, one of the musicians mentioned a family history project which his daughter had brought home from school. She had been asked to enter all her direct-line (common) ancestors into a series

1   For a fuller account of my session with the shaman, see pp. 127–8 of 'The Russian Spirit of Place', *Sky and Psyche*, edited by Nicholas Campion and Patrick Curry (Floris 2006).
2   http://www.assatashakur.org/forum/spirituality-connect-your-center/16359-ancestor-reverence-building-ancestor-shrine.html)

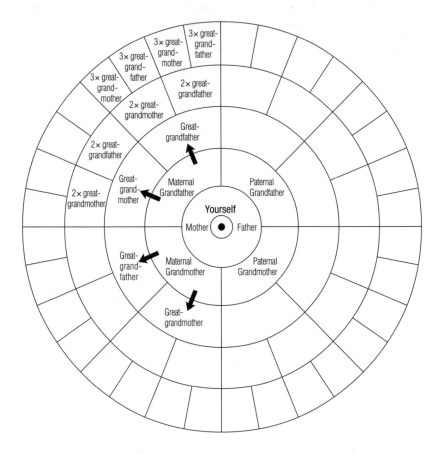

of concentric circles, expanding from a central point to include each generation further back. In this case, therefore, the musician's daughter was named at the central point, and her mother and father were placed opposite each other on the first circle that surrounded her. The second circle would be marked with the names of her four grandparents, and so on, through six circles in total, ending with a final circle containing sixty-four ancestors, all of whom would be the girl's 4 x great-grandparents.

It fired my imagination, and back at home, I tried to draw neat circles divided in the correct way, divisions doubling in each circle. It was tricky, but eventually I achieved a rough template and started to fill it in. This was at a time when I hadn't got so far with my family history, and inevitably I ground to a halt in different areas of the circle. There weren't many 3 x great-grandparents that I could name at this stage, and very few 4 x ones. But the concept, of standing in the centre of circles of ancestors, was compelling. I still come back to it frequently, and sometimes check to see if all those sixty-four are now included. (Not quite.)

Exercise: creating the circles

See if you can create something similar to the circles described above, but I suggest a reduced version to make it more manageable, ending at the circle of thirty-two. I find that thirty-two direct ancestors are plenty, if I want to know them as individuals and discover their stories, and as this diagram works as a visual aid and a tool for connecting with your ancestors, I recommend keeping it within practical bounds.

1. Find a large sheet of paper (A3 size, for example; or, if you use A4, then get it enlarged by a photocopier once you have drawn the template). A square sheet is ideal, but it's fine to use a rectangular one too.
2. Put a firm, well-defined dot at the centre. That will be you! Don't name this, or any other points for the moment.
3. Draw a small circle around the dot (a pair of compasses will help) leaving plenty of space to create further circles beyond. Put marking points at the four quarters of the circle.
4. Continue drawing concentric circles until you have five altogether, plus the dot at the centre.
5. Divide each circle evenly into twice the number of points that the previous one has. They will therefore go as follows: 2, 4, 8, 16 and 32, with the final and outermost circle having 32 evenly spaced points or short marker lines on it. (You may be able to do all this on the computer, if you have the technical know-how.)

6. Write a title on the page, such as, 'The Circle of the Ancestors'.
7. Make several, if not a dozen, copies of your template. You will almost certainly need to fill it in more than once before you have a version you are satisfied with. Keep at least one blank one back, which can serve to make further copies.
8. Begin to fill one page in. Put the name of each ancestor and, if you like and have room, the dates of their birth and death.

Contemplating the circles

9. Now you can start to make use of your chart. What does it feel like to be at the centre of your ancestral circles? Try the following:
10. Look at the finished chart (even if not all the names are complete); gaze at it for a few minutes.
11. Close your eyes and try to visualise it. Call up the names of those you know; this is probably easiest in terms of one circle at a time, your grandparents followed by great-grandparents and so on.
12. Can you see in your mind's eye a circle of sixteen, then thirty-two grandparent ancestors, even if you cannot differentiate each one of them? Which ones stand out clearly? Which are shadowy figures?
13. Acknowledge them all with gratitude and respect for the life they have passed on to you.

This is a powerful exercise, which can produce different types of effects. You may experience the ancestors as protecting and caring. But being surrounded by family in this way might also come across as suffocating or too restricting. There is no 'right' way to experience it, and it may well be that you will find that it varies, if you try out this exercise at different times. After all, this is on a par with family life – sometimes it's the best support we can have, and sometimes it curbs and frustrates us. But if you keep this as an exercise to return to, you may find that your sense of being connected with your ancestors grows, and that in some sense, they become more 'alive' to you. Use the circle as a personal ritual to greet and get to know them.

The Shapes of Your Lineage

There is always a choice as to the way we represent our ancestry, both in the shapes we use to draw it in, and the selection of relatives we include. Each option has its own strengths and weaknesses, emphasising some elements and ignoring others. We have to make such choices, so it's important to be aware of what they involve, and whether they suit our purpose.

Value and limitations of the circle

The ancestral circle is a great tool for reflecting on your ancestry, but not necessarily the best way to map your family history. There is no room for brothers and sisters, aunts or uncles in this model, or indeed your own children, if you have them. It is also, in one sense, an egocentric view of the world – you appear in it as the centre of the family, as though all that effort from your forebears was put into creating this one special person.

If you try the exercise, you will almost certainly find, however, that witnessing the circle with yourself in the centre does make an impact. It gives a strong sense of your complete direct-line ancestry. But it also shows how these ancestors double at each generation, reaching 128 in a span of less than three hundred years for many of us. If you added in all the siblings, the numbers would rapidly soar; put in the siblings' children too and it becomes overwhelming. That's why most charts of family lineage restrict the scale of relatives included.

Following a line

Genealogists do often work their way back through many generations, but usually by following a particular line of descent. Most cultures have a specific way of defining a family line, which is said to pass through certain family members, and through this line other entitlements are often passed down too, such as inheritance rights or the claim to nobility. The official line may descend through either the male or female side of the family, or by those who bear the family name, for instance. In most Western societies, the family name is usually perpetuated by male members of the family, and this is generally taken to be the formally acknowledged line of descent. But one of the first things I learned while studying anthropology at university was that the forms of kinship in human societies are wide and various. There is no one standard way of defining family relationships, though all over the world kinship and lineage is mapped out in one way or another, counting some family members as the key figures of lineage and leaving others out of what is considered to be the direct line of ancestry.

As we have just seen, taking all possible direct ancestors into account does become unmanageable, so this is perhaps inevitable. The lineages that are thus created gather enormous significance in many societies; keeping the knowledge of lineage has often been the province of bards, who could chant or sing the names of generations going back into the mists of time. In Africa, these male and female reciters of the family descent still exist, and are called griots or griottes. Such knowledge must have been valued since ancient times, as many recitations of lineage also occur in the Bible.

This then is the power of the line in genealogy. It is the opposite approach to that of the circle; instead of including all direct-line ancestors, it defines select representatives of the family, through whom our authorised descent may be traced.

CHOOSING YOUR LINEAGE

When you are starting your family history research, the most practical option is usually to take one line of the family and work back through that, from present times to previous generations. The circle has its uses, but your active research will require more definition; just as we talk about 'a line of research' in general terms, we need the same in the case of family history. Choosing one line over another does not restrict you indefinitely though; you may decide to research one line, and later move on to develop another. This will ultimately lead to the branching shape of the family tree, to be considered shortly.

Which line will you choose? In Chapter One, I suggested casting a preliminary vote for either the male or female side of the family. Now we can consider these options in more detail.

THE PATRILINEAL LINE

This is the father's line, and the most common way in which we define family lineage in Western society. Often, this is also the route through which the family surname is transmitted through the generations. There are exceptions to this: both in Iceland and Spain, for instance, traditional naming systems pass on the mother's surname too, though this is becoming eroded to some degree by the pressure to conform to international standards in documents and passports. Other variations frequently occur, as when single mothers choose to give their own family name to their children, or when emigration and a subsequent reinvention of the family identity can erode the former name, and make it harder to fill in the line of ancestry. And in previous centuries, Welsh families used a patronymic naming system, in which the father's given name becomes the surname of his son or daughter. So Rhys ap Morgan and Margaret ap Morgan would be the son and daughter of Morgan; and if he was known as Morgan ap Evan, then his own father's first name would have been Evan. This has caused many a genealogical headache, and I am very glad that my Welsh ancestors, by the end of the eighteenth century, were no longer using this custom!

If the father's line and the family name do go together, this can be the easiest path to follow when tracing family history. If you choose to pursue this route it may prove quicker and more straightforward to chart your family lineage back through the generations, and with time and patient research you may be able to trace it back to the sixteenth century or even earlier. The focus is, of course, on direct-line male descendants; you will probably record women marrying into this line, but include little if anything about their family background. Also, the further back the ancestor, the smaller the part he (in this case) will play in your genetic make-up (see p. 100). Certain problems can arise too, such as an illegitimate child, father unknown, who can bring your patrilineal line to an abrupt halt. But there is plenty to be gained too: you can achieve a clear understanding of your descent through this particular family line for perhaps hundreds of years. You are also likely to share a name with these ancestors, and with other living descendants, which can boost your sense of personal identity and cement family bonds as a result.

Is this a natural or an artificial way for society to trace lineage? It's possible that the existence of a lineage convention does in fact strengthen the family's identity and maybe even their gene pool, by influencing both their actions and their choice of marriage partners. If it's always said, for example, that 'the Dundeals are good at making money, and holding on to it', then Dundeal children will be under pressure to become entrepreneurs, to invest carefully and to choose partners who will reinforce the Dundeal values. Even if not all do this, a good proportion of them are likely to, over the generations. There is an argument, therefore, for saying that a family formed under the patrilineal system of descent and nomenclature will very likely be the genuinely dominant line in our heritage. It may have shaped our personality and influenced our outlook. Additionally, since it's usually the easiest one to trace, it is therefore a natural starting point for many family historians. But it is not the only one.

THE MATRILINEAL LINE

If you are a woman, you may, quite naturally, consider the mother's line, sometimes rather patronisingly called 'the distaff side', to be of more importance. And any of us – male or female – may want to know more about our mother's roots for a variety of reasons, whether personal or circumstantial. There are also cultural counterweights to the dominance of the father's line; in cities such as Liverpool and Birmingham in the UK, where women have traditionally been strong and resourceful, running their own businesses and bringing up children single-handed, families often prize their female line of descent and may indeed know far more about their mother's side than about absent fathers who were away at sea or just plain gone.

The knowledge that each woman was born of a woman is powerful too, and may influence an interest in the female line. When a friend of mine was giving birth to her daughter, a vision came to her of all the female ancestors of her family stretching back through the generations, a long line of mothers of which she was now the youngest living representative. It is a stunning thought, that we women can measure the family journey backwards through the bodies we have emerged from, like a series of Russian dolls stacked one inside the other, leading from mother to grandmother, great-grandmother and so on, right back to the unnamed and unknown women of the ancient past. When my own granddaughter was born in 2009, I was able to put together a series of photographs showing her place in six generations of women, and I can also add two earlier names to this, predating the era of photos, going back to Maria, her 5 x great-grandmother who was born in 1790. I could do this only because I'd chosen to research my matrilineal line; and had this been all I'd achieved from my research, the chance to pass this knowledge on to my granddaughter would have made it completely worthwhile.

Tracing the matrilineal line is not so easy, however, because of surname changes and because society has not previously paid it so much attention. There is help out there: a neat little book, called *The Female Line* by Margaret Ward (see Resources, p. 250), is a particularly useful guide to records. But there is no magic wand to wave for finding the way back through the grandmothers, and it may be a slow, step-by-step journey to discover each woman's maiden name in order to go back one generation further. With female descent, therefore, you gain a line of ancestresses, and the direct-line male ancestors make a brief appearance as partners to the females. It is the counterpart of patrilineal genealogy, and if you pursue them both in the pure version, you will end up with two completely separate lines of descent which only conjoin when your mother gets together with your father.

The family tree

The family tree, as the third main map of genealogy after the circle and the line, enables us to combine elements of both the ancestral circle and a specific family line. It allows for including different lines of the family and for siblings; you can draw it up as broadly or as specifically as you like. The tree is also a beautiful symbol of the family, with its leaves and branches corresponding with the individuals on it and the lines they have sprung from. In a deeper sense, it depicts the family as a living entity – living, breathing and growing over the centuries, with each person's life shown as a tiny, but significant, part of the whole. Like the ancestral circle, it is worthy of contemplation in its own right.

Family trees have often been drawn in a highly decorative way, as well as in stylised, abstract versions. But the core concept of the tree remains, and the idea of the family as represented by a tree connects to an ancient and widespread symbol, known as the Tree of Life. This great Tree is said to grow at the heart of the universe, its branches stretching up to the heavens, and its roots reaching down to the underworld. In between the two, life as we know it exists, with its burgeoning variety of animals, birds, fishes, insects and, of course, people. The myth takes a variety of forms, featuring in many countries and cultures: there is the Tree Yggdrasil in Scandinavian legend, where the eagle above fights the serpent below, and between the two a little squirrel runs up and down the trunk carrying messages and insults between them; there is the mystical Tree of Life in the Jewish tradition, a map of the sacred principles such as love and justice that we find both in the world and in ourselves; there is also a simple motif of a Tree of Life found woven into carpets and cloth in Central Asia and the Middle East, thought to date back to prehistoric times. Then, in shamanic cultures such as found in Siberia, the sacred tree plays an important role, acting as a ladder to the otherworld, to which the shaman must climb in trance. One Siberian story tells of this Tree as the birthplace of human souls; when a child is born, a soul flies out from the Tree as a bird, and when life is over it returns to rest in the branches again.

The connection between the family tree and the Tree of Life is good to keep in mind because it links the sense of our personal life to that of our ancestry, and from there to the whole of human life itself – the common life that we all share. As Bernard, one of the survey respondents, describes it: 'I suppose I feel part of a stream of sentient lives, ideas, feelings, actions, as though I come from somewhere, and am not just a "new start" from birth.'

SETTING UP A TREE

As you prepare to research and chart your family history, give some thought to the type of tree you would like to use. Most people nowadays use a computer to create a tree; genealogical software is developing all the time, and current programmes include an attractive choice of ways to display and print a tree. You will be able to add photos, colours, backgrounds and all sorts of other elements to customise it. Or you can draw up your own tree, with simple straight lines, vertical between generations, and horizontal for family members of the same generation, whose names you can record in little boxes. Paper templates are available too, both decorative and plain. (We'll come back to setting up your tree and selecting relatives for it in Chapter Five, and you'll find details there of suitable software, as well as in the Resources section, p. 255.)

Exercise: visualising the tree

I would like to suggest that you close the work of this chapter by visualising the tree of your family, in terms of a mythic but living and growing organism. Read through the following sequence first, and then try it out, preferably without referring back to the page again until you have finished.

For this, and any future visualisation exercises, sit comfortably in a quiet place, with your back upright and feet resting on the ground. Close your eyes, take your time to relax, but stay alert. Breathe gently, and at a slightly slower pace than usual.

Picture a huge tree growing out of the earth, its roots sinking into the depths below, and its branches spreading up to the sky. This is your family, and you are a part of it, so sense your own connection with it: touch it; feel the contact with its trunk, branches and leaves.

Now step back a little in your mind and see the tree as a whole. See and hear the life and movement within it. Possibly, individual relatives or ancestors may come to mind. Don't try to place them too precisely; by all means acknowledge them, but keep a sense of the whole tree as the main focus of the exercise.

Spend two or three minutes contemplating the tree, then rest for a few seconds before opening your eyes. Gently become aware of your surroundings again. Then jot down any impressions that arose; you'll find it useful to keep a record of such experiences.

Repeat this exercise as and when you choose.

The way is now prepared for you to find the material you need, first from existing family relatives and mementos, and then through external research resources. As you do this, take with you the symbol of the family tree; it can help to support and sustain your quest, and is a reminder that you do not stand alone, but are part of the whole living creation.

CHAPTER THREE

The Gathering Process

Soon after I began to get interested in family history, I travelled up to St Andrews in Scotland to visit my aunt, the widow of my mother's brother, Roy. When Berit heard that I was researching, she invited me to come and look through her late husband's papers to see if there was anything that might help me.

My Uncle Roy's own interest in family history began in the 1930s, when a genealogist unexpectedly turned up at his parents' home in Nottingham, declaring that there might be a drop of noble blood running through the family veins. Roy, who was about thirteen at the time, wrote up his notes of the encounter:

> Lord Lascelles (now Earl Harewood) making enquiries about ancestry. Legal chap took up enquiries and they hunted about in old parish registers etc. at Hemyock ... Found that our line of descent from the Stuart family of Scotland and also from the Dukes of Devonshire more direct than his lordship's!! Wrote to my great-uncle telling him this, and said that if all the various taxes etc. were paid, my uncle in Northampton could have the coat of arms etc. of the family.

The great-uncle, one of the few wealthy members of the family, never did respond to the appeal, so we are still crestless.

Later, Roy became an academic, a professor at St Andrews specialising in medieval French, and, as one might expect, he knew the value of keeping a comprehensive archive. In his latter years, he began to draw together what he knew about his parents' history, checking with his siblings as to what they might remember. He collected his notes on this, along with journals that he'd written in his youth, and all the family mementos and documents that had come his way. Now, sadly, he was gone, but Berit had sorted his papers impeccably. I was very welcome, she said, to browse through them.

I spent a couple of days in her bright Scandinavian-style home (she was from Sweden originally), poring over paperwork, punctuated by a few bracing walks along the sea shore. I was in heaven. Not only was it a pleasure to see my aunt again and to talk over family memories with her, but I had complete access to bundles of letters, piles of mementos and boxes of photographs. It was enough material to keep me enthralled, but not so much that I felt overwhelmed.

I read a letter from my mother's sister, written at the end of the Second World War, on VE Day, describing the local celebrations; I studied a newspaper cutting containing my grandfather's obituary and looked at a birthday card written in a shaky hand by my great-grandmother, Sarah Brown, née Lee, which she had sent to my uncle as a little boy (see Appendix I, p. 244). I also found the preliminary hand-written notes that Roy had made as he attempted to piece the family history together. These contained invaluable leads (which I would later follow up) and sketched brief, but vital, word portraits of certain family members. For the first time, I 'met' my Great-Aunt Florence. (I had never heard of her before, but now realised that my mother was named for her, as Kathleen Florence Owen.) Here is what Roy wrote:

> Auntie Florrie (Florence Brown) kept Post Office in Brington Northants. Met? Dacey, in South African mounted police, who was on a visit to England. Engaged in England. Married. Lived in South Africa (Durban). He died suddenly. She became a stewardess with a steamship line visiting India.

What a story! (And there will be more about Florence and her sister Sophia below and in Chapter Six.)

This and other notes Roy made were like nuggets of gold to me. I returned home with a wealth of material, including a birthday book given to my grandfather by his mother when he was a little boy, and filled in by him with the birthdays of many relatives. This was not only a wonderful keepsake for me, but also a good check system for many of the birth dates I subsequently researched. I had to bear in mind, however, the genealogist's classic adage: don't believe a fact until it's confirmed from more than one source. For example, Grandpa had proudly written down his own place of birth as the USA, whereas, according to his birth certificate, he was born in Somerset. (He could be forgiven for the misunderstanding, since the family was at that time living in America, but his mother returned home to her own family for his birth, then brought him back to the US when he was three months old.) I copied, scanned and wrote down everything that this little archive contained, and right up until the present, some five years later, I am still finding new leads and clues in what it has to offer.

Collecting Family Material

The gathering together of family information and records is a valuable stage in the process of researching your family history. It may not form the very first step in your research, but do include it sooner rather than later. Find out what you have already, and ask your relatives what they have too. Are there old letters, certificates or wills belonging to members of the previous generation? Start by combing through these to see if you can piece together more of the family background. Even if you think you are familiar with them, look again, as they may contain names, dates or addresses that you haven't noticed before, and which could play a valuable part in helping you to trace your relatives and their movements.

Maybe you have objects in your possession that tell a story? I have my grandfather's clock, presented by his colleagues on his retirement as Baptist minister, and a great-uncle's christening mug, painted with name and date. Both are sources of information, as well as forming part of the family heritage. It may only be when you start to work on your family history in this way that you do indeed recognise the heritage that surrounds you.

Joy, one of the survey respondents, found her chief treasure in her mother's bureau:

> I had always been led to understand that a red velvet-covered family Bible was in the loft and was disappointed to find nothing there. However, after my mother's death in 1995, I was sorting through her desk and was delighted to find the two most relevant pages which had been removed from the Bible – they contained details of her father's family, many of whom were sea captains.

Whereas Joy's find led her directly to setting up the family tree, Sheila S.'s was more circumstantial, and shows how some mementos can help to shed light on the personality and lives of our ancestors. Her 2 x great-grandmother, Mary Ann, found herself married to a ne'er-do-well who committed crimes of forgery, but Sheila is convinced that Mary Ann herself had higher aspirations. 'I always feel very sad for her. I feel she was an educated young lady, as I have a book given her when she was nineteen, entitled, "The Ladies' Tale: Exemplifying the Virtues and Vices of the Quality, with Reflections".'

Joan felt in touch with her great-grandmother from an early age, through the sampler she had made, which hung on the wall in the house of Joan's uncle and aunt. My sister-in-law has an even earlier sampler sewn by her 2 x great-grandmother in the 1840s, embroidered in delicate silks. It now hangs in shadow under the stairs, as it needs to be protected from bright light, and when I finally spotted it on a recent visit, I found the 2 x great-grandmother's name revealed in full – something that I had previously spent several hours researching for my husband on the internet. This shows that it's worth asking other family members first, before spending time and perhaps money on chasing up the records. Bear in mind, though, that a memento which appears to crown an ancestor with virtue can be misleading: the curate who was presented with a silver snuff box in 1831 turns out to be none other than Bernard's notorious ancestor Augustus Joseph Tancred, whom we met in Chapter One – the one who eloped with a nun.

Don't Leave It Too Late

As you gather your records and mementos together, do seek help from other family members when you can. Pat was given a box of old family photos after the death of her aunt, but had no idea who was in them. Luckily, she was still able to ask her mother to identify them. Often, however, when it comes to asking older relatives, it could be too late if we put it off. Steve saw the danger, and acted in time:

> About fifteen years ago, after the death of some elderly relatives, I realised that I knew very little about the history of my family and that I ought to do something about it before all the information was lost for ever. Armed only with an old family photograph album and a copy of the Reader's Digest *Explore your Family's Past*, I began to quiz my mother about everything she knew or could remember. Fortunately, she could put names to many of the faces in the album and these were related to her side of the family.

Using this information, Steve was then able to hit the genealogy websites and fill in gaps on the family tree:

> It was like peeling an onion! Generation after generation appeared before me and led me to discovering that my maternal grandmother's sister was still alive. Meeting with her produced even more information.

Steve is the first to point out, however, that this didn't answer all the questions, and that there is nearly always a lot more work to be done. But talking to relatives and sifting through all kinds of memorabilia can yield fantastic rewards.

Gathering mementos may also envelop you in a cloud of nostalgia, so it pays to keep a cool eye on the hard facts that emerge from the evidence. By all means enjoy the sensation of being transported back to your family's past – that's an important element of experiencing family history – but be objective about it as well.

Here are some guidelines for sourcing information:

- Ask other family members if they have any letters, photos or documents that you can see. Make copies or scans of these wherever possible; using a digital camera, if you have one, is a quick and effective way to do this, especially if you can't take them away to copy. Check the photographs as you take them, to make sure they are in focus, and/or take extra pictures just to be on the safe side.

- Look among your own papers, letters and records to see if there is anything that relates to family history.

- Collect together memories and photos that you have of more recent relatives who you've known personally. You might not consider them to be 'history' in the same way, but they can act as a stepping stone to investigating the ancestors that you never met. Their own lives and habits may give clues to those of a previous generation. And even if you don't plan to write up your parents' generation fully in your family history, you'll probably want to include the bare facts, so assemble these; the relatives who we think we know best can easily be the ones we have the least hard information about.

- Take a fresh look at the objects you own: have any of them belonged to family members, and do they tell a story?

- Make a list of the 'hard evidence' from these mementos. A pile of letters, for instance, probably contains more wordage than you can retain clearly in your head, so be professional about gathering your facts, and note down each source and the information that it contains.

- Consider creating a 'chronology' of the dates in your family history. In the early stages especially, this can help you to see who was where when, and provide a useful cross-check by date across different branches of the family. A computer spreadsheet can be an effective way of doing this.

- Enter up new dates and names on your family tree as soon as possible, or you risk forgetting what they are, and make a note of where you found them (either in your files or in your genealogy programme, which usually offers areas where you can record sources).

- List queries that arise, or details to check later, and make a note of any puzzles or stories that you'd like to follow up. That way, you can come back to them at any point.

- Finally, don't beat yourself up about anything you may have thrown away previously. We've all done it! It's impossible to keep everything, and starting from where you are now is a good place.

This stage of your research is likely to provide food and fuel for the journey for a long time to come. You'll be inspired by the various records and objects, and they will give you leads and offer mysteries to be solved that will keep you moving along the trail, perhaps for many years ahead.

Following the Trail

My great-aunts Florence and Sophia are good examples of how you can follow the trail to build up stories of family members. I've mentioned the brief account that Roy had written of his Aunt Florence (see p. 44) and this, coupled with photos in his collection of an eager young woman with shining eyes, inspired me to trace her story further.

I discovered that Florence had started off in service, like many girls of her generation, and particularly in the case of my maternal grandmother's family. She and her brothers and sisters were encouraged to take up steady but humble jobs, which for my grandmother and her sister Florence meant taking up posts as servants. The family had known hard times; they survived an earlier era of famine in the weaving and mining town of Bedworth, near Coventry, and were perhaps only saved by my great-grandfather's decision to join the railways in the late nineteenth century, which gave them new social mobility and a way out of an impoverished industrial area. This decision meant that the family finally ended up living in on the edge of the great Althorp Estate in Northamptonshire, where my great-grandfather Henry worked till retirement as the signalman for Althorp Station.

Through Roy's collection, I learned that both Florence and her sister Sophia had worked as postmistresses in the little village of Great Brington, situated close to Althorp, and in whose church members of the Spencer family (from which Princess Diana came) are buried. Finally, I was able to visit the post office for myself, and found it still open – a tiny shop nestling in an ancient cottage, which stands in a picture postcard setting of perfect golden-stoned houses. I wanted to find out more. I knew that Florence had taken over the job from Sophia – but why?

I had a copy of a cheerful, chatty letter that Sophia wrote to her sister Hannah (my grandmother) while she was happily ensconced in the post office; it talked about the knitting she was doing for the village jumble sale and about the broody hen she was going to set on a clutch of eggs. There was no hint of anything amiss. There was nothing more that the helpful owners of the post office could tell me, so I strolled up to the churchyard. And as with David Sm., in Chapter One, serendipity helped.

I came across two men who were photographing and cataloguing the many graves there. Any Browns hereabouts? I asked them. I wasn't sure if any of the family had been buried there at all, and it was a common enough name, so I wasn't too hopeful. But they led me straight to a grave recording the death of Sophia Brown at the young age of thirty-eight in 1914. I felt a shockwave travel right through me, and tears came to my eyes. Here was the proof that Sophia had met a sudden and untimely end. Now I knew from the dates why this particular letter had been kept; it was the last one that Sophia ever wrote to her sister, my grandmother.

The story of Sophia is still coming to light; if I had written this chapter two months ago, I wouldn't have this information about her grave, nor my subsequent findings from the death certificate which I ordered, revealing that she died of septicaemia. Every new finding raises a new question: how and why did she get that? With the help of the Northampton local-history archive I found an obituary for her in the local newspaper. I learned that: 'Miss Brown was held in high esteem by all who knew her', that she was an organist and 'one of the most earnest workers of the ladies' sewing class'. Plus, it gave all the names of those who had sent flowers – useful both for checking the family tree and for understanding the kind of circles she moved in.

So don't expect all your stories to appear straight away; they may unfold over years to come. I later explored the website connected with the church at Great Brington, and found a complete list of burials which contains the name of another member of the family, a previously unknown great-aunt, who died at the age of six from diphtheria. One discovery leads to another and there is rarely an end to family history. As David Sw. says:

> I think it is true you never really stop with family history. There is always something around the next corner just as you think you have exhausted all the possible research. In my own case I have just found that a 2 x great-uncle (who has been on a long-finished branch of my family tree for over twenty-five years) threw himself off a steamer while heading for New York under an assumed name (my next research job).

Regrets

I mentioned in the previous chapter that a sense of regret and loss – inevitably, I believe – accompanies many of our searches into family history; but although this is sad, it is a good motivator.

You may deeply regret (as I do) that you didn't talk to your parents more before they died, or that you threw out keepsakes which you would give your eye teeth to have back again. I think that grief takes different forms, and sometimes, in an attempt to get through the awful business of dealing with the death of a relative, we may try simply to shovel the past into a bin bag – often, quite literally.

My brother and I were both in the aftermath of marriage break-ups when our mother died; we were fraught, and had little time to sort through her possessions together. I offered to take on the task of look-ing through her box of photographs. If a photo didn't contain a picture of someone I recognised, I threw it away. This was before the start of my interest in family history, so you can imagine how I have regretted this loss, for which I can blame no one but myself. But I have also learned to forgive myself for it. We cannot keep everything from the past, and we must make choices, often at difficult times and under severe pressure.

In a way, missing items create a space that we can fill with new research and discoveries. We are also able to reconfigure our posses-sions, taking stock of what we do have, valuing certain things more than we did previously. The one surviving letter from my Great-Aunt Blanche is all the more precious to me because it was kept by acci-dent – it literally fell out of an old diary kept in my teenage years when I was browsing through it a couple of years ago. Blanche wrote to me faithfully every birthday and Christmas, and I threw the whole of her correspondence away when I moved out of my parents' home. Or I thought I had.

What you recover, after loss, has heightened importance, and may spur you on to track and trace further information in a way that you might not have done otherwise. Acknowledge regret, but don't let it swamp you, and appreciate what it may have brought you as well.

Family Memories

It's a natural step from assembling a family archive to collecting family memories from living relatives. I've mentioned the process of asking relatives to identify photographs, but Ian's research went one step fur-ther, when his mother's funeral proved, perhaps surprisingly, an entirely appropriate occasion to gather in pictures and stories. He was already on a mission to find new photos wherever he could, and his rel-atives were helping out:

> Thankfully, our family wakes are never solemn affairs, but family photographs also helped with the grieving process when my mother passed away. My surviving aunt

and a maternal cousin had come to the rescue of an earlier plea to borrow some old family photographs, and both had sought some excellent examples just in time for the wake. These were passed around the gathered family and friends to much laughter and friendly banter at the various hairstyles and poses, and I'm happy to say that everyone's tears were from laughter – exactly as Mum would have wanted it.

These memories that you now record can also include stories that you originally heard in childhood. Evelyn's mother came from a family of farm workers in Northumberland, and she used to tell her daughter how the family moved around from farm to farm, following the work where they could. From a young age, she would present herself at hiring fairs, where she was usually taken on as a dairy maid or mother's help. This mention of the hiring fairs opens the door to a whole slice of social history, dating back to the sixteenth century when Edward III introduced them in an attempt to regulate the labour market. Evelyn's mother must have been among one of the last generations who offered themselves for hire there. She was able to paint a picture of the scene for her daughter, describing how, for instance, she had to put a feather in her cap once a deal had been struck, to ward off any further offers of employment. Her recollections are an important glimpse into a vanished world, and Evelyn has preserved them in her family history.

Caution Advised

If you have the opportunity to talk to relatives, especially ones from an older generation, go gently. Care is often needed. Ian, who described his mother's funeral earlier, warns: 'Whenever contacting people I always bear in mind that some people prefer not to air long-forgotten skeletons, or have an outlook that prefers to look forward rather than back.'

Alison came across full-scale resistance in her search for family knowledge:

I wanted to find out more about my mother's family and so I wrote to an elderly aunt who had started her own research. She was mortified to learn that I was 'digging up the past' and wrote to my mother asking her to dissuade me. This was mainly because my grandmother had had a baby son before her marriage to my grandfather and she wanted this kept a secret.

What current generations regard as quite acceptable (in this case illegitimacy) or merely interesting, former generations felt was shocking and could not be spoken of. Josie's hard-won discoveries were rejected by her fellow family members when she showed them the narrative she had written: 'A drowning while drunk and the following temperance in the family had to be left out of what I had written, said the committee for a family history.'

Some stories, such as suicide or incest, become too unpalatable even for the researcher, and may also be left lying unaired to avoid distress to living relations. Barbara was halted in her tracks by the following discovery:

One of your questions was about things I wish I hadn't discovered. I have long known that my father's mother died shortly after his birth, and my father was brought up by his grandmother. Apparently, his father rejected him. I know that my parents made several attempts to meet my paternal grandfather and sort things out, but always without success ... I thought I would see what I could find. The birth, marriage and death certificates were easily found. The birth and marriage certificates were quite normal; the death certificate, however, gave the cause of death as 'shot herself in the forehead with a revolver whilst of temporarily unsound mind'. I am convinced that neither of my parents is aware of this, and that it was probably hushed up at the time. I have no intention of telling my parents after all this time and will do no further research into my father's family while they are still alive.

Even if we don't come up against such difficult and tragic circum-stances, this does act as a warning to tread carefully. In the end, each of us has to make up our own mind as to which stones to leave unturned.

Here are some tips to help you with your quest for first-hand knowledge:

- Give your relative some time to think about the idea of talking to you. You could drop a word into the conversation first, or write a letter asking if they would be willing to share their memories with you.
- Meet up at their convenience and in familiar surroundings, whenever possible, so that they are comfortable and relaxed.
- Take a voice recorder with you if you can. Use it openly, but reassure your relative that it's just for reference, and explain that you'll both soon forget it's there at all.
- Take notes, especially if you can't record the conversation.
- Think about your seating position and set it up without fuss at the start. Sitting at an angle to each other is easier and less confrontational than face to face.
- Ask questions, but don't talk too much yourself, unless you need to use a prompt or insert a brief anecdote to keep the conversation going.
- Allow the person time to reflect on their answers if need be; accept silence as part of the process.
- Don't continue for too long. Half an hour is usually plenty, then try to arrange to meet again if there is still plenty to explore.
- If you make a recording, take notes from it afterwards or, better still, type it up. But bear in mind that one hour of voice recording takes six hours of transcription (another good reason for keeping track of the time during the interview).

Family Myths and Mysteries

Family stories, as I've already suggested, often act as a catalyst for further research in family history. Your gathering of information may yield a few more of these tales, but are they tall tales or genuine recollections? As a general rule, the best approach is to gather first, research later. As Sheila M. G.'s account bears out, there may be truth in some tales, although many will be exaggerated or distorted:

> My husband's grandfather died in 1986 but we have him on tape telling his stories, including him meeting Laurence of Arabia in Egypt. He also told of his sister being burned to death in a house fire one Christmas while he was out shopping with his parents and older brother. The story was that she had set light to the house while reading, probably by swinging the gas lamp round and catching light to the curtains.

But Sheila M. G.'s investigations subsequently proved that Laurence was not in Egypt at the right time, and that the old man had given an inaccurate version of his sister's death: 'Searching for a child of about eight years old, able to read and be left on her own, turned out to be a red herring. In fact, the poor girl was aged three, and her clothing caught fire while playing with mother. She died three days later in October 1902.'

Angela, who was pressed by her grandfather before his death to take on the task of researching the family history (see p. 6), traced one legend to source and found it somewhat adrift of the truth.

> One story in the family was that, like so many others, we were descended from royalty. Well, I found that hard to believe, so started to delve. The story was that my father's maternal grandfather, born in 1847, was the illegitimate son of the Duke of Cambridge. There are papers held by another member of the family admitting him to Christ's Hospital, together with a letter signed by the Duke of Cambridge. On investigation, it

turns out that he was sponsored to attend Christ's Hospital by one of the hospital's four gentlemen patrons, who took it in turns to sponsor a child, and my great-grandfather's was the Duke of Cambridge. On informing one of my aunts of this discovery, she refused to believe it and continued to maintain that she was descended from the Duke of Cambridge and a German princess!

Unsolved Mysteries

This leads us to the question of existing family puzzles, which are also worthy of investigation. Here's how Ruth answered the survey question as to whether any interesting stories or discoveries had emerged in her family research: 'Aforementioned great-grandfather's wooden leg. Must find out if that was from the war.'

Elaine longs to find out the truth about her great-grandmother, Alice:

> The family story says that Alice was illegitimate. The story goes that her mother was housekeeper to the local squire and bore two children, Alice and her brother (name unknown). When the squire died, Alice and her brother were educated by the family on the condition that their mother (also name unknown) would never see them again. I do have a very old piece of paper on which is written, 'To my little Alis, who I shall never see more, in hope that she will be a good girl.' I cannot find an Alice Morrish, an Alice or a Morrish daughter of the right age in the right area on any 1861 census. On the marriage certificate the father's name is blank. She appears on the 1871 census, aged 16 as a children's nurse. Place of birth – unknown! Subsequent census returns give a different place of birth each time. Now, how does one unravel that one?

My suggestion, as I said earlier, is to keep any tall stories or unsolved riddles along with your other family history data, and wait until the time is right to take them further. You could drive yourself crazy trying to validate them before you've constructed a firm family tree. And as you continue your search, you may well find that other clues turn up which will help you to track down their origin.

Having said that, do enjoy your family legends and stories! They are tantalising and will tempt you to go further. Some of them come from the dark recesses of family memory, and may not be so pleasant, whereas others gleam brightly, and have immediate appeal. Either way, both form the warp and weft of your family history, and should be treasured accordingly.

Crafting the stories from your family history requires good detective skills in teasing out vital clues and sifting truth from the stuff of legend. But it does also require us to develop a research technique, to grapple with large amounts of data and to know which sources can yield the relevant information. This is the next task on our journey.

CHAPTER FOUR

Researching the Past

Finding factual data is a vital ingredient in your search. Until you actually know who your ancestors were, and have some basic information about their lives, you can't build a picture of them or understand your own place in the chain of generations. In this chapter, we'll look at the specific types of record to search for, and where they can be found, while in the next chapter, you'll find advice on how to manage your research, organise your findings and build your tree. If you are about to construct your family tree for the very first time, these two chapters will give you all you need for your research; for more experienced family historians, taking stock of the research methods reviewed and reading the tips and experiences quoted from the survey respondents should freshen your perspective and bring new ideas into play.

A Toolkit for Research

What follows are general guidelines for conducting family history research, which you can use as a starting point, and as a foundation for further explorations as you gain more experience. After becoming familiar with these principal resources, you will be able to develop your own particular lines of enquiry, and shape them to your needs – according to the geographical area you're researching, for instance, and the nature of your specific ancestors. These guidelines have been kept quite broad so that they won't date too quickly (resources for family history are currently developing and expanding at a rapid rate, especially on the internet) and they should allow you to approach your enquiry with confidence.

Three essential tools needed to support your search are:

- access to the internet
- at least one good genealogy reference book
- family history magazines.

These will help to keep your research on track and up to date. Between them, they should act as signposts to all the avenues you might wish to follow.

Using the internet

I'm assuming that you'll be able to use the internet for much of your factual research. (If you don't have a computer of your own, you can use one in a library or archive.) These days, in terms of records and information, it doesn't make sense not to go online, unless you really have no choice. It won't condemn you to spending all your time in front of a computer screen, and in terms of the overall family history project, the hours spent online will at least be equalled by those engaged in research expeditions, visiting museums and archives, studying photos, talking to cousins and other rewarding 'live' activities. Among my survey respondents, only a handful have never used the internet, and these are usually long-term family historians of advancing years, whose knowledge has been hard-won through countless patient hours of searching by traditional methods, and who don't wish to learn new tricks at their stage of life. As for everyone else in the survey, even if they began their research offline, they have by now embraced the new technology and found it indispensable.

As Alison reports from Australia:

The World Wide Web has made research so much easier, particularly if you are living overseas. Some fifteen years after my initial research, I decided to look at archives on the internet. Suddenly, new discoveries were made, stories emerged and these elusive ancestors began to take on a more personal profile.

Angela backs this up:

> Today, I use the internet for most of my research. Apart from it being quicker, it is also very convenient not having to travel to repositories around the country. In the early days of my research there was, of course, no internet. Everything was done manually. It was very laborious, with every register or microfilm having to be searched page by page looking for references.

There are still professional genealogists around who maintain that the older pre-internet ways are best, and they may find that their tried-and-tested methods still work best for them. But this is not recommended for new entrants, or for those who have the choice to upgrade an ongoing quest by going online. Fran affirms that the internet is not only valuable for finding 'hard' data, but can round out your research in a remarkable way:

> Don't believe the people who denigrate the internet as a resource. It would be hard to overestimate the value of websites like Ancestry and Genes Reunited in putting me in touch with relatives, close and distant, who shared stories, photos and information. All sorts of fascinating stuff crops up, from old postcards to estate agents' details of an old family home.

RESEARCHING ON SITE – PROS AND CONS

While hearing from people who have worked online does certainly whet the appetite for a browse through the websites, we shouldn't lose sight entirely of the experience of researching in the physical rather than the virtual world. Angela reminds us of what we may be missing online, despite the internet's undoubted advantages.

> At Essex Record Office, I was researching my husband's paternal grandmother's family, and was handed the original registers for Debden going back to the 1500s. The fact of being allowed to hold and search through these old books was a great privilege. They had a smell all of their own that screamed 'age' at you, the sound of the pages – made of thick parchment – as you turned them and they crackled, the elaborate writing, sometimes faded, sometimes looking as if it had only been written yesterday, was a real joy to see. It was so time-consuming, but so rewarding to be able to touch the old parchment documents created hundreds of years previously.

I hope that you will be able to experience some of the pleasures of handling old documents directly, as visiting archives is certainly still to be recommended, as will be explained later in this chapter. Increasingly, though, items such as parish registers and old newspapers are kept locked away for their preservation, and since archives themselves now supply many of their records on microfilm, the contrast between researching online at home and in an archive may not be as distinct as it once was.

Sandra points out that for her it was not all antiquarian bliss, and that pilgrimages to record offices, in pre-computer days, could also be intensely frustrating. (All the UK records she mentions are now housed in other locations, such as the National Archives at Kew):

> It could be very disappointing to visit the census offices in Portugal Street in London. There were not very many seats and you just had to wait until one became available and then you had to trawl through whole microfilms hoping to find your family. Once I took ages doing this only to find 'Family away for the night' written in at the address. At St Catherine's House you needed strength to cope with the enormous books of birth, marriages and deaths in very crowded spaces. It was a little less hectic searching for wills at Somerset House.

Nowadays, both the national indexes for birth, marriage and death records and full UK census results can be searched online by name, date, place and other criteria. So it's not just the fact that you can choose to conduct research operations from your living room, but also that you can usually home in on your ancestors directly, by using a selective search and without having to go through every entry in the records.

NOT COMPUTER LITERATE?

If you are not able to work with a computer, you can visit archives, libraries and record offices to look at material yourself, either in original form or as microfiche. The reference books suggested below can act as guides to help direct your search. For places that you can't visit, or where the record is computerised, you may be able to get basic help from librarians or archivists in looking up essential records;

> sometimes local family history societies will offer a free or very inexpensive 'look-up' service in this respect. It's possible too to pay a professional genealogist to do the research for you, although this will obviously be charged at hourly market rates.

Reference books

Can you remember the date at which wills began to be recorded nationally in England, and do you know where they might be located before that date? How do Scottish records differ from English and Welsh ones? What is a Chelsea Pensioner, and how do you go about searching for one? Where do you look for an ancestor living in India or Australia? A good comprehensive book will help you track down the information you need.

However broad the internet is in its scope, you'll still find it useful to own at least one general but detailed reference book on family history which can set a trail that you can follow, and give you appropriate indicators in specific cases so that you can navigate to the right resources. Just thrashing blindly around on the internet for military records, for example, might prove to be an exhausting waste of time, whereas a reference book could give you an overview that would help you to understand the whole issue of where such information is stored for different branches of the armed forces, for different wars and for different periods of history.

A number of current titles for general family history guides are given in the Resources section (see pp. 249–50), and any mentioned below can be checked there.

TIPS FOR CHOOSING A FAMILY HISTORY REFERENCE BOOK

- Check for an up-to-date edition.
- Make sure that the book fully embraces the concept of internet research (even recent titles still occasionally

fulminate about the intrusion of computing into the sacrosanct world of genealogy, and refuse to recognise more than a handful of internet sources).

- Select the level of detail that suits you. Some books go into enormous detail (e.g. *Ancestral Trails*) whereas others (e.g. *Who Do You Think You Are? Encyclopedia of Genealogy*), provide clear general guidance on the main areas of research, such as probate, census, etc.
- Take your country location and/or that of your ancestors into account, and try to find a book which caters for this.
- Consider buying or borrowing (your library may have a selection) a more local or more specific reference book as well – one that relates to your ancestry by origin, religion or trade (e.g. Afro-Caribbean, Quakerism, or railway workers).
- Try to read and absorb at least some sections of the book ahead of your actual research sessions, so that you have a route map to hone your direction.
- Consider creating notes from the book, to act as instant checklists while you're researching.

Family history magazines

Each month, I look forward to the arrival of the family history magazines which I subscribe to. (In my case, these are *Who Do You Think You Are?* and *Your Family Tree*.) I browse them, reading some articles in detail, marking up items of interest, such as new websites to explore, and scanning the pages for mentions of locations or topics that might relate directly to my family. Over the five years or so that I've been researching, I've realised that these magazines are an invaluable resource. They are, in my view, the best way of keeping up with current developments in family history. They will also inform you of family history events, tell you what new databases have gone online, and contain unique, specialist articles covering specific regions, trades or ethnicity which could just propel you in the right direction for locating your ancestors. Free CDs may also be included, which can contain full texts of historic books, software trials and unusual local records.

Places and Resources to Search

Armed with your basic equipment package comprising internet access, reference books and family history magazines (an effective albeit odd-sounding trio) you now need to know what to look for and where.

It will be easiest, in fact, to cover the 'where' question first. Here are the primary resources for you to investigate:

- Websites
- Record offices, archives, museums and local-studies libraries
- Family history societies
- Cemeteries and churchyards
- Genealogy fairs
- Family history talks, classes and workshops

Websites

The number of genealogy websites is expanding all the time. Your family history magazines will help to keep you up to date with these, while the addresses for all the websites mentioned in this book are included in the Resources section (see pp. 255–6), along with a wide range of other tried-and-tested sites, listed by category.

The following are the main types of relevant website.

GENERAL FAMILY HISTORY

The major websites for general purpose use in the UK are Ancestry and Find My Past, which contain UK census records, birth, marriage and death indices, some military records, shipping lists and other types of specialist data. Their records are not confined to the UK, however, and, particularly in the case of Ancestry, include many from across the world, especially America and Canada. These websites are constantly updating their records, so if you stay with them for a year or more, you will see changes and new facilities appearing quite frequently.

For full and continued use of these, to search and view all original records, you will need to take out a subscription. Different deals are available, some with restricted geographical zones of use, for instance, and for different lengths of time, ranging from a few days to a year. You can also opt for a pay-per-view system. You may want to try out the site first on a short-term basis, and decide how much use you are likely to make of it before committing yourself, but if you are going to research regularly, the most economic sub-scription is for a whole year. Personally, I prefer to spread my search wide without worrying that precious credits are going to be used up on looking at the 'wrong' relatives; I've always found the full subscription good value, and the pay-per-view system expensive by comparison. You may also be able to get limited access through a library or archive.

There are other good general genealogy websites which you'll find listed in the Resources section, and by the time this book is pub-lished, there may well be more. Most offer the facility to build or upload your own tree, and to search for possible connections in other people's family trees too. You may also be able to email other members, but you can rest assured that your privacy is guarded, and no one will be able to access your personal data; the website will forward emails to and from you with no address visible.

Ancestry is probably the outright leader in the field, and has various useful extra features. If you use Family Tree Maker software, for instance, Ancestry links the names you enter to records on its website which might correspond to one of your ancestors; this is indicated by a green leaf appearing next to the person's name on your tree. It also has a publishing branch, My Canvas, which you can use to create a family history book (more on this in Chapter Nine).

Although I sometimes let my membership lapse for a little while, I've always come back to these two websites and have made really good use of my subscriptions. Ancestry has also acted as a point of contact for 'new' relatives (see Contact Websites section, below). Joining two major websites is something of a luxury, but each has data which the other doesn't, and this can help in finding elusive ancestors whose details may have been incorrectly logged on one of the websites, as I'll explain later in the chapter.

Another major resource is the Family Search website, run by the Church of Jesus Christ of Latter-day Saints. This is an extraordinary phenomenon – and it's also free! Its basis rests in the Mormon belief that those who have died can still be brought to Christ by performing the appropriate temple ritual, and that their lives and names should be recorded in a genealogical form for this purpose. Thus the Church's members have gone to enormous lengths to compile data from genealogical records throughout the world, and a good proportion of this information is available to view on their website. Many family historians make extensive use of their website, and you can, for instance, find some excellent transcripts from UK parish registers. Where family data is uploaded by individuals who use the site, though, it becomes less reliable, and most genealogists advise caution when taking information from it. Nevertheless, it's a remarkable resource, and can be a way to take a line of ancestry back a generation or two further than you thought possible.

CONTACT WEBSITES

These are primarily orientated to finding others who may be researching the same ancestry as you. Ancestry is useful in this respect, but the acknowledged leader is Genes Reunited. Although you can use some of its facilities for free, membership is cheap and allows you to contact other members directly, something you're almost certain to want to do. I have discovered several new cousins from different branches of the family this way. There is also Lost Cousins – a free and friendly website, with an excellent electronic newsletter, which is fast becoming popular, and where family members that you upload from the British census will automatically be matched with similar entries from other people's trees.

UMBRELLA WEBSITES

These act as a hub, listing other websites that allow you to find the kind of specialist or regional internet site that you need. Again, there are several of these, of which Cyndis List is the best known, and for the UK the very useful Genuki, covering British genealogy, local history and topography, with links to other records and sites.

ARCHIVE WEBSITES

These are becoming indispensable for specific countries, and the individual websites for National Archives in Britain, Ireland and Australia, and the National Library of Wales are primary resources for tracing records relevant to these areas.

SPECIALIST WEBSITES

Sites for Jewish ancestry, Commonwealth war graves and Staffordshire pottery workers are just some of the many specialist websites. Umbrella sites, plus leads in magazines and books, or just a Google search, may help you to locate them.

INTERNET FORUMS

I'll elaborate further on these in the next chapter, but these are a brilliant means of finding out what you need to know about a certain place or topic. Just post your question, then wait for the answers to roll in! RootsChat is among the best-known internet forums.

Record offices, archives, museums and local studies libraries

All these offer a rich repository of documents and records and/or artefacts. They are professionally run, often with very helpful staff who can assist with your enquiries. It's beyond the scope of this book to describe them all in detail, but here are some suggestions to help you get the best out of them:

- Visit specific English and Welsh county record offices for the particular region you're investigating.
- See if there is an online catalogue available before you go, so that you can select records to search for and perhaps order these in advance.
- Phone before a visit; some archives only have limited seating and a high demand for places.
- Prepare for your visit by sorting out your family tree and queries to research – it's all too easy to realise when you get there that you've forgotten a vital date that you need for your search.
- Bring ID for admission, be prepared to leave valuables in a locker, and have a pencil ready for making notes (pens are usually forbidden). You can probably take in a laptop, if you wish.
- Take your digital camera, as the chances are that you'll be allowed (sometimes for a small fee) to photograph records and other photographs – a time-saving way of logging information.
- Try specialist museums – e.g. mining, weaving or agricultural – for insight into your ancestors' lives.
- Don't be scared to ask for help. For the majority of archivists, this is what makes their job rewarding.
- Look at the books housed in local studies libraries which often include hard-to-find titles which can help you in your search; this is usually where local newspapers are archived too.
- Consider visiting one of the Family Search centres, run by the Church of Jesus Christ of Latter-day Saints (see mention of their website above, on which you can also locate a centre for your area). There you can check whatever databases and transcripts they have on hand for free, and order in any other microfilms kept by the Church at a modest charge, to cover the costs of posting these to the centre.

Family history societies

These are based regionally, and often have their own library, journal and a service to help members to connect to each other to share information of mutual interest. Some even have volunteers who will offer a 'look-up' service for little or no money, to assist other members who live at a distance. The membership fee is usually very modest. You can locate UK family history societies, and some in other countries too, at http://www.ffhs.org.uk.

Cemeteries and churchyards

A trawl through the relevant burial grounds for your ancestors, even without very specific aims in mind, can yield helpful information. I wandered through the graveyard of Llanbister Church in mid-Wales, armed only with the knowledge that the parents of my 3 x great-grandmother had come from there, and I quickly found a host of graves bearing the Kinsey name. I couldn't see anything directly relating to my ancestors, but it led me to the discovery that the Kinseys were very prominent in that area – a complex group of families whose members came from different levels of society.

Genealogy fairs

These offer opportunities to buy books, CDs and local records, to browse old maps and pamphlets and to talk to stallholders and, perhaps, visiting experts. The annual *Who Do You Think You Are?* family history show in London has become incredibly popular in the last few years, and you can book short consultations there with professional researchers for free, and talk to specialists visiting from official archives and record offices who may help you to solve a problem. There is usually a great atmosphere, too, so it's a place to renew your enthusiasm if you are flagging in your quest.

Family history talks, classes and workshops

These can also be a means of increasing your background knowledge, and learning about specific factors which may help you in a particular search. In the case of lectures, put your questions to the speaker before or after the event if they don't relate directly to the subject of the talk. I've had brief, but valuable, conversations this way which have given me useful leads and have also – importantly – helped me to eliminate false paths of enquiry.

What to Look For

Now let's move on to considering some of the primary records that you're likely to look for. These are listed below, and while most of the examples I give are taken from British sources, I've made the checklist as generic as possible, so that you should be able to search for the same type of records in different countries.

- Census entries
- Birth, marriage and death records (often referred to as BMD records)
- Wills and probate
- Military records
- Burial records
- Emigration/shipping lists
- School records
- Voters' lists (electoral rolls) and phone directories
- Old newspapers
- Property documents
- Local directories
- Trade or professional records
- Assorted legal and official documents
- Criminal records
- Historical maps
- Old photographs and postcards
- Books and pamphlets

This list is by no means exhaustive. Many genealogy websites and local archives will have special categories of their own which may be worth exploring. To pick up further ideas for investigation, it pays to scan the home pages and newsletters of the websites, and to browse the catalogue of any local archives that you're visiting.

Below, I provide a detailed guide on how to trace ancestors through the first three types of record, namely:

- census returns
- birth, marriage and death (BMD) records
- wills and probate.

This is followed by brief descriptions of the others.

Census returns

British censuses were recorded at ten-yearly intervals from 1841 to 1911 and, with the exception of the 1911 census, these are available to view free of charge on general genealogy websites. (Later ones are not yet accessible, being restricted under privacy laws.) They are often the first port of call for family historians, as they are easy to search online and give valuable details about individuals. Census entries give an address, and name every member of the household who was resident on that particular night, including babies, servants and visitors, along with their age (often approximate), address, status (married, single, etc.) and, from 1851, their occupation and place of birth. The 1911 census is even more elaborate, listing the number of children born to a married couple and the number of rooms in the house; it also includes the signature of the householder. At the moment, there are specific charges for accessing this particular census through its designated website at www.1911census.co.uk, or via pay per view or with an additional subscription at Find My Past. Note that Find My Past does not include Scottish census returns, but that Ancestry does have transcripts of these; as with other Scottish records, the main hub for them is at www.scotlandspeople.gov.uk (see also under birth, marriage and death records in the next section).

At the time of writing, Family Search has just put up most of the censuses for England and Wales on its website (free to view) and two censuses for Ireland have recently become available online without charge. These are the 1901 and 1911 censuses, and can be viewed through the National Archives of Ireland at www.census.nationalarchives.ie.

When searching the census online, you can usually do a general search of all available British censuses, or select a specific one – the 1881 census for Wales, for instance. The way you enter your search criteria and the range of records you choose to search inevitably has an effect on the results that you get. There is the facility to put in both the name of the person you are searching for and some details – date of birth, place they were living, etc. – but there is no firm rule as to what works best. Searching this type of record has a technique all of its own (see box for examples). The amount of information you give to define your search may need to be expanded or reduced to pinpoint the person or family you're looking for.

SEARCHING AN ONLINE CENSUS

Here are two extreme examples of ancestors from my own family tree – John Brown and Selina Gristwood – for whom I tested a search for on two different websites: Ancestry and Find My Past.

John Brown

If I merely enter 'John Brown' into the search box, without choosing a specific census, or listing his date of birth or indeed any other information, this brings up a veritable flood of results (in the case of the Find My Past, it's 72,000, while with Ancestry, it's over a million – and that's just their UK and Ireland records). Both websites will also be flexible to a certain degree with the search, and may include J. Brown, John Browne, and even wider variations, such as simply Brown with any other forename. In answer to my search, Ancestry's site says plaintively, but quite correctly, 'A little more information will give you better results.' It recommends: 'Try adding a county, province or country ... Try adding a birth or death date; even a guess might help.' So if you have a common name to look for, you will certainly need to restrict your search criteria, which, in fact, means extending the amount of detail that you offer to define the person you're looking for.

Selina Gristwood

If, on the other hand, I enter the unusual name of 'Selina Gristwood', and opt for the 1871 census, then Ancestry offers me just one exactly matching result for that name, the right one for Selina (an ancestor by marriage) when she was eight months old. Obviously, I need a little more information to be sure that this is indeed 'my' Selina, but in this case I happen to know that the place of residence (Windsor) is correct, and that some of the other members in the household tally with her family. So there is no problem in identifying her.

Find My Past, however, can't come up with anything under this name. Why so? It turns out that on this particular census, her name is spelled as 'Selena'. Ancestry has made allowances for this variation, and has automatically provided me with this result in response to my request for 'Selina'. If I now enter that particular spelling to Find My Past, or else tick the box on its search form which authorises it to include name variants, the entry pops up.

So you can see how sometimes it doesn't pay to enter every detail that you know about your ancestor, since it may be recorded differently on the census (their place of birth might be listed as the local town rather than the specific village, for instance), and by asking for an exact search, he or she may slip through the net.

With practice, you'll discover what works best both on different websites and with the type of data that you have. The census image was originally written out by an enumerator, or local official, and has been transcribed for a website database, often by a volunteer. Both listings are fallible, so you may need to try another website, or search in a broader way if you really get stuck. Some of my ancestors were described as born in Ireland, for instance, because the person who transcribed for this website didn't realise that the Kerry they referred to as their birthplace was a little village in the middle of Wales!

Most of the time, though, the census offers a wonderful opportunity to locate families and individuals from your ancestry, as it can both fill in essential information and reveal fascinating details about their lives. A good starting point is to take one of your more recent ancestors, but one who was born long enough ago to appear on the 1901 or 1911 census. I've already mentioned that I chose my maternal grandfather as my very first example, and was surprised to find that he was at the time training to be a grocer, since his profession later became that of Baptist minister. (The phrase Baptist minister may seem to crop up rather often in this book, and I should explain that it's because there were three generations of them in my family – Edward Owen, followed by David Richards Owen and, finally, Bernard, my grandfather; see Appendix I, p. 244.) As Bernard was a teenager living at home at the time, I was also able to see him in context with some of his brothers and sisters, noting the trades that they were working in – grocery and drapery predominantly. Later I was able to tie this into the pattern created by his mother's family, who had built up clothing and dairy businesses, and for whom shopkeeping was a way of life.

From the details given about Bernard's father and mother in the census, I was able to take extra information about their ages and places of birth to pad out my search criteria, finding them then in the preceding censuses, and going even further back to discover their respective parents and grandparents. In this way, on Bernard's father's side, I traced four generations of the Owen side of the family through the census, right back to my 3 x great-grandparents, who were born in the eighteenth century. From this example, it's apparent how the seventy years of censuses at our disposal in Britain offer a golden opportunity to build a family tree, and to get to know the families which compose it.

Birth, marriage and death (BMD) records

Until 1837, there was no official centralised registration in Britain, and life events were recorded mainly in parish registers, if at all. Even after the 1837 watershed, not everything made its way into the formal records until 1875, so a search after 1837 but before 1875 isn't completely guaranteed to be successful.

BEFORE 1837

As a general rule, for pre-1837 births, marriages and deaths you will need to search local parish registers. In this case, it is the baptism rather than the birth that is recorded, so keep in mind that your ancestor might have been anything from a few days to a few years old when he or she was baptised. If your ancestors were nonconformist, they may still have used the parish church for these rites of passage (at times, the law insisted on this), or there may be records surviving from their own chapels and churches. Usually, though, these nonconformist records are patchy and may be hard to trace, or be restricted in access.

Contents of specific parish and nonconformist records are increasingly being digitised and made available online, but you will need to check individual websites or Google the parish itself to find what is available. They may also be bought as booklets or CDs, which have often been transcribed by family history societies. A very good way of checking if a particular UK parish register is available to purchase is by visiting www.parishchest.com. You can then usually order it online directly. Ian points out how useful they have been to him:

> As a large number of my paternal ancestors were from Oxfordshire, the local FHS society have produced a series of reasonably priced CDs of parish register transcripts which

has saved an awful lot of mileage, again providing the means to search when I have a spare half-hour, and providing the ability to return to the subject easily.

Most old English and Welsh parish registers, apart from the current ones in use, have been removed from the church in question to an archive, usually a county record office. In Scotland, they are housed centrally at the General Record Office. In a record office, you will generally be given a microfilm or microfiche to view rather than being able to handle the original parish register, since they are precious and irreplaceable. There is also a system of recording known as 'Bishop's Transcripts', the full listings of baptisms, marriages and funerals which were turned in to the diocesan office every year (in theory), and if these survive for your parish, they are well worth consulting if the register isn't accessible, or if portions of the register have been lost or names missed out (it happens). They may not contain all the accompanying details listed in the parish register though, where, for instance, the father's occupation may also be recorded along with his child's baptism.

Parish registers have been kept in England and Wales since 1538, and Bishop's Transcripts since 1598, and the survival rate overall for these is good, giving genealogists a chance to trawl through several hundred years' worth of life events for a family whose parish is known. Scottish parish records began in 1553, but fewer have survived from the earlier years.

AFTER 1837

Once civil registration began on a national scale, records were kept in a more reliable form by each locally appointed registrar, a system still in place today, as all of us know who have gone to the register office to record a birth or death, or to celebrate a marriage. Official members of the clergy are authorised to issue their own certificates, and, along with those from the local register office, these are kept in a central archive by the Registrar General.

You can search BMD records online in family history websites, and once you've located the entry you need, along with its registration area and reference number, you can order copies of certificates online from the General Register Office if you wish. It's much cheaper to do this via their own website, www.gro.gov.uk/gro/content/certificates, than through other family history websites. You can also request a certificate from the relevant local register office, which may sometimes speed up the process, or allow you to get help finding an elusive record.

It can be difficult in any case to be certain that you're ordering the right certificate, as the details given in the index are scanty; a common name such as 'John Brown' (see p. 74) could throw up a number of possible candidates in the birth records, for instance, even when you know the date and place of birth. Most family history researchers are resigned to spending money at some point on the wrong certificates, in order to find the right ones by a process of elimination.

INFORMATION ON BMD CERTIFICATES

BMD certificates give specific extra information. For England and Wales, the parents' names and the mother's maiden name are listed on a birth certificate, while on a marriage certificate you will find the groom's occupation, along with the names of the fathers of both bride and groom, and on a death certificate there is the address at the time of a death (which could be a hospital), along with the cause of death.

REGISTRATION IN SCOTLAND AND NORTHERN IRELAND

Scottish registration follows its own procedures, which began in 1855, and its records are known as Statutory Registers. These are held alongside parish records in the General Register Office of Scotland, located in Edinburgh, which is very convenient for researchers who can visit in person. Otherwise, the chief website for Scottish records is www.scotlandspeople.gov.uk, a reasonably priced and very well-organised online database. Scottish certificates contain even more detail, and marriage certificates list occupations of bride and groom, and the maiden names of their mothers, which is a real boost to tracing the family back further.

In Northern Ireland, BMD certificates can be ordered from http://www.nidirect.gov.uk/gro.

DO YOU NEED FULL SETS OF BMD CERTIFICATES?

Some people like to collect every certificate relating to a direct-line ancestor, while others are more selective, buying certificates chiefly to find out new information or to confirm details of their ancestors. My own approach is mainly the second one, unless I feel a particular emotional connection with an ancestor, and want to have a firmer memento of his or her existence. Collecting full sets of certificates seems to me to miss the point; like an obsession with getting every date and name in place, it can cause one to miss out on the human stories and the vital spirit of ancestry. Getting your facts accurate is one thing, but glorying only in hard data is quite another. Most of the certificates that I've purchased over the years actually mean something to me, and the rest were generally bought to prove a connection. Oh yes, and there were a few – but not too many – mistaken ones too. I've generally found that if I'm patient, and wait till I'm at the right point in my research to trace a birth, marriage or death of a particular ancestor, I can find the record without too much trouble.

Wills and probate

A will can give fresh and unexpected information, telling you about family members and the possessions of the deceased, as well as giving intriguing clues to the character of your ancestor. However, finding a will is a strangely archaic procedure. I puzzled over a number of descriptions of how to do it in family history books and journals, before deciding that the only way to find my way through the maze was to try it out for myself. I soon discovered that this involves an engagement with the courts of Britain, designed to protect the rights of its citizens and uphold justice, rather than to present a user-friendly interface. It is not straightforward, nor comparable with other avenues of research such as archives and record offices, and it isn't usually the first one to try out when you begin exploring your family history. But I do recommend investigating it when you are ready.

STRANGE TIDINGS AND CURIOUS BEQUESTS

Wills can act as a spur to further research, especially as they sometimes raise more questions than they can answer. One will that I
discovered states that Daniel Brown, my 3 x great-grandfather who was
a watchmaker from Coventry, 'thereby forgives his son James his
debts'. James is my 2 x great-grandfather, and this has left me curious.
Why had James, a silk dyer, needed to borrow money? Was he strug-
gling to make a living, or did he have extravagant habits that he
couldn't support? As yet, I don't know the answers, but the questions
encourage me to keep digging to see if I can find out more.

Wills also shed light on rather intimate and sometimes quite curious aspects of family life. Another 2 x great-grandfather, Charles
Reynolds of Hunmanby in Yorkshire, made elaborate arrangements for
the passing on of his piano to two of his daughters, who were, in fact,
stepsisters. I learned from this that they were living together:

> I direct my piano shall remain in the joint possession of my
> daughters Mary Stephenson Reynolds and Emily Sethering-
> ton Reynolds so long as they shall remain unmarried and
> live together but in case they shall cease to live together then
> it shall remain in possession of the oldest of my said two
> daughters until one of my said two daughters shall marry.
> Then I bequeath my said piano to my daughter who shall be
> unmarried absolutely.

It's clear that he wanted there to be no argument in the matter – and
what a sad vision it conjures up, of the last unmarried daughter in sole
and lonely possession of the piano. However, I'm not sure that either
of them ever married, so perhaps they stuck together as living compan-
ions for the sake of the piano!

I was also determined to see the will of a maiden great-aunt who
I had never really known, but who had left me a significant inheritance when I was a child. When I read the will, I was touched by the
way it revealed her thoughtfulness and kindness to others: her gramo-
phone and wireless left to a Home for the Blind, and all residual
income to the Great Ormond Street Hospital for Children. One of the

chief delights about a will is that you never know just what it may contain, and where that might lead you, I discovered that a great-uncle had requested two commemorative benches to be placed on hills where he loved to walk; this gives me an excuse to visit the hills sometime soon, and see if they are indeed there.

FINDING A WILL: PRE-1858

So how do you go about finding a will in the UK? First of all, bear in mind that a large proportion of the population never made a will at all. It is always worth having a look though, and sometimes one of your ancestors will surprise you with the fact that he or she did make one.

As with the BMD registration, centralised records started at a relatively late date, in this case 1858, the year when the Principal Probate Registry was established in London. If a will was made before 1858, it had to be 'proved' through one of the ecclesiastical courts, and there is no overall record of who made a will and where, or indeed if it has survived at all. Some copies moulder away in solicitors' vaults for decades, and are finally turned out, either to be thrown away, to be turned into parchment lampshades (fashionable in the 1940s) or perhaps sold at a flea market. I have bought a couple of wills this way, not related to my own family, but just for the pleasure of reading them and researching the original testator a little further.

Perhaps you may be lucky, and for this an online search of archives can yield results. The National Archives has a helpful guide to starting your search for a pre-1858 will at www.nationalarchives. gov.uk/records/research-guides/wills-and-probate-records.htm, and their website can also be searched by name, which will both show you wills in their own archives and give you a link to others held elsewhere, for instance in county archives, if they have been catalogued digitally. This is how I found Daniel Brown's will (see p. 81) and the local record office was then happy to make a copy and send it to me for a small fee. Some wills are even available in digital format and can be downloaded for a modest charge.

If your ancestor is Welsh, the prospects are brighter, since in 2009 the National Library of Wales digitised over 90,000 pre-1858 wills, all of which can now be searched for online and read in full at no charge.

All in all, it's a fishing trip to find an early will, and best to assume it's a matter of luck as to whether or not you will get a result. Any comprehensive genealogy reference book should give you further details of the complexities of will retrieval from this period.

FINDING A WILL: POST-1858

After 1858, all wills were proved through the national probate registry system. This also includes so-called 'letters of administration' – records of the administration process to liquidate an estate where the person died without leaving a will. Although wills, like BMD records, were registered at regional offices, every will does end up listed on the National Probate Calendar, which can be searched.

But before you breathe a sigh of relief, I quote from the official guide to the registry: 'The only place where there is a complete set of calendars available for public inspection is First Avenue House in London.' You may indeed view incomplete sets at eleven other local probate offices, or on microfiche at many county archives, but they run out at a certain date. Up until recently, there was nothing online either, so for a full search, you will either need to visit the London office in person, or instigate a search by post. However, help may now be at hand, since the Ancestry website has recently uploaded details of the Probate Calendar from 1861 to1941, which can be searched by name as well as by year, even though it doesn't cover the entire time span of the Calendar. Family historians have welcomed this new facility with open arms, and report that it has improved their search enormously.

Following the official advice further, we learn with dismay that a postal search can only be initiated through a special unit of the York Probate Division, and although a link for downloading an application form is included in the web page given on the next page, no instructions are accepted by phone, and there is no online service for ordering wills. As a recent post from Sylvia on the 'Who Do You Think You Are?' family history forum says: 'The service is not easily accessible to people residing out of the UK ... sadly HM Courts is still in the dark ages with regard to ordering and payment for probate copies.'

It was after this revelation that I decided to make the trip myself, to the London Probate Office at First Avenue House in Holborn, and to treat it as part of the rich tapestry of family history experience, rather than as a chore. And so it turned out to be. Will-making is after all a solemn business, and the Dickensian atmosphere and hushed tones did make an impression, reminding me of the transience of the lives now reduced to an inventory of possessions, and also instilling a certain gratitude for a national registry that records and guards these precious reminders of its citizens' lives. Wills may also, of course, be the gateway to a fortune, so there are good reasons to validate and protect them. The process of searching out wills, some of them belonging to relatives who I had known and loved, proved more moving than I expected, and I had moments of hesitation as to whether I should pick and pry into their lives in this way. It was a salutary lesson in discovering that it is sometimes the driest, dustiest repositories where you will be most touched and even unnerved by investigating your ancestry. But with my aim in mind, and a firm respect for those who had passed away, I located and ordered the wills that I needed.

The process itself is relatively simple. The calendars are kept in large printed volumes, and you can pick out the one you want by date for the year and alphabetically for the surname you require. The entry itself in the calendar gives very useful information about your ancestor, including their full name and final address, the date of death, the value of their estate and the person to whom probate was granted. Often, the occupation of the deceased is given too. From this, it's but a short step to order a copy: simply fill in the application form and hand it, with the volume itself, to a member of the counter staff for checking. There is a small flat fee and a choice of a one-hour service, a five-day collection service or a postal one of seven working days. You can also order a copy of a will from a local probate office if you can find it listed in the calendar kept there, or if you already know the full details.

Scotland, Northern Ireland and Eire have their own probate registry offices and systems. For details of these, the regional ones in England and Wales, and a general guide to getting hold of copies of wills, see www.hmcourts-service.gov.uk/cms/1226.htm.

TIPS FOR SEARCHING FOR A WILL

- If you plan to visit the London Probate Office, it may be worth waiting until you have a complete list of ancestors whose names you'd like to check, since this can be done quickly once you're there, and you can order all the wills on the spot.
- Search the Calendar beyond the year of death, since it can often take a year or two for the will to be proved.
- Remember to search by the married name of a female ancestor – you will be used to thinking of her by her maiden name in terms of family history.
- Check out the internet links above to fill in the detail of the probate system.
- For pre-1858 wills, try a general internet search, or through the National Archives website – you may be lucky and locate a will this way.

Other records and documents

MILITARY RECORDS

These are among those most eagerly sought by family historians, and, as suggested earlier, you may need to turn to a reference book for detailed specialist advice as to what to look for, and where. It will depend upon which branch of the armed forces your ancestor served in, and in what war or at which period. Among the wealth of documents available are medal rolls, service records, pension entitlements and regimental diaries.

By way of example, after an intermittent search over several years for my own ancestor Edward Owens, who served in the Napoleonic Wars, I was able find a variety of details of his service, both about him specifically and about his regiments. These included his exact postings, a physical description of him, records of his admission to the Chelsea Pensioners, his inclusion on the Corunna Medal Roll, letters to the general in charge of his regiment and the regimental 'returns' which gave precise details of where his battalion was stationed. This involved two visits to the National Archives at Kew and one to the National Army Museum in London. I also contacted the regimental museum and had wonderful help from a volunteer there, who checked just about every other detail available. Given that Edward Owens joined the army over two hundred years ago, and was a humble foot soldier rather than an officer, this is a remarkably full record. It does indicate, however, that each ancestor will present a different challenge, and you will need to plot a course to trace their service and find all the supporting information available. As someone with no great interest in military matters, I found this challenging, but not impossible, and the more I grappled with the task, the more I enjoyed it. It does take time though and it may not be possible to rush uncovering the full story of a military ancestor.

If you subscribe to a general family history website, such as Ancestry, you will find scope for searching military records there. It's worth reading any information the website offers, to understand what is and what is not included, and to use other sources to fill out the story. Again, the National Archives has an excellent A–Z list of research guides, which includes those on specific aspects of military history; click on any one of these titles to see a comprehensive list of the records they hold on this theme, with explanatory notes.

If you have ANZAC ancestors who fought for Australia or New Zealand in the First World War, you may be able to find their full records online at the National Archives of Australia (http://recordsearch.naa.gov.au), all viewable for free. I discovered two of my great-uncles this way – they had emigrated from England in 1913, only to find themselves signing on for service there and sailing back to Europe with their Australian fellow soldiers. For Albert Ewart Owen, who was killed in France, the records run to thirty-five pages, and contain a poignant list of the items in his possession when he died, including his mother's diamond ring, and a book of Longfellow's poems.

BURIAL RECORDS

As distinct from death certificates, burial records are listings of where and when people are buried in a particular cemetery or churchyard.

You may find some of those that are relevant to you online, or you may need to contact the particular church or the local council to determine whether a particular ancestor is buried there, and to pinpoint the exact plot. Also check what family history suppliers have to offer at www.parishchest.com. Transcribed records also include memorial inscriptions, or MIs, as they are known.

EMIGRATION/SHIPPING LISTS

Available at certain family history websites, these cover passengers leaving or arriving at certain ports over particular periods of time, including the main British and American ports, plus that of Ellis Island in New York, and Canadian and Australian ports. Although they may not always be comprehensive, and the level of detail therein varies, these records can be an excellent resource for pinning down your ancestors' departure and arrival dates. I have discovered from these exactly when my great-grandfather emigrated to America, as well as the ship he and his new wife sailed on, and the port they left from (Bristol). I also had the surprise of seeing his brother's name alongside theirs in the passenger list. You can check the ships your ancestors sailed in through further links, or via a general internet search, and sometimes see photographs of these as well. I traced their vessel, the *Arragon*, discovering both an oil painting of it, and reports which revealed it to be a terrifyingly unseaworthy vessel that finally ran aground on a rock, a few short years after David, Mary and John had arrived safely in New York.

As for my Great-Aunt Florence, who left the UK for South Africa to get married, I found that Florence's brother Tom and his wife accompanied her on the outward voyage, and I have managed to trace all her subsequent visits back to the family in the UK over the next thirty years. This has been helpful in tying in other family dates and photos – and also revealing how little she travelled with her husband while he was still alive!

Note: the records listed below are, broadly speaking, to be found at county record offices and local studies libraries; you may also find some of them online through a general family history website, or via a Google name or place search.

SCHOOL RECORDS

These include admission records and log books. These may have restricted access, however, as some record offices keep them 'closed' for one hundred years, so you'll need to check out the availability of specific examples. In these chronicles of school life, you may find lively details of the day-to-day running of the school, including mentions of naughty pupils, perhaps with your ancestor among them.

VOTERS' LISTS (ELECTORAL ROLLS) AND PHONE DIRECTORIES

These are particularly useful for trying to trace living relatives or descendants who may be listed for recent years.

OLD NEWSPAPERS

Either local or national newspapers can be searched for details of your ancestors' doings. If you are looking at original or microfiche copies without the resource of an index, get as precise a date as you can for your search – for an obituary or accident, for example – otherwise it will be very time-consuming to read through many editions. Online newspaper databases are usually fully searchable by name or keyword, though they may not be totally reliable and consistent in this respect (see Resources section, p. 260).

PROPERTY DOCUMENTS

These abound in archives, and some can also be traced or even read in full online. Many online archive catalogues include a précis of each document, which can sometimes tell you all you need to know without the necessity to see the full set of deeds or mortgage transfer. In general, they help you to see what kind of property your ancestor was living in, whether as tenant or owner, and details as to its garden or land, and to where it stood among neighbouring properties.

LOCAL DIRECTORIES

These are an excellent source of information about residents and tradespeople, especially in the nineteenth and early twentieth centuries. If your family ran a business, you may be able to find out precisely when it was set up and how long it lasted, as the directories were issued at regular intervals.

TRADE OR PROFESSIONAL RECORDS

These are a wide field, and you may need a separate guide to tracing any which survive for the particular trade you're interested in. There are records for factories, postal workers, merchant seamen and so on – some official, some from private companies and some as local collections. Check any general family history websites to see what they have on offer, keep an eye on family history magazines for clues and look in local archives for regional trades, for which they may have special records.

ASSORTED LEGAL AND OFFICIAL DOCUMENTS

These include apprenticeship records, binding over young men and women – often children, in fact – to learn a trade or craft. These can usually be found in local record offices, and are often well indexed by name; you can also look for marriage bonds (an alternative way of securing a marriage licence, as opposed to banns of marriage) and legal disputes. You may also find parish relief and workhouse records relevant to families who had fallen on hard times.

CRIMINAL RECORDS

These may be found in various of the resources listed, such as newspaper databases (as accounts of court cases), among legal records and on some special websites (for example, www.blacksheepindex.co.uk). Proceedings of the Old Bailey in London from 1674 to 1913 are now fully available to search and view free online at www.oldbaileyonline.org.

Simply by using the family surname, I discovered through a newspaper search a philandering ancestor, and was able to read very full accounts of his appearance in court and his attempts to wriggle out of responsibility for seducing a young neighbour and getting her pregnant; her mother was now suing him for loss of her daughter's services. His defence was that the mother kept a brothel, and that both the girl and her sister were frequently ready and eager for an intimate encounter!

Bear in mind that although the passing of time can make this kind of discovery less shocking, and that it can even be entertaining in a way (Virginia found a bent customs officer in her family tree, soliciting bribes of wine), some very unpleasant crimes can come to light; Sheila M. unearthed an ancestress who was hung for poisoning a child, for instance. And you may also be disturbed by the harsh punishment meted out for minor crimes committed by the poor, such as transportation to Australia for stealing a coat, or a hungry child being locked up for taking food.

HISTORICAL MAPS

These are useful for checking how a village or street layout looked at a certain period. Specialist maps, such as local tithe or enclosure maps, may help you to confirm more precisely where an ancestor lived, especially if you already have the name of their abode from another record.

OLD PHOTOGRAPHS AND POSTCARDS

While these may not show your ancestors (though they might, if you're lucky), they can be a valuable source of information about the places they lived in, and the occupations they carried out. I've studied photographs of Victorian grocers' shops to see how my own ancestors might have gone about their business, since several of them were in this trade, and I did, in fact, find an old postcard showing one of their shops, with the family name painted on the end wall of the street in Windsor where they traded.

BOOKS AND PAMPHLETS

These can provide you with excellent background information and include local guides to villages and churches, books on social history, military campaigns, trades and professions, costume, food and furniture in previous centuries, folklore, old architecture and other aspects of the life and times of the family you're researching. Never pass up the chance to buy a locally published edition when you're visiting an ancestral area or a specific museum, library or archive; many minor works by local historians are little mines of information that you cannot easily find elsewhere. Even with the wonders of internet ordering, such books or pamphlets often go out of print quickly, or are not available beyond a few local outlets. Treasured examples among my own collection include a study of the village of Hemyock in Devon, a booklet on the ribbon-weaving trade in the Coventry area and an account of the nineteenth-century famine in the town of Bedworth.

TOP TIPS FOR SEARCHING

- 'Google your family names once a year in case something new has turned up.' Josie
- Remember that you can switch to an 'image only' view when you search online – useful if you're looking for pictures and photos. The same goes for maps.
- 'Sometimes the tiniest scrap of information may come in useful later. Keep a note of anything possible and refer to it from time to time.' Margaret
- 'Do not take literally everything you read – dates, names, etc. Remember all the information has been input by a human being and therefore is not guaranteed to be accurate.' Valerie
- 'I always advise people to double-check and cross-reference all their facts.' Maggi
- Allow a wide variation when searching for names, since spelling wasn't always consistent.
- 'When looking at the census returns, look at previous and following pages. You might find close family living near by.' Elaine
- 'My approach to research, and which I would recommend, is simply to be as thorough as possible in exploring every source, and not giving up.' Virginia

- 'Once you have found a 'root' place (where your ancestors have lived for generations), then join the local family history society, as you will be able to tap into lots of local knowledge this way.' Melanie
- If you have no luck searching a specific parish register for a family whose location you know, try adjacent parishes. The official book which lists these is *The Phillimore Atlas and Index of Parish Registers* – a pricey tome, but copies are held in most reference libraries and record offices, and staff will often give you a photocopy of the page with the relevant map on it.
- 'If a topic comes up, Google it to find out more.' Sheila M. G. (This could relate to any detail of your ancestor's life or to national events which affected the family.)

CHAPTER FIVE

Managing Your Research

As you begin to amass data about your ancestors, you will need to devise strategies for managing it. Although this might sound dull, organising your material can, in fact, be a satisfying and meaningful experience in its own right, especially where building the family tree is concerned. We'll take a look at this first; then later in the chapter we are going to consider ways in which you can seek help from others to further your research, and strategies you can adopt to keep it on track as well as fresh and interesting in your mind.

Building Your Family Tree

The family tree stands at the heart of family history research, and as it grows, you'll feel a pride in your accomplishment at adding to it, and integrating all the elements it contains. It is a symbol of life and, in particular, the life of your family and of your ancestors. Taking pleasure in the form of your tree and the sense of lineage that it communicates is an important element of family history itself. So, right from the start, think about how you would like to portray the tree. Your approach may well change as your project grows, but at each stage, choose a method of presenting your tree which suits the data you have and the way you'd like to see it displayed.

The family tree on paper

At the start, you may find it easiest just to write down the names of your ancestors on paper, to get a rough idea of how the generations shape up. Using paper and pen or pencil is no bad thing in the initial stages, as it helps to train your memory and to perceive the growing shape of the family. It doesn't matter at all if the results are somewhat scrappy and untidy.

In practical terms, you can use the normal method of vertical lines to represent descent from one generation to the next and horizontal ones to show siblings and spouses. An equals sign (=) is the standard way of representing a marriage, when placed between the relevant pair of names.

DRAWING YOUR FIRST FAMILY TREE: MARKING THE MOMENT

When you draw out your family tree for the first time, it's a significant stage in acknowledging your lineage. Here's a suggestion for marking the moment:

- Wait for a quiet half-hour, when you are unlikely to be disturbed, and sit down at a table or desk with several sheets of blank paper and pen and pencil. You can also use coloured markers, if you like.
- Close your eyes for a moment and conjure up an impression of the ancestors surrounding you, from different times and generations. Let it be a rather fuzzy impression, without too much definition.
- Now affirm your sense of yourself at the centre of this, while still maintaining the ancestral sphere around you. Experience this and let it settle for a couple of minutes.
- Open your eyes, and write your name towards the bottom of the page, in the centre. Put a box or draw an oval around it, if you like.
- Add your parents' names above your own; then, using the lines as suggested above (vertical for descent, horizontal for the same generation, and = for marriages), connect them to

yourself and to each other, adding in any siblings that you have, your grandparents, aunts and uncles, great-grandparents, and, if you have space, great-aunts and great-uncles (brothers and sisters of your grandparents).

• Give yourself plenty of space on the page, but don't worry about any of this being too meticulous; you can use slanting lines if it helps, and if you make a mistake, overwrite it and keep going if you can. You can do a fair copy later. If you don't know the name of a particular relative, add a defining label, e.g. 'maternal grandmother'.

• Now take a look at your first and fundamental family tree; reflect on its branches, the sense of descent through the few generations that you've recorded. Enjoy the moment! And don't throw this version away; keep it as a memento of your journey into family history.

You may decide to go on using paper diagrams of your family tree during the early stages of your research. It's also a good way to sketch out single branches of the family when you first identify them. And you can spice up any rough charts with notes. Here's a brief example: it comes from three pages of handwritten notes which fell out of a second-hand book on genealogy that I bought from a charity shop. The relationships between family members are indicated by simply drawn lines.

> Uncle Ted + May adopted Joan (daughter of Joan died child-birth)
>
> Aunty May in service to judge. Grandad had lied about age – got judge to get him out. Also had bad knees to get discharged.

And so on, through various scrawled mini-trees, notes, dates and addresses. Maybe these are the jottings of someone who was talking to an elderly relative, or perhaps they were the first fruits of research.

Although they are not a thing of beauty, I find them intriguing and full of life, even though this family history is, strictly speaking, none of my business!

NOTE ON NOTES AND SKETCHES

Do keep any early notes, diagrams and jottings that you make, however rough they look. They are a part of the record of your own journey through family history, and may also contain snippets of information that you can return to later. Everything handwritten or hand-drawn in this way also has its own qualities which say something about the mood and energy of the person who created it. For your own personal archive, returning to look at early notes and trees will remind you of the way you set out on your quest, and will probably give you a strong sense of how the journey has developed since then. And it's good to include them in papers that you intend to pass on to the next generation. I've found my uncle's notes inspiring in that respect.

Family-tree software

You will probably find that you want to create a computerised version of your family tree quite soon after you begin researching. There are some excellent software programmes on the market, which are regularly updated. Leaders in the field are Family Tree Maker, Family Historian and Roots Magic. There are also free software tree-makers, which you can track down online, or via a family history magazine bulletin. Alternatively, if you sign up to a website such as Ancestry or Genes Reunited, you can choose to build your tree directly on to the site. However, it's actually easier and more secure to create your tree independently of a website; you can upload it very easily later, since nearly all computer-generated family trees can be exported in the universally recognised 'gedcom' format.

It can be tempting to buy a cheaper, outdated edition of a software programme, but when I tried this several years ago, I found it awkward to use and poor in layout. Once I had upgraded, however, I found the software (in this case Family Tree Maker) was a joy to use, and had far more aesthetic appeal. Buying a current version need not cost a fortune though, if you look out for special offers.

A good tree-maker will do all the hard work for you of arranging the layout, and configuring the lines of descent and cross-relations throughout the tree. There are many extras and features on all contemporary programmes; for instance, mine allows me to display my tree in varying layouts, such as 'fan', 'bowtie' and 'hourglass'. And it tells me what the exact relationship is between any other person in the tree and myself as 'home person', from 'second cousin two-times removed' to '4th great-grandfather'.

On my software, as with all the major family-tree programmes, you can upload photographs, write notes about a person and list data about various features of their lives – for example, residence, military service, education and so on. It's possible to record almost all the details that you know about your ancestors on your computer-generated tree. However, if you opt for this approach, be extra careful to save copies, and/or keep paper records too.

You can also select visually appealing backgrounds and generally have fun with the design element, along with 'publishing' reports on a selected individual or a family branch. This is particularly useful, since once your tree grows large, as it will do almost inevitably, it becomes pointless to try and print out the whole map, and it is much more practical to choose a branch or set of notes for which to create a hard copy.

Growing your tree – but how far?

Once your tree starts to grow, the numbers of relatives included on it may rise to several hundred quite quickly – mine now contains 957 names, and that's mostly just on my mother's side! So where do you stop? Everyone has their own criteria, but the following points and suggestions may help you to decide:

- Keep the number of names on the tree overall in proportion to the number of ancestors who you want to record in extra detail. In order to highlight them, you will need to include other names too, to fill in the family lines, and as a rough guide, I suggest entering about twice as many ancestors who will simply appear as names and dates as those who are more significant to you. I have, at present, about six hundred ancestors who are just 'leaves on the tree', and around three hundred for whom I have recorded more personal information. This works well for me, but test it out and see how you find it.

- Restrict the number of siblings that you enter further back than your great-grandparents' generation, otherwise this can grow a tree too far across its lateral branches, especially in an era when families tended to have many children.

- If you have personal contact with cousins beyond your own immediate line (e.g. third or fourth cousins), you may wish to include their branches so that you can see the connection with your own.

- The same goes for a more distant ancestor who is particularly colourful or interesting.

- Think how far you would like your tree to include non-blood relatives. While including spouses of your blood-line ancestors is a good thing, do you want to have their family trees included as well? I often put the parents, and sometimes the siblings, of a person who has married into the family, to get a better picture of them as an individual, but I am now ruthless about excluding any further relatives.

- You are also likely to want to put in descendants too, although these may have to be restricted once you're on to the grandchildren of your third cousins! But it will mean a lot to your own children, nephews, nieces and so on, if you include them and their children too.

- Be very wary of data on other people's trees, especially those posted on the internet (for instance, on the IGI index of Family Search or on Ancestry). Sometimes, they are completely unreliable, or perpetuate mistakes they've copied from other trees.
- Don't merge your tree with anyone else's (i.e. upload all the data from it automatically) unless you are absolutely sure that this is what you want to do. There may be mistakes that can trip you up, or very distant relatives (or those who are not even related to you) which will clutter up your tree. Merges can be difficult to undo, especially once you've added more data of your own. (I have learned this the hard way.)
- If you do have access to a useful tree that someone else has created, I recommend taking the time to enter up each individual separately on to your own tree, making a deliberate choice as to whether or not to include each one in your genealogy.

Ian sets out his practical approach:

I guess I started as most people do, by looking at how far back a particular name goes back and the geographical migration. From there, I started looking at the siblings of ancestors to give the family a more complete picture and have recently moved on to their spouses, as again, this gives a better picture of how they lived. I've had to rationalise what is included on my tree, however; I quickly noticed on some Ancestry users' trees that the content runs into tens of thousands of entries through numerous marriages. I therefore made a conscious decision to stick to the spouses of siblings – with the exception of the last two generations. Cousins have been purposely excluded as the content then would become unmanageable.

KEEPING YOUR TREE MANAGEABLE

Deciding on how large you allow your tree to grow will depend partly on how many generations or numbers of ancestors can have meaning for you. It's tempting to claim a pedigree dating from the mists of time, but what degree of kinship does this actually involve?

One family history magazine recently ran a feature on a celebrity who is a direct descendant of Robert the Bruce, the Scottish king, some nineteen generations back. By my calculation, that means he was her 18 x great-grandfather, one of an astonishing 524,288 direct-line ancestors which she could claim from that generation. In other words, her royal 18 x great-grandfather is only one out of half a million of her forebears in that generation whose blood and genes went into creating her. If you add in all her other grandparents and great-grandparents who have lived between then and now, the numbers go up to over a million. It's a sobering thought.

Charts and family-tree forms

You can create beautiful trees by hand, if this is your preference, either by designing your own template or by buying a ready-made chart form. Check what is available free on the internet (though you may be limited by the size of paper you can print out), and also what genealogy suppliers have to offer. Advertisements in the family history magazines are a good source for locating these suppliers, and if you visit family history fairs, you can see examples and make your choice from traders there. You can also have data taken from your computerised family tree and put into an attractive poster or chart by some of these companies, which is a great choice for a commemorative gift.

Just bear in mind that any chart, even a large wall chart, probably cannot contain all the names that you discover in your ancestry, so you may need to limit your choice to direct-line ancestors and descendants.

Organising Your Research

Everyone who undertakes some family history research will have at least some idea of how to file and store the material they unearth. My survey respondents would like to encourage you in this, even if it's an ideal they haven't all quite managed themselves! As Melanie puts it, 'Inevitably, as you get further back in time your tree gets huge, so you must start organising your material right from the start, before you get swamped.' And Charles urges that you 'keep your records in good order! Mine are a mass of papers that one day I will sort out!'

I don't want simply to copy here some of the rather pedantic articles that I've read on how to archive, label and digitise what you accumulate. In my experience, it's difficult in any case to adopt any one method that will last you right the way through, since your material will outgrow the first, or even the first three ways you choose to organise it. So instead, here are some brief tips which you may find helpful:

- Ring binders and box files are useful for storing material by category or family.
- Notebooks are your best friends in archives and during field research – use them for jotting down facts, leads and queries. Date them and keep them for future reference.
- Card indexes are beloved by many writers and researchers (but not by me!).
- Computer spreadsheets can be useful for listing records found, certificates acquired, and even a family chronology.
- Text files, photos, and scans on a computer need good organising within folders as you gather more material.
- Scanning photos, as well as keeping hard copies, provides extra security and may be useful for emailing to other relatives and researchers. Try keeping a file of key photos

which you can access quickly for this, and perhaps a set at a lower resolution, handy for emailing.

- Acid-free storage is recommended for preserving old documents, newspapers, etc.
- Back up all your computer files. Always.
- Consider printing out emails, since you may acquire some wonderful, detailed ones from other family members along the way. It's all too easy to think of emails as ephemeral, but they could be the heritage of the future.
- If you have time to spare, indexing key articles in family history magazines may help you to follow up a relevant article when you need to.
- Keeping your whole collection of pamphlets, maps and possibly family history society journals handy in one box, preferably upright, means that you can rifle through them easily and quickly to find what you need.
- Prepare reports and printouts from selected parts of your tree before going to archives for research. Having these for handy reference can save confusion.

Getting Help

Family history can be a remarkably co-operative venture. I am by nature an independent kind of researcher, but I've discovered what a pleasure and a relief it can be to share searches and findings with others in genealogy, and to accept their help as well. As Ian says, 'Don't be afraid to ask for assistance as there are a lot of very helpful people out there.'

The main sources of help are:

- other relatives, including newly discovered ones
- archivists, museum curators, librarians and other professionals
- local historians
- professional genealogists
- family history societies
- forums.

New leads from 'new' relatives

We've already looked at how you might talk to your existing relatives (see p. 55), and consider what the family collective memory has to offer. However, you will probably find that you also grow your family tree with 'new' relatives too, which can be one of the great joys of family history research, as well as a rich source of information.

Finding 'new' relatives is aided enormously now by the internet, though is not confined to it. Back in the days when I was a teenager, for instance, my father placed an advertisement in a newspaper and unearthed a branch of the family who had emigrated to Tennessee in the USA in the nineteenth century. They were thrilled to be 'discovered', and before I knew it, we were heading off on a trip to America, something rare and highly exotic in the pre-package-holiday era of the 1960s. We experienced southern culture and hospitality at first hand, and I also saw the inside of the local hospital when my grumbling appendix chose to become acute. Fortunately, one of our new relatives was a surgeon there, so the treatment was excellent, to say the least – and covered by our travel insurance! My parents kept in regular contact with these relatives afterwards for the rest of their lives, and both sides benefited by being able to fill in details of our joint ancestry.

Since I began my own family history research, I've been in touch with over twenty new relatives. With the discovery of others who share your lineage, remarkable new information often appears. My third cousin Debra, in Ohio, for instance, was able to give me the key names from the Owen line after we'd 'met' on the Ancestry website; since then, we have swapped ideas, photos and data for several years. From other cousins, I've obtained a complete family portrait of my Owen great-grandparents with their twelve children, and also photographs of this great-grandmother's parents, the butter-makers from Somerset, whose faces I never dreamed of being able to see. Another newly found cousin in New Zealand helped me to solve a family legend about a runaway heiress (see pp. 167–8) and from others again, I've heard first-hand anecdotes about family members, which have helped me to understand their characters better.

I've tried to repay these relatives' kindness by circulating my updated findings as they came to light, and eventually was able to offer everyone online access to the volume of family history that I've written (see Chapter Nine).

Asking for help, and offering it to your new relatives, can pay enormous dividends. I can say quite categorically that I would not have been able to complete the spread of ancestry now recorded on my family tree without this assistance.

TIPS FOR CONTACTING NEW RELATIVES

- If you find someone through a website, proceed carefully until you are confident that the new contact is indeed your relative. Restrict your communications through the website email (which protects your personal details) until you feel ready to give them your own email address.
- Ask if they have any photos of your joint ancestors which they could, preferably, email you.
- Offer to share data or photos with them, but keep in mind that it may be better to do this in stages, rather than send everything at once in a rush of enthusiasm. This helps to establish a reciprocal basis for sharing, and again protects you until you know the person better.
- Bear in mind that it may not be possible to maintain all contacts on a permanent basis, and that both you and they may send a flurry of emails only to drop out of sight thereafter.
- Not everyone will warm instantly to your quest. Some relatives, despite the fact that they are researching family history themselves, may have reasons for being reserved or unhappy about their ancestry – perhaps if they are the descendant of an illegitimate member of the family who was spurned by the rest, for instance.

HANDLING SENSITIVE MATERIAL

It's also worth thinking carefully before sharing sensitive material. I mentioned earlier how I discovered the newspaper report about my 2 x great-uncle who had seduced his girlfriend and then abandoned her when she was pregnant (see p. 89), and who subsequently went on to marry more respectably, as he and his parents saw it. When I discovered the account of his antics, I had a moral dilemma on my hands. I was in touch with two of his descendants, one through his legitimate line, and one through the illegitimate one. Would they want to know about this? The report of the court contained some highly personal insinuations, and insults traded between the two sides were colourful, to say the least. On the other hand, did I have a right to keep it from them? In the end, I emailed both gentlemen and told them I had found a rather lurid account of our ancestor's doings, which put no one in a good light, and did they wish to see it? Both of them were eager to read it, so I forwarded it on.

This seemed to work out reasonably well, but there is no standard way to handle such a tricky situation, and you may have to make the difficult decision not to go any further. One of my cousins found that her American in-laws were Scottish in origin, not Irish as they'd believed, which would have been a huge blow to them. And one of the survey respondents discovered what looked like incest in the family tree of a person she was helping. In both cases, the researchers decided to maintain a silence over such sensitive issues, and found tactful ways of deflecting the search.

Archivists, museum curators, librarians and other professionals

Just occasionally, you still come across an old-style, fierce dragon of a librarian who will huff and puff when asked to help you with a query, and imply that it is not worthy of attention when she has so many more important things to do. Fortunately, however, this is now rare, in my experience at least.

On visits to record offices, I've eavesdropped on a number of conversations (see p. 1, for example) and have heard archivists being unfailingly kind and helpful to visitors. They make space at tables when, in theory, they are fully booked, they assist novice computer users to view the census, or point researchers to the specialist records they need. One lady responded to my phone call to the archive by fetching the nineteenth-century minute book for the Baptist chapel in question, and reading out to me the relevant entries with as much relish as if she was enjoying a mystery story! (There was indeed a bit of mystery about my great-grandfather's sudden appearance and disappearance as minister there.) On another occasion, I travelled all the way home to Gloucestershire from Wales before realising that I'd left my cardigan in the archive there. I rang up, and the chief archivist offered to pack it up and send it on to me; it arrived the next day without charge.

Given that these professionals often go the extra mile, and exceed our expectations of help, it seems only fair to respect their workload, to make requests politely and never to insist on help that they cannot easily or willingly provide. If you do find one who is unobliging, my advice is to swallow any unpleasant taste and simply approach another who looks more friendly. These are people who know their resources well, and even if you have good research skills, you shouldn't feel you have to do the whole thing without some assistance.

Local historians

Local historian is a broad term, and, nowadays, many intelligent retired people take an interest in, and become, if not professionals, then experts in the history of the area in which they live. Most are only too delighted to share their knowledge with you.

You will come across local historians at talks, in libraries and other institutions, and even, sometimes, quite by chance while you are out and about on the trail of your ancestry. A friend of mine visited the village where her mother was born, where she was especially interested in tracing the story of her grandmother, who ran away from her husband one night, taking the baby with her. She got talking to a man there who turned out to be an expert local historian. He knew all about the escaping young mother and the scandalous divorce which followed, and was able to fill in plenty more details about the background of the grandmother's life in the village.

Likewise, I found unexpected help when I was visiting the Blaenavon area in Wales, to learn more about a coal-mining ancestor. As I stopped outside his old home – a little terraced house – a man emerged from it who turned out not only to be the father of the current owner, but also a real fountain of knowledge himself about the area and its history. He showed me round the house, and told me about the way the landscape and the mines had developed. It turned out, too, that he had helped another descendant looking at the same house several years earlier, and still had her email address. I was then able to contact her in the United States and greet her as another long-lost cousin! It pays to talk to people that you meet.

Professional genealogists

If you need help on a professional basis, perhaps because you live far from the area you're researching, then there are many professional genealogists able to offer a service. You can locate them through the small ads of family history magazines, through noticeboards at archives and libraries or through a professional body such as the Society of Genealogists (www.societyofgenealogists.com/professional-research/). A few of my survey respondents used professional help, with varying levels of satisfaction. As Sheila M. put it: 'No hope of visiting with the distance, and cheaper in the long run to pay for research.' It will help, of course, if you can hone your search as much as possible to start with, so that you are able to present specific requests. Research is usually payable by the hour.

Family history societies (or FHS)

These have already been mentioned in Chapter Four (see p. 71) as an excellent source for research, and there is usually a register of 'Members' Interests' where you can contact those with similar lines of research and then trade information. I've had very productive exchanges with several individuals this way, two of whom were researching the same local name as myself – the Kinseys of Llandinam in Montgomeryshire. Although we can't find any evidence that we're directly related, we've been able to fill in more details together to chart the spread of that particular family name in the area.

FHS may also offer a 'look-up' service for their members, where those on the spot will check records for those who are not, either for a very small fee or for free.

Forums

There is a large community of helpful family history researchers out there, who may be able to help you with any local or specialist queries that you have, or even with a specific family line.

Irene recounts her experience of using RootsChat (www.roots chat.com):

> This site has been particularly helpful because at any time, day or night, when a question is posted in the chat room, there always seems to be someone who is able to assist. I pondered the lives of these helpful people, and wondered whether some of them were perhaps disabled and this online activity was their social life but, on the other hand, one lady I was communicating with suddenly had to leave

'the room' to feed the baby! Maybe it's just due to the fact this is an addictive hobby! Similarly the chat room of Genes Reunited has solved one or two queries for me in the past.

David S. echoes this: 'I would advise anyone to join RootsChat because not only is it free, but I have found there is always someone willing to help.'

When I discovered that my 3 x great-grandmother, Maria Kinsey (see Appendix I, p. 244), had accompanied her husband Edward Owens on at least part of his active service in the Napoleonic Wars, I wanted to learn more about women as camp followers in this period. With some trepidation, I ventured on to a specialist military forum (www.napoleon-series.org), where probably the world's keenest enthusiasts swap highly complex information about their researches. I need not have worried; there was room for a novice like me, and traces of others who had also come on to the forum with need of basic guidance. The experts flocked to answer my questions, and gave me leads to reference books where I could learn more.

You'll find forums on many general or specialist family history websites that you visit, and most family history magazines run their own forums (see the Resources section, p. 256). In addition, you can search by subject for other forums which may not be directly related to family history, as I did with the Napoleonic Wars.

TIPS FOR USING FORUMS

- Check out the dates of posts relating to subjects of interest, since it may have been months or even years since that discussion was active, and any new question you post may not receive a response. Start a new thread if that's the case.
- Don't be afraid to ask simple questions, but do make it clear what you want to know. For instance, I was uncertain about the various military divisions – battalion, regiment and so on – and because I didn't ask for clarification, some of the answers I got were confusing without this knowledge.

- Always thank people for their time and help.
- Don't swap personal email addresses without good reason, or display them openly online. Keep other personal details confidential too, and adopt a user name online.
- See if there are any queries which you can help to answer.

THINKING OUTSIDE THE BOX

Vicky takes her quest beyond the normal avenues of enquiry – and gets results:

> Chat to anyone who might give you a clue – welcomers in churches, family history fairs ... We left a note on a well-tended grave which my father had thought in the 1970s was a cousin's – it was. The note was found. That one lady had four children, they had ten, and they've had twenty-six. Forty relations in no time!

So don't be afraid to try out new ideas for locating people; you can even knock on doors if need be. Bernard is an old hand at this:

> I have found cold-calling (through letters or phone calls) on people with some of the unusual family names has been very productive and also welcoming, in some cases leading to lasting friendships across national boundaries. Though sometimes initially suspicious, most people have responded warmly once they get over the 'Do you want money?' phase. Knocking on doors has been part of this direct approach and more often than not has resulted in a cup of tea and genuine interest in my quest, rather than a cold brush-off. I have gathered much valuable information this way.

Helping Others

If you share information with others, this will of course be helpful to them, but will also give you a sense of community within the family history sphere. You could become a volunteer at a local archive and, in so doing, learn a great deal more yourself, as Joan recounts: 'I did a lot of my research when I worked as a volunteer at the Lancashire Record Office, going every Wednesday morning and working on the Probate Preservation project and spending time in the afternoon doing my family history and learning the ropes.'

If you have spare time to offer from home, then there are ongoing transcribing projects to which you could contribute (listed on websites or in family history magazines) by entering up data from old records. Charles, for instance, transcribes for FreeBMD (www.freebmd.org.uk). As well as helping to provide an invaluable resource, this may also earn you credits on the website, or an early viewing of newly digitised records and documents.

I often offer a session on my home PC to friends or relatives who are just beginning their family history, using my subscriptions to websites to help find the first historical data for them. Not all turn out as expected – I had to tell my sister-in-law that her family were not Welsh through and through as she'd believed, since one of her key ancestors had sailed over from Cornwall and never went home again! However, provided there isn't anything seriously amiss, there's nothing like the glow of satisfaction you'll experience if you can help another person put a missing piece of their jigsaw into place.

Research Strategy – Tactics and Tips

Your quest to research your family history may well last several years, if not decades. It's an emotional journey as well as a practical one, and also involves considerations of time, energy and money. So it's useful to revisit your objectives every now and then, and the route you intend to take. Once you've passed through the first stages of research, you may need to review and modify your initial aims, as discussed in

Chapter One (see pp. 17–25), and devise strategies for handling the various aspects of the family history experience.

In this next section, I'll set out what seem to me to be the most significant elements of the search, adding my own tips to those suggested by my survey informants.

Setting your objectives

It isn't necessary to set your goals from day one. The opening phase of trying out new search tools and filling in chunks of your family tree without too much thought for where it will lead you can be a joyous, stimulating one. But before the tree grows too fast, or the unsorted paper records turn into untidy heaps, it's probably a good idea to figure out where you'd like your quest to take you.

Earlier, we considered choosing just one side of your family to research to start with (see pp. 36–40), and this is one of the first questions that can come up again for review, once you're launched on your research. Is there another branch that you'd like to switch to now? Or a particular trail you wish to follow back in time as far as you can? Or possibly, you may, by this time, be able to see a pattern emerging which you can make use of to vary your lines of research while at the same time keeping to your overall goal. I, for instance, began with the rather hazy objective of researching my mother's line, but have since then defined and investigated various branches of it, knowing that I can switch at intervals from one to another without losing the thread. I also now add in a little light research on my father's side too, to supplement the areas he left out when he carried out his own research about thirty years ago.

LEAVING SOMETHING FOR OTHERS

When I was a volunteer at a hospice, helping with a Life Stories project, I often sat talking with a woman patient who was an expert on weaving. As well as her own memories, we discussed weaving and textiles, which I was interested in too. One day she grew sad. 'I haven't finished my notes. I was going to leave all my findings to my students,' she said. 'Now there isn't time to do it – I've only got some of it ready to pass on.' It was such a poignant moment, and I didn't know what to say. Then I realised that it wasn't so much about giving her personal comfort, as trying to help her see the value of the work she had done in the wider sense. These students would have a great opportunity. 'They'll be glad to have somewhere to go, to follow the lines of enquiry you've set up. It's giving them a chance too,' I told her. This seemed to give her some peace of mind. I hope that it did help, since she died a couple of weeks later.

And this does have a bearing on family history too: just as leaving a family tree for the next generation can be an incredible gift, so leaving certain areas of it unexplored can be a great blessing to those who come after you. Don't expect to finish everything off completely in your lifetime. Even if this were theoretically possible, you would be barring family descendants from the excitement and satisfaction that you have experienced in your search. Whether or not they take up that challenge will be up to them. Maybe you'll see no signs of interest during your lifetime – my father certainly didn't get much of a response from me – but later on, perhaps, they will suddenly develop a passion for family history and seize on your legacy with enthusiasm. What you leave will be of immense value, and what you haven't completed will be a spur that takes them on a life-changing journey.

Getting involved

Many of us find that we start to get involved, and sometimes too involved, in our ancestors' lives. What begins as an interesting exercise can begin to occupy our waking thoughts, and sometimes even our night-time ones too. 'My ancestors have really come alive for me ... I often wake up in the night thinking about them,' says Norma. Elizabeth H. too confirms her involvement: 'I have grown to care a lot about these ancestors of mine.'

So how should you handle this experience if it comes your way? I suggest two guiding principles: the first is to acknowledge it, and accept that it can happen; the second is to keep it within reasonable bounds, and not allow it to overwhelm your everyday life.

We in the West are in some ways disadvantaged in this respect, living in a society which lacks a mechanism for including our ancestors in our lives, which is unusual within the history and spread of human culture, as illustrated by a television programme I saw recently about an African tribe. Their days are spent gathering and harvesting food, fetching water and keeping their village clean. Sometimes though, one of them will break off work to walk over to a particular tree and pray to the ancestral spirits they communicate with through these trees, asking them for blessings. And at a certain time of year, all the villagers rise in the middle of the night and perform a long ritual with song and dance, invoking the ancestors in their wish for a fruitful growing season. It may seem strange to compare our sedate twenty-first-century genealogy with tribal rituals and beliefs in ancestral spirits, but perhaps the gap between our world and theirs is not so great after all. Or at least, it need not be, if we can find a new place for ancestors in our lives that is in keeping with contemporary life.

It is not uncommon to discover in the process of doing your family history that your own ancestors do begin to play an active role in your psyche, even if you attribute it simply to an overheated imagination. But family history is, after all, the stuff of imagination: we engage with recreating our ancestors' lives from the facts that we discover, and, as we paint their portraits afresh in our minds, they may take on a kind of life of their own and – horrors! – even seem to 'speak' to us. If you experience something like this, I recommend not being alarmed by it. It's not a sign of insanity and it need not upset your religious faith or overturn your values. What is lacking, though, in contemporary society, is a place for it (apart from the graveyard and the family photo album), and this is something we may need to develop afresh if the current enthusiasm for family history carries on growing.

I'll make a few suggestions relating to this later, in Chapter Eight (see p. 218), but for now, I just recommend keeping your investigations in proportion to your other work and activitites, and not abandoning other interests for the sake of spending more and more time on your family research. It can become obsessive – it's such fascinating detective work, after all – but try to limit your involvement, and turn your attention fully back to the things of today when you finish your research sessions.

TAKE A BREAK NOW AND THEN

It's normal, and healthy too, to drop your research from time to time and have an ancestor-free spell. I have, several times, reached saturation point, when I simply couldn't look at another census return or plot another name on the tree, and dropped family history for months at a time till I felt ready to continue. This may be partly to do with the need to absorb and integrate the information gathered, something which may require time away from active research. It can also be due to technical overload, using websites for long hours and trying to fit all the details together with furrowed brow. Whatever the reason, I suggest leaving your search alone when it gets too much of a burden. Give yourself time off, and don't even bother planning when you'll return to it. The interest doesn't need to be kept artificially alive – it will almost certainly return of its own accord, when you are rested.

Your outlook

Your readiness to take a break when needed can actually be part of a mature and rounded outlook which has patience, tenacity and acceptance at its root. After all, if you have confidence in the value of your research, you can accept the need for a pause without worrying that it means you're giving up, just as you'd be ready to take holidays from your regular line of work. This quiet, underlying persistence is something that our respondents recommend, especially in the active progress of research. 'Have plenty of patience!' says Dorothy. 'Perseverance and lateral thinking have their place. Go back to problems after the passage of time when a new angle of search may present itself,' suggests Lorna A. While Elizabeth W. recommends: 'Tenacity by the bucketful! Keeping good records of stuff done. Going over the same stuff again and again will throw up that little gem of info.' And as Virginia sums up her advice, 'My approach to research, and which I would recommend, is simply not giving up.'

Research tactics

Good tactics will help you to develop a perspective on your research which will minimise wasted effort. They help you to see the wood, rather than just the trees.

CHECK YOUR FACTS

The survey respondents were insistent that the one thing needed above all in research is the careful checking and cross-checking of information. Angela speaks for many of them when she says:

> One piece of advice I always give to people is never believe you have the correct individual or that the event you discover is correct until you have at least confirmed it with one other source. If in any doubt whatsoever, always check further until you have either proved or disproved the information before taking the next step. It is too easy to believe that the first piece of information is correct and then you can waste so much time, and probably money also, researching the wrong individual and family line.

Within this general brief, Melanie recommends tracing wills as a good source of data against which to cross-check other records. Christopher, a long-term and very experienced researcher, says: 'My system has always been to verify each step of my family history from original records, especially when dealing with information gleaned from the internet. This is something I would advise all family historians to do.'

ALLOWING FOR PROBABILITY

But what if you can't get that ultimate proof that your findings are absolutely correct beyond any shadow of doubt? Robert does not believe this is possible in any case: 'You may have as minute a record as you like, and yet there is often no incontrovertible proof.' I agree with this; there are plenty of instances where you will have to 'take a view'. You may need to go on the weight of evidence, the amassing of several probabilities rather than one completely verified fact. What would such 'incontrovertible proof' be, after all? Can we ever know for sure that a child is the true son or daughter of their reputed father? There is always a chance, even a tiny one, that something has been concealed, or false information put on record. As researchers, we need to be sure within reasonable bounds, but to a certain degree we have to take our findings on trust, if we've followed sensible research procedure.

In my own research, I have had to take it as very probable, but not absolutely certain, that my 2 x great-grandfather, Revd Edward Owens, is indeed the son of Edward Owens, the soldier. I haven't yet been able to trace a baptism for him, but the weight of other evidence, including family records, naming patterns, dwelling places and so on, tips the balance towards that relationship.

Where close family links are at stake, you will want the evidence to be as firm as possible, even if it is not as complete as you would like it to be, but when the project is not so vital (as with the research I carried out on the origins of an old sampler in my possession – see p. 188), you may feel that it's perfectly acceptable to be less rigorous in your checks. The important thing is to be clear about this; do indicate whether your conclusions are certain, probable or only possible, and retain all the evidence so that later on you can check it or take it further if you need to.

THE DYNAMICS OF SEARCHING

The way in which you search, in terms of how you use your energy and attention, is rarely discussed, but I think this is an important topic: the approach you use can be crucial to the task in hand. I've been researching material for books for several decades, and I've learned that both a broad and a focused way of combing through information has its value. These techniques, which are primarily techniques of consciousness, are quite close to what Buddhist meditation refers to as 'concentration' and 'mindfulness'.

In mindfulness, the mind is allowed to encompass a wide field of attention, whereas in concentration it focuses on one point at a time. They are not entirely mutually exclusive, but whereas in meditation a balance of the two may be both desirable and achievable, in applied activities such as research, it's more usual for one to predominate over the other. Both have their value; the important thing is to recognise what each means, and to vary them accordingly.

Within an internet search, a broad or 'scattergun' approach, as I call it, can be very useful. Scattergun means that you roam around websites, trying leads here and there, with the aim of finding something substantial – and hopefully exciting – along the way. It's a natural outlet for pent-up energy and enthusiasm, and can yield brilliant results if just one lead comes good with an unexpected hit. It's akin to lateral thinking in that you may make intuitive leaps that result in finding information that you would never have done with a patient, step-by-step search. We may be becoming better adapted for this too, since, according to current research, the use of computers may actually be changing the way our brains are wired: reports say that we are now very good at scanning and taking in a wide spread of information; the downside, however, is that we may also be losing concentration and the ability to focus on detail.

Whether or not this is true, internet searches often mean that you have to skim, scan and surf, otherwise you would become bogged down in hopeless websites and dead-end searches. The disadvantage of this approach in terms of family history research, though, is that you can spend a couple of hours in this way with nothing to show for it at the end, except an ill temper to vent on those around you. My suggestion is to use this tactic, by all means, but deliberately limit your time at it, and perhaps restrict it to every second or third session.

For single-line, methodical enquiries, either on- or offline, marshal your existing facts and leads first, so that you can focus on the most likely path to follow. Go steadily through the data, leaving no stone unturned. Keep track of where you've been, and list all the leads you've followed, even if they turn out to be blind alleys. This kind of research dynamic may be essential if you're trawling through lists of names in parish registers, for instance; if you miss that vital name because you're skipping pages, you may have to come back and do the work all over again. The pace here is likely to be slow, and the attention to detail meticulous.

With practice, you may find that you can switch from one mode to another more fluently, learning when to browse fast through unpromising material and restricting the flow when you reach data which needs more thorough checking. Both instinct and logic play a part here: when to turn elsewhere without finishing the document, for instance, and when to keep plodding on to the very end. It's quite healthy to encourage your brain to switch in this way, and you will soon tell by your results whether or not it is paying dividends. Using the idea of mindfulness and concentration to help you, as already described, you will probably find that you begin to work quite naturally with these different types of attention, and will be less tired as a result.

FAMILY NAMES

Tips from a number of survey respondents encourage us to be broad and flexible in our use of family names, and to search in imaginative directions.

This is Valerie's view:

> I subscribe to a very good family history search site which contains a wealth of information, but have struggled at times to find the people I am looking for, only to find the surname has been transcribed inaccurately e.g. Ellis = Ellitt; Goate = Coat. It is a good idea to look up your family member on several sites. I have found relatives this way.

Lorna A. puts her point simply, saying, 'I've learned to ignore spellings of names', while Elaine suggests a way of interpreting and using names as leads: 'Up to about 1900, first sons were usually named after father and second sons after grandfather – or vica versa. Same principle applies to daughters. Unusual second names are usually the mother's maiden name.'

Naomi uses family names as a springboard to search for contacts:

'I always contact anyone with a name I recognise. There are only a few that lead anywhere, but one produced a fifth cousin!' And Ron has discovered a wealth of associations by using his family name as a search tool, and suggests that those with unusual names could do likewise:

> Look on the street maps where I have found Lampard Terrace, Lampard Grove, Lampard Close. Find out as much as you can about when, and why the name. It is fine for us who have a relatively uncommon name, but will not work for all. Look at the atlases too. Knowing my bunch came with a leader from Strasbourg in the 1500s, I found Lampertheim as a northern suburb. In that Lampertheim there is a Lamperthof (Lampert's farm) that I saw earlier this year. It is clearly a hotel from a converted farm. There is another Lampertheim, and other references in the same area (Lampertwald, Lamperwald). All lie between the bases of Calvin and Luther. A lucky strike for us with a queer name perhaps.

Even without an unusual name, though, there may be local links with your family name in the area they lived in. I discovered that 'Walkers Gate' estate in Wellington, Somerset, is named after the dairy that my ancestors, the Walkers, used to run on the site.

NAME PROFILING

An easy and interesting way of checking out the spread of a family name is to use a surname profiler. Run by the National Trust, www.nationaltrustnames.org.uk/default. aspx is a free site where you can look up the geographical distribution and frequency of a surname as recorded in the UK either in 1881 or 1998. Commercial CDs, with more detail on, such as the facility to look up forenames as well, are also available to buy inexpensively. These profilers won't give you details of individuals, but they can help to show the general areas where families of this name live and thus perhaps give clues to the ancestral areas they occupied. It is worth trying even the more common names, like the Browns in my own tree, since I can see at a glance that they are not spread evenly throughout the UK, as I expected, and are hardly present at all in the far west, the far north or in Wales.

FAMILY STORIES

The importance of collecting your family stories has already been mentioned, and whether they turn out to be legend in large part doesn't diminish their usefulness, as my respondents point out: 'Never despise oral reports. I have never found one entirely wrong yet,' says Ron, while Josie's advice is to 'assume that there is a grain of truth in any family legend – it just may have happened in a different generation'.

And Angela pays tribute to the family tradition which finally led her to success after a frustrating struggle with inaccurately recorded official data: 'I ordered the certificate, and when it arrived it confirmed all the oral history that I was already aware of, so I knew it was the correct one this time. If I had not had an oral family history with all the names of the women who married into the family, I could well have barked up a very long and very wrong tree!'

YOUR OWN WEBSITE

Starting up your own website based on your family name is something that can pay dividends. It can be a place for posting new discoveries and swapping information with other relatives and, of course, it can draw in new contacts from your extended family who have probably found their way to it by the kind of name search mentioned above. Again, as in Ron's geographical searches, this may work best for if not unusual, then more distinctive names. As Ken D. recommends, 'If you are able to do so, set up a website like mine. People are so happy to help and share information. My website is literally shared across the world.'

Making Mistakes

Question nine of my survey on p. 10 is, 'Have you ever made any serious mistakes in your tree, which you've had to undo, and if so, how did this affect your research?' Ruth, a newcomer to family history, answers: 'Not yet, but give me time.'

It can happen to us all. You're priding yourself on a beautifully set-up family tree, with hundreds of names, lineage clearly displayed, dates all in order. Then you decide to take another look at the records for that direct-line ancestor whose information was hard to confirm. Maybe you entered it up in the early days of building your tree, when you had less experience, and you never quite got round to checking it. You find it's wrong, after all. This is not your ancestor. How many other names and links will you have to check and remove now?

At least Ruth is aware of this possibility from the start. About a third of the survey respondents admit to significant mistakes which have hampered their progress. These fall into five clear categories:

- Incorrect assumptions and guesswork
- Other people's mistakes
- Names and their problems
- Inaccurate dates
- Computer problems

On the plus side though, making mistakes does tend to create solutions for better research practice, as we'll see in some of the examples of errors that our informants confess to committing.

Incorrect assumptions and guesswork

Valerie's reply to the question above was very direct:

Oh yes! Researching my husband's family – his grandfather married a Benjamin – I started to look for Benjamins and put together a lovely family tree. Until I got a copy of their marriage certificate and found I had been barking up the wrong tree! So I had to scrap the research I had done and start along the right track. Lesson learned: always get firm confirmation of relatives before trying to trace ancestors. BMDs are invaluable and they are cheap compared to the time wasted researching wrong families. Worst of all for me, I had passed all the information on to another Wright family member, so had to go back and admit I was wrong!

It can be very tempting to enter up data before you're as sure as you can be that it's correct. Relying on guesswork and assumptions about family members has thrown other respondents off track too, like Irene:

It is so easy to fall into the trap of believing you have correct dates only to find at a later stage the dates were coincidental. It's amazing the number of people who have the same names, dates of birth, identical places of birth as the relative you are researching. It is so important to check and recheck dates, etc.

Some of our family historians have learned from their mistakes in this respect, as Teresa reveals:

I did make one mistake when I started researching my maternal grandmother's family and thought I had the correct person. Fortunately, before I went too far, I approached the research officer at my local genealogical library for help, and he pointed out that he thought I had the wrong family. This caused me to reassess the information I had and to look for a different spelling in the surname which proved correct. It happened early in my research, and only made me more careful in checking all documents matched before assuming I was on to the correct person.

And mistakes can lead to better practice. After Virginia put a wrong family line into her tree, she resolved not to enter up information in the future until she could verify it: 'Now I tend to develop a working hypothesis, and then try to prove it.'

Other people's mistakes

One of the biggest causes of error is that while you may be a careful researcher, not everyone else is. 'There are many possible mistakes which can occur from taking information from other people,' says Sheila M. G. wryly.

Many of the family trees uploaded on to the internet are not accurate, as mentioned already, and may be riddled with data that has been passed on from one person to another without any further checking. It's even possible in some cases to construct your tree almost entirely from chunks of other people's trees, which might end up being as fantastical as some of the lineages constructed in earlier centuries, full of improbable royal forebears and ancestors drawn from myth.

'There are many problems with data that has been wrongly put into sites like Ancestry,' as Keith points out. And Fran too admits to the lure of easy internet searches, although she did not suffer too badly: 'Early on I was seduced by existing trees on Ancestry or Genes Reunited. The only effect was some drudgery in retracing my steps to provable facts.'

Lorna W. came across a problem using the International Genealogical Index (IGI), the resource that is a part of the Family Search website, to which anyone can upload information.

I have made some mistakes researching my husband's family in Scotland. Using just the IGI, I found the surname Warren occurred quite a bit in the Inverness area, and because of names and dates that seemed to correspond, I assumed this must be the family from which he was descended. However, once I had access to census records, via the internet, I realised I had been completely wrong, unless there is a link much further back than I have been able to go.

It's not always internet data that can throw us off track, either. Tam runs a One-Name society, for the study and correlation of a particular sur-name, and found that he was often making wrong input where he relied on the declarations of the people who submitted the information. He has been able to turn this to good use, however, for his work on the One-Name project: 'False lines are just the data for other lines of research.'

Ian has proved that even if mistakes are sometimes inevitable, a good research method can at least enable you to put things right:

> My initial search starts with the various websites (Ancestry, IGI, CWGC and Great War Forum to name a few) as they are easily accessible, but then having found some possible answers, I trawl through the local library or county record office for the proof to back up the detail. This has proved useful in the past, as one investigation wiped 150 names from my tree in one hit, once the real evidence was uncov-ered. It did at least prove that my process works.

Although all our researchers managed to correct mistakes made, it may not be so easy getting others to correct theirs. Sheila M. reports on her own experiences with other people's trees, which were little short of fictitious, debasing her own efforts; she also highlights the prob-lems of stopping your own family information being circulated:

> I have been in contact with some other Wooltorton researchers; in fact, the latest one is in the USA (contacted via Ancestry) and claims to be connected to William the Conqueror and other notable persons! I have become more reluctant in recent years, since, probably due to *Who Do You Think You Are?* [the TV series], my research has been 'bas-tardised' and passed on as proven to quite a few people. One chap has added everyone he can find up to 2005, including newborn babies. It took several emails to get him to remove myself and family from the websites where he entered his tree. He also worked on assumption and married people off because it 'seemed right'.

Names and their problems

We've already touched on the question of the spelling of names, and how this may vary through different records and periods. When it comes to making errors through names, though, there's also the possibility of misidentifying a person with a similar name to that of your ancestor and claiming him or her for a long-lost relative before being too sure of the facts. Michael, searching for one of his great-grandparents, a Thomas Alfred Moody, found himself going in completely the wrong direction:

> I looked at the census returns in 1881 for him but he didn't appear in any of them ... However, the 1881 census did reveal that there was an Ada Moody, aged eight, who had a sister Alice and whose father was Alfred Moody ... During the Victorian period, people often adopted their second Christian name, so the absence of the first name Thomas did not concern me too heavily.

Armed with further information, Michael concluded that this Alfred and his wife Maria were almost certainly his great-grandparents, and he enthusiastically followed the trail further:

> Their ancestors led me to some interesting people including the Caffyn family who were very prominent in West Sussex back to the seventeenth century. I was very pleased with myself and I would have happily continued in my ignorance until the 1911 census was published.

Unfortunately for Michael, this demolished his hypothesis at a stroke, and he concludes somewhat wistfully: 'It is with a tinge of regret that I have had to jettison Alfred Moody and the Caffyn family, but I suppose accuracy must prevail. So look at the 1911 census carefully; you never know what you may discover.'

The same applies with any new sources that shed a different light on your data; you may have to sacrifice cherished work if they don't support your findings. So it pays to be cautious, and, in the case of names, to check thoroughly, and not to be surprised if unusual-sounding but similar names turn up, even in the same locality. I was trying to link one Lancelot Lee into my own family tree; no problem, I thought, with such a striking name. However, there are at least six Lancelot Lees in the 1901 census alone; by 1885, Tennyson's 'Idylls of the King' had been published – poems relating stories of King Arthur in which, of course, Sir Lancelot features – so it's not surprising that a number of romantically minded parents chose this name for their sons.

Inaccurate dates

My 3 x great-grandmother, Maria Kinsey, was born in 1782, as indicated by the parish records. Or was she? According to her death certificate issued in 1855, she was seventy-five years old when she died, which would put her birth back to 1780. But wait – the parish register is for baptisms rather than births, so could she have been two years old when she was baptised? A look at the marriage records to check shows that she was married early in 1799 to Edward Owens, no age given; so if she was actually born in 1780, this would make her a more mature nineteen, rather than a young seventeen-year-old bride. But then again, her last two children were born in 1824 and 1828. Could she really have been forty-eight at the birth of the last one, another Maria, who died of scarlatina aged only thirteen? And so it goes on. Despite four official records here, there is no overall consistency as to Maria's age.

Keith sums up the issue in a nutshell:

The big problem is dates. These can vary, and be just guesswork. And the other problem is birth and christening dates being mixed up. Deaths and burials the same. And the real problem is that many people never remembered just how old they were. My father died aged ninety – not true, he was only eighty-nine.

Does it matter? For very conscientious genealogists, it does. For those of us who would like to be accurate, but would happily allow a reasonable margin for variation, it may not be so important unless we start building other theories and relating other data around specific dates that cannot be verified. The danger is that you will start believing what you've entered on your own tree, even if you put it there more in the spirit of optimism than certainty. After entering in scores and even hundreds of names, you may not necessarily remember which were speculative. Ideally, always include the word 'about' with a date if you're not certain (family-tree software will usually reduce this to a convenient format for you, such as 'Abt.'), and indicate the source of your evidence or suggestions. You can also use 'Before' and 'After' to signify dates by which you know the person was born, married or dead. I have not always obeyed this rule, but now I wish I had!

Computer problems

Sheila M. highlights how a home PC too can be the source of problems, even to the extent of losing the whole of one's research. More of a disaster than a mistake, perhaps! But she also shows how even this very black cloud did have its silver lining:

> Experience teaches, as they say, and one nasty one was my PC getting a virus or something and I lost the lot, but then I did go through and re-enter information and found additional overlooked information. Now I try to reassess information after a time lapse, and usually find something missed, probably due to excitement in the initial find. I am, I'm afraid, a somewhat impatient person! I am still trying to go through and put some order into my chaos.

SAFE STORAGE
I make no apology for repeating the advice to save your work carefully. Always back up files on your computer, either to disk or to a

dedicated external device. Once you have many photographs and large files, it makes sense to use the latter. You can buy a relatively inexpensive and easy-to-use device, and back up all your files on it with just one command. Seek specialist advice if you'd like to find even more secure off-site storage which won't be lost, for instance, in a house fire.

Repairing the damage

Very often, the way to repair wrongly entered data is simply to remove the offending items, and painstakingly restore what you know to be correct, a process that Sheila M. G. referred to earlier as 'drudgery'. David Sm. had such an instance: 'I have recently made a mistake on my maternal grandfather's side and I am still undoing the consequences of this mistake. It also means redrawing my family tree.'

Whether you use computer software or write out your tree by hand, it's an unwelcome chore to redo your hard work. Melanie has had the problem twice, 'both times caused by identical names and place of birth and similar birth dates. I just had to take the tree back to the break and start again, saving the "incorrect" line in a separate tree. In both cases, the incorrect and new lines joined again higher up the tree.'

If you're not certain how one potential branch of the family connects with the rest, it's possible to start a separate mini tree with no links to the main one. Later, if you find the right connection, you can merge it into your tree. And, once again, even a knotty problem can bring unexpected rewards, as Kate found: 'A couple of times I have gone off at a tangent and put people who have married into the family into the wrong families. I have rectified this and solved other mysteries in the process.'

Mistakes involving other researchers can produce a battle of wills as to who is right, as Ken D. reports: 'I had an interesting, friendly challenge with a cousin of mine doing family history. We both "found" our great-grandfather Edward Davies – but they were both different Edward Davies's. I won on the "place of birth" issue!'

Not all altercations are so amicably sorted, however, and in some of those reported, one can imagine the challenge and counter-challenges these may have involved. Sheila M. tells us: 'Another chap working on the Bishop family tree sent me his information which threw mine into confusion, although I had relevant certificates, etc. When I asked for copies of the certificates for proof, he said he hadn't purchased any!'

Josie has found it difficult to present her own findings to those who have an attachment to earlier and less accurate research: 'The greatest diplomatic problem is disagreeing with pre-internet research, where something key was missed in faded microfilm, or the info was not available. But the researcher is now dead, and their family won't have anything amended.'

It seems that in the computer age too, requests made to other internet users to remove wrong family history data are often resisted or ignored. Norma reports: 'Many family trees on ancestry.co.uk are inaccurate and I can prove that from my mother's first-hand experience. I always leave comments on the website when I find mistakes, but some people would rather not know.'

This may be due partly to the fact that, once on the websites, information posted can be hard to correct in that format. Irene struggled to undo what she herself had posted: 'On one occasion I had to seek the help of Genes Reunited to undo a simple date error as I was unable to correct the mistake myself.' Keith, too, couldn't change a mistake about the gender of one particular relative: 'Was unable to correct, so it still stands today.' William confirms this problem: 'My serious mistake was to put Mary Goldthorp of Shepley, 1757, on Genes Reunited, which I have found impossible to correct.'

If you build your tree on a site such as Ancestry and Genes Reunited, you may have limited control over it. So, returning to the advice given earlier: keep your family tree offline in your own software programme, then post the version you want online, which means that you can remove or delete it when you wish, replacing it with an updated or corrected version.

TOP TIPS FOR AVOIDING MISTAKES

- Get sufficient proof of names or dates before entering them on your family tree.
- If a date is uncertain, indicate that it's approximate or unknown.
- Add in your sources where possible, so that you can trace where you found the data if a query arises.
- Remember that people may share the same name, and even the same year and place of birth, so don't assume that someone is necessarily your ancestor until you have additional evidence.
- Treat other people's trees, especially those posted on the internet, with great caution.
- If you do make a mistake on your tree, bite the bullet and remove the data as soon as possible, plus any related links. You can always keep them to one side, in case they can be reinstated later.
- You will probably find that other people take data you've posted on the internet into their own trees, and may use it erroneously. Ask yourself if it is really worth the trouble of confronting them and asking them to change it.
- Build and edit your tree offline in your own software programme. Don't create a tree online unless you have to.
- Always back up your work, either with paper copies or on disks or external memory, or both.

The Budget

Finally, in this section, we return to the budget, first mentioned in Chapter One. If you followed the suggestions made there (see pp. 23–5), you will already have some idea of roughly how much you are prepared to spend in a year. Most family historians expect to spend a certain amount annually on their interest or hobby, but whatever this is in your case, we're all looking for ways to save money in these cost-conscious days.

Here are some ways to help curb your spending:

Free trial offers

Some subscription websites have free trial offers which you can make good use of, especially if you prepare your questions in advance, so that you can focus your efforts in the limited time.

Software packages

Similarly, some family-tree software programmes may come bundled with a free subscription; when I bought Family Tree Maker, for instance, I was given six months' subscription to Ancestry.

Family history magazines

These are full of money-saving tips which are right up to date. An edition I've just received at the time of writing has a feature on 101 ways to save money on your family history research.

Ordering with caution

This is something to keep in mind when you send off for BMD certificates and other records. Be sure that you've covered the range of records in which you might find your ancestor. In other words, don't rush to order a birth certificate for Joseph Albert Bloggs until you've checked carefully that there are no other possible baby Bloggs that could be contenders. If there is more than one, try the most likely candidate to start with.

Using your library

My library has produced a bookmark which says: 'There's more to your library than the books. Who are you? Discover your family history. Ask a member of library staff to discover more.' Take them up on it! You will almost certainly be able to get a 'library' version of Ancestry on their computer system, and maybe more besides.

Make your trips worthwhile

Taking trips to ancestral stamping grounds is half the fun of family history. See what you can combine: village settings, local graveyards, visiting a cousin, calling in at regional archives or museums, for instance. It's possible to pack a great deal into a one- or two-day visit, and if you treat it as something of a holiday as well, then you will feel that you are getting good value for money.

Books and magazines

These can be read in or borrowed from libraries, and sometimes found in charity shops. Don't, however, limit your research with the not-so-useful out-of-date editions. It's worthwhile investing in at least one really good, new reference volume.

Swap information and certificates with other researchers

You can make very good photocopies via a home printer of certificates and the like. Use your scanner too, and your camera to take digital pictures of photographs. This is the age of information sharing.

Invest well

Even though you are keeping an eye on your budget, do spend the money needed to get the kind of records and back-up that you need to grow your tree and build your stories. Sheila M. comments, 'I have found that many researchers are rather conservative in respect of money. But what a waste of time not to prove information!'

I would add: pay out for what brings you fulfilment and may prove a lasting legacy for your family. This is a heritage that you are creating.

CHAPTER SIX

Living Portraits

Suddenly I was seeing things through different eyes. No longer were they names on paper, but were taking shape before me. I saw people with jobs, different dress, houses or lack of them, misfortunes, habits, nicknames, relationships, neighbours and lifestyles I had never seen before. Each aspect opened a door into a new chapter, often a very colourful one. Stories emerged that made my hair curl, sometimes with joy and often with embarrassment, but that was life, and life wasn't easy, to say the least.

Ann, a 'Lancashire Lass'

Ann's new vision of her ancestors emerged after she began to delve into her family history research via the internet. Up till then, she had only heard more recent family stories gathered from her grandmother, head of five generations and known affectionately as 'the Oracle'; the earlier ancestors were merely names on scraps of paper until Ann was able to spread her wings and follow the ancestral trail back into the deeper past.

Creating portraits of individual ancestors, connecting with the places they inhabited and even studying the objects they owned is one of the essential elements of family history. This chapter is about enlivening the past in this way, in order to embrace an approach to family history which is more than just names and dates.

Unlike the plotting of the family tree, where we aim to enter data as consistently as possible, with a degree of symmetry and certainly with precision, the chance to build portraits comes intermittently. The spotlight that you shine on the past will illuminate the features of some ancestors, and not others. But this in itself gives a wonderful texture to the tapestry of the family history, with each individual portrait akin to a 'close-up' in a film, contrasting with the general spread of ancestors in the 'long-shot' panorama.

Ancient Faces

In the first century AD, a remarkable new development took place in a place called Fayum, about forty miles south of Cairo. Here, skilled artists began to paint portraits of individuals, to serve as memorials. After a person's death, such a portrait was placed by their relatives in the atrium of their house for a year or two, in the midst of ongoing family life, before being buried with them. These pictures are at once vivid and lifelike, and at the same time eerie, ghostly echoes of those they commemorate. Visiting an exhibition of these portraits is itself a haunting experience, as I can vouch, and an author who has studied them comments that in their presence, she never feels alone.

These ancient faces seem to conspire to keep the past alive. We have our own more recent tradition of portrait painting, of course, and grand family mansions are often hung with paintings of ancestors both noble and scandalous. But perhaps these are created more to mark the past than to live on in the present, as the Fayum portraits do.

Do we want to bring our own ancestors back to life, or is that a step too far? Perhaps each person has to answer that for themselves. In family history though, doing research to help us to put flesh on the bones, and to see certain ancestors as individuals, is undoubtedly important, so whether you want to write about an ancestor as an interesting individual case study, or take them to your heart as family, I would certainly recommend creating such portraits where you can.

Painting Portraits

Sometimes, when all you have to start with is a name and a few sparse details, it can take a lot of work before you've built a convincing picture of a relative. At others, all it takes is just a few vital snippets to turn a bundle of information into a living person. I mentioned my Great-Aunt Florence earlier, and how I had discovered more about her as a postmistress, as an emigrant to South Africa, and as sister to Sophia who died tragically young (see p. 50). In her case, she was already taking shape in my mind, when I acquired two extra elements which transformed her into a reality. These were the photos from my uncle's collection, and an unexpected contact with a great-nephew of her husband's, via Genes Reunited. Taken together, they worked magic!

The great-nephew provided a scan of the card sent out with her wedding cake in 1924, plus further photos of Florence and her husband, along with the news that Stephen Michael Dacey ('Mike') was rather a bad lot. Our family memory classified him as a member of the South African police force, but his provenance was somewhat worse, as it turned out that he had been in a band of armed mercenaries who roamed the land shooting recalcitrant Boers. Now I could take this into account when studying photos of Florence; early shots show her as an eager-faced young woman with shining eyes, arms draped affectionately around the shoulders of her nieces and nephews, one of them my mother. She'd got herself out of a servant's position and taken on the challenge of running a post office, and developed a real love of philately, according to my uncle, whom she encouraged to build up a stamp collection. But the photos taken after her marriage show her face as more set and resigned, and those with her husband don't look at all happy. Although still sturdy and strong, the joy has vanished from her eyes. Florence had been an adventurous girl, but what had promised to be the biggest adventure of her life – sailing away from a sleepy Northamptonshire village to a new life in South Africa – had turned out to be a difficult challenge.

Mike died early, at the age of forty-one, apparently from a tropical disease, leaving Florence perhaps happily liberated to follow her own path again. She became a cabin stewardess, sailing between South Africa and India.

The final spark that ignited her presence for me as an individual was a first-hand account from the mother of the great-nephew, who had remained friends with Florence even though they were not related by blood. Florence visited her in the 1950s (a visit I was able to date from the shipping lists posted on the internet) and the mother remembers how thrilled Florence was to see snow lying on the English countryside – something she hadn't experienced for so many years.

This example shows how 'hard' facts (census reports, BMD certificates, passenger lists and so on) act as the 'bones' of the ancestor, building up a framework. But it's usually when we add the 'soft' aspects – photos, anecdotes, letters, for instance – that we glimpse the 'real' person and feel we can start to get to know them as an individual. Some genealogists might argue that this is not evidence enough, and it's true that we interpret these findings, and perhaps do so to some extent according to our own preferences or bias. But knowledge of each other as human beings is never a precise science, whether we are getting to know a person who is alive or someone who died many years ago.

Even with relatives that you knew as a child, you may come to view them in a very different way once you look into the family's past. Sue was very close to her grandfather as a child:

> When he retired, my grandparents moved to live in the same village as we did, and I started to go to church with him every Sunday morning. On Remembrance Sunday he would always sit holding my hand, and tears would creep down his cheek.

Sue didn't understand the full story until later, when she saw the letters he'd sent to her grandmother from Belgium in the First World War. On 3 April 1917, just before the Battle of Vimy Ridge, he wrote to his wife:

> When I did get back to the shelter, the first job I made was to read your letter, and my darling I felt as if you had written it so I could have it just when I felt the need of it and you

most ... I have no one here at all to give me a cheerful word or the smile of love and sympathy that I need so much. I feel absolutely on my own fighting right and left against all sorts of evil, and the only helping hand I get is through your letters.

After seeing the letters, Sue says:

Reading these letters has not changed the way I saw my grandpa, but reinforces what a kind, thoughtful, gentle man he was. He loved nature, poetry and his garden. The best grandpa I could have wished for.

A more distant ancestor, in terms of the past, is the notorious Revd Augustus Joseph Tancred, Bernard's 2 x great-grandfather, who we first met in Chapter One (see p. 12), and who is now springing back to life as a result of the research Bernard has done. The Reverend Tancred was born in Cork in 1802, and is said to have to have eloped with a nun. He has become an object of fascination for Bernard: 'The quest for "AJT", as I like to call him, has been something of an addiction these past thirty or so years.' And his persistent research has turned up a few more scandals surrounding this intriguing rogue of an ancestor:

Not surprisingly, a man who may have eloped with a nun did not stop there. When Evelina, the woman who bore his children, and who may have been his wife, and may have been the nun, died in Grahamstown in 1847, he sought the comfort of a second wife, identified a likely candidate and applied for a marriage licence. Whether this was by an early form of internet dating or not, he seems not to have had sight of the bride-to-be until he turned up at her family home and found the goods not up to scratch, as if contrary to an imaginary Trade Descriptions Act. What did he do? Petitioned the governor for a refund of the cost of the marriage licence. Moving on to pastures new, he then married the under-age daughter of a Dutch farmer in the northern

Cape, where he became the local MP. His escapades in the Cape parliament became legendary: challenging members to duels, brandishing the mace, walking out into the street and trying to sell the Parliament building itself. As one obituary comments, 'With a more evenly balanced mind than Dame Nature would appear to have endowed the subject of our present notice, he might, and most assuredly would, have risen to a much more enviable position among his adopted countrymen than that to which he attained.'

Speculation and discovery

Getting to know an ancestor often leads to more speculation, as Sheila M. discovered regarding her grandfather:

Family history had it that he was sacked by the Metropolitan Police for hitting a man who called him a b—d. In actual fact, he was a bookies' runner and lost his twenty-one years' pension when forced to resign in 1933 (info from Metropolitan Police records). He had served in the Norfolk regiment as a lad with his five uncles, then in the police and back to Norfolk regiment for the First World War, where he became a sergeant before being demoted to a private. That's one big regret – his military records were in the burned ones. [Over 60 per cent of British records from the First World War were destroyed in the Blitz. Some that remain are damaged by fire.] Love to know what he was demoted for.

Sometimes one detail can act as a key to an ancestor's choice, and the changes that it made to the family, even if it does not bring total illumination about the individual. As Janet reports, 'I found out that my 2 x great-uncle James, who had vanished, went on to Cuba and Jamaica and his family ended up in New York. He married a black woman, so our family changed colour, which was all very interesting.'

It isn't always so easy discovering enough personal information about an ancestor from further back in history, as there are less likely to be personal memories passed down about him or her, and letters, diaries and so on are rarer. However, sometimes just putting the story-lines together brings enough elements into play to achieve the transformation from a name to someone who you can imagine as a living person. Finding a famous ancestor certainly helps, as records are likely to be much more fruitful and accessible.

Mick was lucky:

> I have a famous artist ancestor, Thomas Webster RA. Not a direct ancestor, an uncle, but you can buy prints of his work and old postcards too. Webster was the leader of what was known as the Cranbrook Colony in Kent, who were into genre painting. I have managed to buy three letters of his that he wrote, I have an original sketch and one of my walls is full of prints of his paintings. Webster also painted a picture of his parents too, my direct ancestors! I have also visited Webster's house in Cranbrook ... his studio is still preserved and has a wonderful ceiling designed by an eminent architect of the day.

I can vouch for the interest of Webster's work, which shows scenes of the day especially relevant for family or social history. Although these are romantically depicted, themes like *A Letter from the Colonies* nevertheless give a marvellous impression of how ordinary people lived, with the cottager's family waiting eagerly but anxiously for the messenger to hand over the letter, and to read news – maybe good or bad – from the emigrant family member so far away.

Witnesses to your ancestors' lives

There's a chance that you might be lucky even with a more humble ancestor too, by tracking down accounts that relate directly to your ancestors, recorded in the observations of other people. Just recently,

I was reading *Kilvert's Diary* again – the journal of the Reverend Francis Kilvert, who was posted to Clyro in Radnorshire from 1865 to 1872. I realised that this was only a few miles from where my Baptist minister ancestor, Edward Owen, was living in Painscastle, and although Kilvert was in the area some twenty years later, there could still be tales or descriptions relevant to Edward's time there. To my joy, there were! Kilvert himself paid a visit to Painscastle which he described at length, commenting on the recently opened post office, the gathering of the older men of the village outside one of the pubs, where they regularly chewed over the state of the world, and the meeting with a reclusive vicar of the parish. All this came along with a vivid and extended portrait of the village, which helped to give me a real flavour of the place in the mid-nineteenth century. But there was an even more relevant report. Kilvert was fond of chatting to the elderly of the parish, and often recorded their stories of times gone by. On 21 May 1871, he writes:

> After Church visited some of the cottages. Elizabeth Pugh told me that when she was living at Little Pen-y-fforest she used to go to the Baptist and Independent Chapels at Painscastle. Stones were regularly thrown into the Chapels among the congregation during service, and once a dog was hurled in.

So the chapel where my 2 x great-grandfather used to preach was not quite the simple, peaceful place of worship I had thought! My own visit to the village hadn't revealed any of its tumultuous past, but now here was an eye-witness account of the conflict that took place within the village itself, presumably between church- and chapelgoers.

Kilvert's Diary is full of colourful, detailed accounts of the neighbourhood folk, rich and poor, and if one of these should be your ancestor, you have a goldmine of first-hand information which could bring him or her to life in a way you may never have dreamed possible. So it could pay to search out other published memoirs and diaries relating to a particular area relevant to you, or perhaps to someone working in the same profession, or making the same journey as one of your forebears. Although some volumes may be in print as mainstream books, as Kilvert's certainly is, there are also examples of private memoirs and journals uploaded on to the internet which could prove valuable to you. There's an extract from one of these in the next chapter, relating to the story of a girl who stitched a sampler which is now in my possession (see p. 193).

Tales of the unexpected

The family history trail doesn't merely offer rosy views of a halcyon past. Even though the exploits of ancestors are events in the distant past, their impact on you may turn out to be not so much heart-warming as shocking or upsetting. If you do choose to investigate your ancestors' lives, bear in mind that almost inevitably one or two less salubrious personal details will come to light. At least four survey respondents discovered suicides in the family tree – one a grim tale of an ancestor cutting his throat with a pair of scissors in 1881 (Sheila M.), another of a son who jumped off a dinghy into the sea, weighed down by the boat's anchor (Charles).

Unsavoury tales of bigamy and incest have to be taken in, and one may wish that the character in question didn't have 'a face' as in a portrait, but would retreat into anonymity again. Virginia didn't relish what she found out about her great-grandfather, who 'turned out to have been a very bad lot'. She asked me not to give the family name in this case, so sensitive an issue would it be with surviving family members:

A clerk, he was sent to prison in 1876 for forging a railway pass, which he had used to take his wife and two toddler sons on holiday from London to Matlock. When he died in 1904, his wife bitterly told the coroner that he had been a drunkard for over thirty years (all their married life), had sold all their possessions to pay for drink and had not worked to support his family for twelve years. He had been abusive to his wife and children when drunk, such that on occasions they had locked him out of the house. None of this was ever known to my mother's generation; I discovered it in newspaper reports.

Even where the family is aware of misdemeanours, an unpleasant ambiguity can remain about the truth of the story, as Jeanette relates:

> We had a tale in the family of my husband's great-grandfather throwing his wife down the stairs when she was pregnant and killing her. I researched this and found from her death certificate that she was suffering from a chronic kidney condition and being pregnant hastened her death after she miscarried.

Was she pushed? Or was the husband accused unfairly of precipitating her death? It would be hard now to ascertain the real facts of the case, but suspicion will always remain.

In cultures that practise ancestor veneration, different views prevail as to whether a 'bad' ancestor should be admitted to or excluded from the family ranks. In his article 'Ancestor Reverence: Building an Ancestor Shrine', relating to the Ifa religion of African origins, Awo Fa'lokun Fatunmbi states in his internet article:

> Most of us have some ancestors who would not be welcome at the altar because of a lack of character development. It is necessary to exclude these ancestors and to make it clear that no communication with them is desired. Before sealing the space with water [as part of the ritual], call the names of those who are to be excluded from participation and firmly express your reasons for not making them welcome.

But elsewhere, I have come across injunctions to include all your ancestors who are part of your line; once passed from this world to that of the spirits, they are considered to have transcended the misdeeds they committed and to have an equal power with other ancestors, which means that they can be of potential benefit to their descendants.

I have never personally come across a case of a contemporary individual being 'haunted' by an ancestor uncovered through family history research, but nor do I mock such a possibility. At the very least, we can become over-fascinated with certain ancestors, and if we dwell too long on acts of theirs which were cruel or destructive, this could certainly affect us. And if many traditional cultures are right when they say that the living can be in contact with the ancestral world, then we should keep our connections to our ancestors as healthy as possible. It's important in any case to maintain a good balance between life as lived now, and what we feel or conjecture the past to be.

The last word on this subject goes to Bernard, descendant of the entertaining scoundrel 'AJT': 'AJT seems very alive to me. I feel he is laughing behind my back, chuckling, "Catch me if you can", for I have never yet discovered his parents, birth, marriage or grave.'

TIPS FOR CREATING PORTRAITS

- Be prepared to create the portrait from a variety of materials, ideally including records and documents, photos and family memories or first-hand accounts.
- Note even the smallest anecdote or oral recollection about an ancestor. This will help to bring him or her to life.
- Study photographs carefully, for they can reveal many clues, both in the detail and also in the character of the subject.
- Allow time to 'get to know' the person.
- Keep a grip on the 'hard facts' – dates, events, etc. – to give your interpretation a firm basis.
- Keep an open mind about any ambiguities of personality or action. Individuals can be contradictory, and you will get a more rounded picture if you allow for that.

Lucky Breaks and Synchronicity

Just as ancestors can almost magically change from being names on scraps of paper to fully rounded human beings who occupy a vital place in our imagination, so the slog of the research trail can also transform, on occasion, from a diligent combing of the evidence, to an activity where astonishing things can and do happen. As mentioned in Chapter One, this is a process sometimes referred to as 'synchronicity'. This could be called a lucky break, but is often accompanied by the sense that it is redolent with meaning, and resonates with other circumstances in an unusual way. It has happened to a number of the survey respondents as part of the process of discovering ancestors and ancestral places.

Mick tells his story:

I tracked one of my great-grandparents' children to a small village in Dorset, called Milbourne St Andrew, so a few years ago we decided to make a visit. We chatted to someone over a hedge, and told our story. Amazingly, he knew about it, and also the fact that there was someone who was still alive in the village who knew my great-grandfather's daughter, Mary Ann Fletcher. It resulted in one of those magical moments in genealogy, when I opened an envelope that contained a picture of Mary Ann, a document that told of her apprenticeship and the story of some of her life in Dorset. I now have Mary Ann's Bible and also a bookmark that she made that went with it.

Evelyn relates a string of such synchronicities; here are two of them:

One day I walked round the Harris museum at Preston – just to have a walk after poring over books in the library – and saw an attendant watching me, so I thought I'd better look more closely, and found a certificate for a child of thirteen, allowing her to leave school for beneficial employment. It was for my aunt!

Another chance was in a churchyard near Preston where a friend and researcher from Ireland asked me to visit and record coats of arms of her family. I found them on the outside walls; to photo them I stood on a brass plate of a grave – realised the names were for my great-great-aunt and her husband and son, and the dates were exactly right!

Evelyn seems to get her 'lucky breaks' particularly when she is helping others. For Ken D., on the other hand, powers of intuition play a part:

The strangest experience I ever had was visiting a church-yard in Mary Tavy, Devon. We were going on holiday to Cornwall and made a detour there, as I wanted to visit the church and see if I could find any family 'Michell' grave-stones. We did not have a great deal of time, so I had to be quick. What happened next is unbelievable, and I cannot explain how it happened. There were about 250 or so grave-stones there. I went to the oldest part, and only the backs of the gravestones were facing me. I was 'attracted' to one stone in particular, which was the very one I was looking for!

Finding Your Family Connections

As we call on our ancestors to reveal themselves, and search the places where they lived, does this in some sense reawaken family connections? Does our intention to shake the dust off a family's past somehow invigorate the identity of the family?

Part of growing your family tree is often the discovery of 'new' relatives, which in turn can lead to new connections, friendships, encounters and the trading of information. Perhaps one of the secrets of traditional cults of ancestor veneration was that by honouring the ancestors, the existing family is also kept more alive, and that a current of vitality runs between the ancestors and the living family members. Whether you see this as a matter of the spirit or simply a practical consequence of digging around and discovering links to past and present – or indeed, both – the rediscovery and renewal of family bonds does play a significant part in the process of 'doing' family history.

Alison's story in this respect is so remarkable that I'm quoting it in full. She discovered the existence of a new relative via the Lancashire Family History Society, and in 2007 was able to fly over to England from Australia and meet him. But this was only the start:

Another amazing meeting took place that year as well. I joined Genes Reunited and listed the family members I wanted to find more information about. My mother had been asking me for years to try and find her cousin who she felt sure had emigrated to Australia with her family. I had no luck tracing the family, some of whom were still living. The cousins had been very close, but after a number of years lost touch through the tyranny of distance and letter writing.

One day, I had an alert in my mailbox. Someone had contacted me through the Genes Reunited site and it appeared we had the same great-grandfather. I responded with a few more details and it turned out that we were, indeed, related. The contact then said she was excited to find a living relative, but she now lived in Australia. I casually responded that I also lived in Australia and gave her my private email address. She then replied that she had retired and with her husband was sailing up the Queensland coast and they were now in a place called Townsville. That is where I live! You can imagine my amazement, and so I asked her to ring me and we should meet for coffee. She duly rang, we made a date and then I asked where she was living and couldn't believe that she was living on her boat which happened to be moored behind ours and along the next pontoon. I could see her boat every time I went to the marina.

This was incredible. I was keen to meet her and was astounded to discover that she was the lady I had been casually greeting and whose dog I'd been patting for the past year or so – and I never knew we were related! She was the daughter of my mother's cousin. She had changed her name by deed poll and, yes, this very woman was the person my mother was looking for all these years. She had known her as a baby, had visited each time she was on leave in the UK and taken Chinese dolls as gifts. When I remarked on this Kym said, 'Oh, so you're the people from Hong Kong – I still have one of the little dolls your mother gave me!'

Alison's story shows that your relatives may be closer at hand than you would ever guess, and that the ways in which you might find them in real life can be stranger than fiction. Is there a genetic pull operating here? We may never know exactly, but through the family history research that we do, we help to create the framework in which such extraordinary – even magical – connections can occur.

EXTENDING YOUR SENSES

You cannot automatically create 'magical moments in genealogy', as Mick puts it, but you can help to create the kind of conditions in which they may occur. One way of doing this is to encourage your intuition to come into play, so that you're not only working from the intellectual, fact-finding part of the mind, but allowing all your senses to be aware and alert. By being open to possibilities, and gently encouraging them, you also give yourself the chance of generating the discoveries and the contacts that you yearn for, in terms of searching for your ancestry.

Exercise: a gateway to knowledge

Our senses are the gateway to knowledge. Here is an exercise to try at any time when you have a moment to spare. You can do it in almost any surroundings, though it will be easier if you practise it first in reasonably quiet ones:

Stand or sit – it doesn't matter which. Let your thoughts go, and instead of thinking, reviewing, etc., become aware of the living sphere that surrounds you. Do it in the round, and include what is behind you, as well as what is in front and beside you. First of all, just observe the impressions that you are receiving. Then check out how each of the classic senses of sight, sound, touch, taste and smell is responding to this environment. Finally, notice how alive this sphere feels, and whether you are picking up other subtle and more delicate perceptions from it. Don't try to interpret them; using this kind of 'back-of-the-head' awareness will, in itself, help you to open up intuitive powers and generate new circumstances.

Ancestral Landscapes

Hiraeth is a poetic Welsh word that means a longing for home, whether that be the place you come from, or the ancestral landscape to which you feel you belong. Robert expresses such a yearning eloquently, and in his case north Wales is both where he has spent time, and where his forebears originate:

I suppose what the family history means to me is very much tied in with my love of north Wales. All my childhood holidays were at Nain's [Welsh for grandmother] in Harlech. Days on the traeth [beach], walks in the hills around Cwm Bychan and trips on the narrow gauge railways conspired to engender in me a deep feeling for the area; and there were always local folk whom my dad knew, and a constant awareness of the language in the background. When I discovered just how deep were my ancestral origins there, all became clear; and by then I had become a hill-walker and was even to spend a little while as a volunteer myself on the new Welsh Highland Railway. I have always hankered after Gwynedd, but for a long time had not realised that it was, after all, the hiraeth. My father eventually passed away at ninety, and I laid his ashes to rest in his beloved Llyn Cwm Bychan, among the craggy hill-sides his forebears had farmed through the centuries. When my turn comes, I hope to join him there. Yes, it is a land that calls to me. Calls me home.

In family history, even if a terrain is not part of your personal past, you may still be able to take the opportunity to explore the ancestral landscapes for the first time. Such a journey can even be in the nature of a pilgrimage; many of the respondents who've undertaken such a quest, sometimes travelling thousands of miles to do so, have found it deeply meaningful, as we'll see shortly, and as Norma describes here:

> My ancestors have really come alive for me. They lived a long way from where I now live, but I can't wait to visit the places where they lived. I have a photograph of my 2 x great-grandfather as the 'wallpaper' on my computer. He was born in 1824 and died in 1899, so never in his wildest dreams would he have imagined that this could happen.

Why visit old haunts?

Sandra's experience touched her deeply: 'It has been very moving to visit the churches where they have been baptised and married, and to find their graves, and to read what their families have said on them.' And Geoff's travels proved very enlightening for him:

> An aspect of family history which I have found to be very interesting has been genealogical tourism. I have visited

villages associated with my family and on one memorable occasion went to the church where my great-grandfather married in 1827. This was a country church and seemed to have been very little changed over the years. I have also visited the site of the house in Sheffield in which my great-grandfather and family lived, and have discovered that this was in the heart of what was the industrial area. It must have been a smoke-filled noisy nightmare of place, particularly for country dwellers. Site visits such as these can increase understanding.

These quotes from family historians who visited places and burial sites associated with their ancestors reflect two of the principal reasons why such expeditions can be so rewarding. There is the emotional component, which Sandra expresses, and also that of developing greater understanding of our ancestors' lives, as Geoff points out. And both help us to feel a stronger connection with those ancestors, as indeed does the very act of treading on the same ground. As Josie says, 'I have enjoyed visiting the villages and knowing that their eyes had seen those hills and walked those paths, and that they were christened at this font.'

Preparing for a trip

Our family historians are also keen on good preparation. This helps you to make the most of your visit, and to locate tricky-to-find houses in advance. As Virginia explains:

> It's important to get a sense of place – study maps of where your ancestors lived and worked, and if possible visit. I knock on the doors of houses where my ancestors lived, and generally get a warm welcome. In return, I provide histories of their houses.

And Charles's groundwork really paid off:

Hampshire Archives in Winchester proved a goldmine in tracing the Hampshire Shoyers [the family name]. We have copies of the deeds renting their cottage from Edward Austen, brother of the author Jane Austen. From the original enclosure map we were able to locate the exact location of the cottage and visit the site – now in thick forest.

Even though you may not be researching in archives or poring over records when you make your visit, I recommend getting together a selection of notes, tree diagrams and dates beforehand, so that you can, if need be, check whatever comes up – a headstone, place name, date of birth and so on. Good maps are invaluable, and in the UK a large-scale Ordnance Survey map can be tremendously helpful. You can also switch to an OS view of local areas on certain websites, such as Bing Maps (http://www.bing.com/maps/) and find historical maps on sites such as Genuki. This can make all the difference between finding an old family dwelling and driving around in circles.

Careful preparation then can be a good basis from which to experience the chance encounters, offers of help and surprises which your field trip will almost certainly bring. Here's an extract from my journal account of a trip made to mid-Wales in May 2009, with the aim of locating the farmhouse where the father of Margaret Richards, my 3 x grandmother, lived at the beginning of the nineteenth century:

We traced 'The Gate', which was once the home of David Richards, with the help of a friendly local farmer – it helped that we were staying with my third cousin Anne Evans and her husband Philip, a music teacher who is known by just about everyone in the area as 'Anne the Music'! I had already done an internet search, which showed that it's now called Gate Farm. It is situated on a B road between Caersws and Trefeglws, a few miles out of Newtown. We drove up and down the road a few times. Could the small, dilapidated, tumbledown cottage with rusting machinery and overgrown with weeds be The Gate? As with all my expeditions into Wales so far, we found the man at the next farm only too happy to tell us that it was – everyone in the Welsh countryside seems keen to have a chat and will gladly give you bits and pieces of information. He also filled us in with the history of the place; it has recently been inherited by several younger members of a family (not the original Richards family) after the elderly owner died.

Even at its best, the farm could never have been prosperous, except in the sense of making someone a modest living as a smallholding in pre-industrial days. The position is superb, with fabulous views to the hills, but it comes with only twenty acres, and looks as though it was a two- or three-bed cottage with a couple of stables and a small barn. I am not sure how much of it dates back to David Richards's time, but judging from the dip in the roof and the bulge in the walls, I think it's very likely to be the original cottage patched up. Patched up it certainly is, with corrugated iron, odd bits of brickwork and the like. The small stable or dairy has an old-world feel to it, with wooden latch doors, and again this is likely to be original. David was a tenant farmer and it's probable that it belonged in the Richardses' period to the 'Park', a more substantial farming estate over the road.

The younger members of the current family of owners drove up while we were there and said it is about to be sold, and will be converted, so maybe, ramshackle though it is, we were lucky to catch a glimpse of the old 'Gate' before it's changed beyond recognition.

Take your time

Take plenty of time to explore these ancestral landscapes, if you can. You never know just where you will want to linger, or who you might meet. One thing leads, mysteriously, to another. Don't be rushed if you can help it. However, even if you do have to squeeze in a trip en route elsewhere, or must return to pressing commitments, take the chance to make the journey and make the most of every moment.

Alone or in company?

There's no firm guideline as to whether you will find it easier to travel alone or in company. I have done both; I've visited ancestral sites with my husband, a wonderful companion and someone to share my inner thoughts with (not to mention taking over the driving when I get tired). I've also travelled with an easy-going friend who enjoys the sense of adventure involved in ancestor-hunting, which made it fun. But at another time, I've stood alone on my great-great grandmother's grave, lost in a sense of silent communion with her, and could not have made conversation with anyone else.

If you do take a friend or partner, remember that your sense of timing is likely to be very different from theirs. You may well want to linger by a grave, or a view, for what seems to them to be an interminable length of time. You'll need to have the freedom to set the pace, as you can't tell in advance what will grab your attention or pull at your heartstrings. There may be moments when you need to fall silent, and others when you want to talk nineteen to the dozen. It's best if you can mention these possibilities in advance.

Taking chances

Careful planning, coupled with an attitude of spontaneity during your trip, can be a winning combination. Geraldine advises being as brave as you dare:

> I went to Cornwall last summer to look for the family home of Richard Langmaid, which my parents had told me about. I was told that it was a big house, on the top of a cliff, at the mouth of the river, with its own beach. The name had changed, but we found it, and taking courage in both hands, knocked on the door and introduced ourselves. To my absolute amazement, we were invited in and shown around the house by the owner. She was a charming lady and knew a little of the history of the house. It made me feel very

emotional. I was so glad that my husband – and the dog! – made the decision to knock on the door, and would suggest to anyone else to do the same. The worst that can happen is a curt refusal.

Be a keen observer

While you are on 'safari', keep an eye out for anything that might be of interest or importance later. Take a camera with you, shoot plenty of pictures, and make a few notes, since later you might forget details or sequence. Write up your 'field notes' as soon as you get home, or if you are on a longer visit set aside time in the evenings to note the day's findings, even if you're tired. It pays huge dividends.

A good motivation is to send out your trip report in a narrative form as a bulletin to other family members. If you are excited and enthused by your journey, and convey that through your writing, then they will be too, which will help you to feel that you're doing something creative and rewarding by keeping them posted.

Writing up my account of visiting The Gate proved useful three times over: it captured my impressions while they were still fresh, it served as a bulletin to send out to other family members and I was also able to use sections from it in my full family history when I wrote it up in book form later. Time well spent!

The return from a trip is also the time to cogitate on what you've discovered, mull over what it means to you and, perhaps, link it in to existing material, as Virginia recounts:

My aunt knew that her great-grandmother Margaret Hodgson came from the Woolhouse Farm on the moors above Barnard Castle, in Co. Durham. I found that the Hodgsons had farmed there for three generations. I have visited the farm several times, and it still looks like the pencil sketch my aunt had, which was probably drawn by one of Margaret's sons. The farm feels in some way like my family's spiritual home.

Genealogical Tourism or a Pilgrimage?

It's evident from the accounts I've received that visiting ancestral haunts is much more than a fact-finding mission for family historians. It can feel more like a pilgrimage, in which the sense is one of walking on hallowed ground. The pace slows, the senses are keener, and that sense of longing to be connected with what is just out of sight, the people of our ancestry, is experienced. I'll now let extracts from two of these accounts speak for themselves.

Ken Z.'s grandparents were born in the Ukraine, but emigrated to Canada in 1907. After the Ukraine achieved its independence in 1991, Ken made two visits to the country trying to visit his ancestral village, Nebyliv. The second time, he and his wife Liz managed to reach it:

> Finally we approached Nebyliv. The village is located in the foothills, in the shadow of the Carpathian Mountains. Everything was green. People were hoeing potatoes and cutting hay. The fields extended up to the forested mountains, which began a half-mile away and climbed to the sky.
>
> We crossed a wide, rock-strewn river into a village of single-storey houses. When we stopped at a store across from the church, I hurried out of the car and snapped a few photos. There was no assurance that we would return that way, or that the golden domes would be glistening so beautifully in the sunshine tomorrow.
>
> A few minutes later, we drove down a narrow, bumpy lane, and stopped in the shade of tall beech trees. A wooden picket fence surrounded the little farmstead on the edge of the village. In the centre stood a small yellow cottage, a stable and a storage shed. Split firewood was neatly stacked around the walls of the stable and shed. In front of the house were a large, meticulously cultivated garden and an orchard of apple, plum, pear and walnut trees. Behind the house, a hay field stretched to the river. The house and farmstead seemed to have changed little since my grandparents left 102 years ago.

An old woman opened the door of the house and slowly began walking towards us. As she approached, she ignored everyone else and fixed her eyes on me. Aunt Yulia greeted me like a long-lost relative, with a hug and tears.

'Welcome back to Nebyliv,' she said. Two branches of our family tree had come together again after a century apart. I had finally returned to my roots.

She welcomed us into her house, and led us to a table covered with a feast of beautifully arranged plates of food. The small dining room was filled with family. I rose to offer a few words of greeting and appreciation. I tried to express my deep emotion with my limited vocabulary. They toasted the guests from Canada, and I replied with a toast to the hosts, our family and our homeland.

As a memento of my visit, Yulia gave me a hand-embroidered Ukrainian table runner, but the souvenirs I collected myself – four walnuts and a bag of rocky clay soil – were much more precious to me for they had come from the fields my people had worked for generations.

Jim and his wife Gayl made an epic trip from the United States to the British Isles, to try and find Gayl's ancestry, which had previously eluded them:

We learned that Gayl's ancestors had lived in all the countries of the Isles. On these Isles where we had just walked, they endured constant conflict from tribal feuds to clan rivalry to wars among dukedoms and kingdoms that over centuries gradually evolved to country and empire. They shared the vision that led to the Isles becoming the cradle of modern democracy, human rights and civilisation. We know by their actions that they acquired great knowledge and skills and directed their passions to realise this vision.

Lifting Gayl's ancestral veil has made us thankful for and blessed by our ancestors. The great German poet and philosopher Wolfgang von Goethe expressed our sentiments well when he said, 'Blessed is he who thankfully remembers his ancestors, joyfully tells of their work and joys and who feels honoured to quietly enter his ancestral ranks as an essential link in a precious chain.'

Family Heirlooms and Neglected Treasures

The final section in this chapter is about objects that you or others possess, which were once a part of your ancestors' lives. Many of us have items which have been passed down from earlier generations, or which were owned by close family members who have now died. In the context of family history, it is well worth identifying and recording these objects, pinpointing who their owners were, and the story or history that goes with them. This adds to a sense of connection with these individuals, and the lives that they led.

Some people may have almost too many 'treasures' to count, while others may have very few, so this task can vary enormously. Where there are a great number, you may have to be selective. No one wants to live in a museum, either, so it's important to do this in a way which means you can still use them in your daily life, if appropriate, or see them as part of the background of your home if they belong to you, rather than tiptoeing around each china cup or piece of furniture as if it is sacred.

Check what you have at home

You may think you know what you own – but do you? You know about the chesterfield sofa that your granny passed on to you when she had to move into a retirement home, but what about the humble china basin stashed at the back of the cupboard that your mother once made the Christmas pudding in? We tend to identify heirloom items, such as jewellery, watches, paintings and antiques, and ignore the items from everyday life such as tools, kitchenware, boxes of beads and buttons, books and coverlets. Could there be more lurking in your domestic environment than you realise?

Check what your relatives may have

Now this may be a more sensitive issue. If you start asking your siblings what they still have from your parents, grandparents or aunts and uncles, they may become highly suspicious of your motives. Perhaps there was a slight tussle twenty years ago during a family share-out, when you were awarded the leather-bound set of Shakespeare plays, and your brother the carriage clock which you had always fancied. Quite naturally, emotions are bound up with family objects, and even asking to see a particular treasure could provoke a defensive reaction.

You will know your own family circumstances, but I would suggest mentioning ahead of time that you're doing the family history, and want also to make a record of items which have been passed down, so that any future generations can also share the knowledge of where they came from. Your sibling or cousin may then be quite relieved that they don't have to take on this responsibility and, hopefully, will be happy to let you see and photograph any objects. Ultimately, however, whatever is theirs is theirs, and such access can't be forced.

Ask 'new' cousins what may be around

Using the same tactful approach, you may also wish to ask any 'new' cousins who you've encountered through family history research if they have, or know of, anything relating to your joint ancestors. I have been fortunate enough to see, touch and photograph three pieces of polished oak furniture made by my 2 x great-grandfather in Wales. Cousin Harold also has the mallet said to have belonged to this Baptist minister-cum-cabinet-maker. In this instance, Harold had already told me about the furniture, but if this hadn't been the case, I would have waited till I knew him much better before asking if anything had survived. Once it comes to objects which have value, people are – quite rightly – wary of revealing their existence to a comparative stranger, even if they are distantly related.

Making a record of your heirlooms

Much depends upon what you have the time and inclination for, but as a part of creating your family history, you could take up any or all of the following suggestions:

- Write a brief description of the object in question – who owned it, what period it dates from and where it is kept at present.
- Write down some of the associations or stories connected with it.
- Make a hard copy of any writing that you do, rather than just saving it in a computer file.
- Take and print out a photograph to go with the description.
- Research an object's provenance, e.g. in the case of an antique necklace or military medal.
- Make a separate file containing details of some or all of the known objects that have belonged to your family and ancestors.
- Highlight one or two objects, and write a much fuller account of what they signify, in terms of the life of the person who owned them, memories you have in connection with them, or the provenance of the objects themselves in terms of their make, value, use and/or place in social history.

If you decide to write up your family history (see Chapter Nine) then this could form part of the material, especially vignettes of a few chosen objects as in the last suggestion. A fuller record will also act as a guide to those who inherit in their turn, and will help them to decide what to keep and what to dispose of.

The impossibility of keeping everything

It's been said before, but I'll say it again: you can't keep everything, and you shouldn't be too hard on yourself if there are objects which you have neglected or got rid of in the past, and which you would now regard as treasures.

When my mother died, I remember the family gathering at which we all tried to decide which items to keep out of the household ornaments and furniture, and which we would put into auction. I looked at her china cabinet with the two china budgerigars which my father had bought for her during a particularly happy phase of their life, and the Venetian glass sherry set which I had helped to choose on a family holiday in Venice when I was a teenager. I didn't want any of it, nor did my brother, my children or my two nieces. We all took something for ourselves, and that was enough. At the time, it felt too predatory and painful to try and retain more, and even now this seems like the right decision, although there were less significant items that I wish I'd kept – her book of recipes, for instance.

It's hard to know how you will feel and what you will want ten or twenty years down the line, and in one sense, it's healthy to clear away the debris of someone's life as you lay them to rest, and honour that life. Living with a welter of objects that belonged to another person can be suffocating, and the old cliché of having to 'move on' does have validity.

So by the time you come to write your family history there will almost certainly be a history of your own, during which time you didn't take up every opportunity to acquire possessions that once belonged to your relatives. Or you may have lost, sold or damaged those that you did inherit. I won't recount all my misdemeanours in that department but, believe me, there have been many, especially where jewellery is concerned. Anything that you do retain will, however, be doubly precious because it becomes an heirloom with scarcity value.

WHERE TO KEEP, WHAT TO LOSE?

Certain items may seem too trivial to record, and may be of no real interest to you, even if they have come down through the family. What about that battered Latin textbook once owned by your great-uncle, for instance? It's a subject you detested yourself at school and you've put the book away in the box destined for the charity shop – if anyone out there should happen to want a Latin textbook, that is. But hold on a minute: even if it's never going to be revered in your own lifetime, would it be of interest to future generations? If so, consider keeping it in a family archive that you can pass on. Only you will know if you have the room and the inclination to do this, but please at least consider every family item that you currently own in this respect before throwing it away. I speak from experience!

And is it legitimate to include objects belonging to relatives from your own lifetime, who are now deceased, especially your parents? Is this genuinely part of family history? Once again, you will know where you want the trail to start and finish, but for most of us, the generation immediately preceding ours is highly relevant to the whole family story. They are, or have been, the link between us and our ancestry, so just as their memories and anecdotes form a vital part of deciphering our ancestry, so the objects that they owned can also be a part of this history.

A PSYCHIC READING

Those who are gifted psychically sometimes feel that they can 'read' the history of an object by holding it, or see into the character of the person who owned it – a process known as psychometry. If you are interested in this approach, you could ask for a reading from a psychic or clairvoyant who specialises in this; it's an aptitude which can be trained, and although it can't be taken as absolutely reliable, it may throw up some interesting insights.

Reaping the rewards

Undoubtedly, making a record of objects can be an emotional experience, but along with the sorrow of loss that you may re-experience, there is also the wonder and delight in handling something owned or made by an ancestor. The record will also form part of the family archive for future generations, and perhaps in years to come this gathering and preserving of family knowledge will be considered essential, rather in the way that traditional societies carefully preserved the details of family lineage in oral form. You may, in fact, be ahead of the trend by making a heritage archive.

CHAPTER SEVEN

Finding Gold: Unearthing the Lives of Your Ancestors and Others

I like detective stories and solving puzzles, so family history appeals to me in this way.

Isabel

The allure of having a mystery to solve, and being both detective and participant in the quest, is an irresistible draw in family history. Every colourful story or racy anecdote discovered becomes something that both enhances our ancestry and adds to our own sense of identity. Such stories are often the essential kernel of family lore, passed down through the years to be relished and embellished by each successive generation, and although the truth of the matter, if we finally discover it, may not be exactly what we expected, there is still great satisfaction to be gained in investigating such tales, and an enrichment of our heritage when we finally add into it what we have uncovered.

In this chapter, we consider the stories that emerge through family history research – how to pin them down and how to distinguish fact from legend. Later in the chapter, I'll also show how we can apply the same technique for uncovering lives and stories to individuals who aren't part of our own ancestry – for instance those named in samplers, wills, churchyards, house deeds, christening mugs and the like. These 'other lives' can strike a chord with us too.

Who Do We Think We Are?

As stories emerge from the mist, various mysteries may still remain, or even arise as a result of our research, causing us to question what we once thought was certain. Susan's experience attests to this:

> My 2 x great-grandfather had been dead for four years when my great-grandfather was born in 1854. He is listed on the birth certificate as deceased – and he was well and truly deceased, so couldn't have been the father. My 2 x great-grandmother was a publican on the 1851 census, so perhaps she was overgenerous with her 'favours'. Which leaves me to think, 'Who do I think I am?'

Issues of establishing true paternity can be some of the hardest to solve, but although her discovery leaves Susan with a major question, it also becomes a story in its own right. Stories can involve speculation, as well as hard facts. It's one to put in the family annals – a good-time great-grandmother running a pub, who had a more colourful past than originally suspected.

Many families already have a fund of stories which have been passed down, but are incomplete or appear to be semi-mythical. When the family historian gets to work, however, he or she may discover a wonderful tale underlying the snippet or legend. It's often commented that most family folk stories have a grain of truth in them somewhere, and I have certainly found this to be the case. But even if they are partly fictitious, they can also act as one of the greatest incentives to explore one's ancestry and, if finally brought to light, can shine like nuggets of pure gold. They may be tragic, joyful or humorous, but they are always fascinating.

So if you have such a legend lurking in your own family, I recommend that you do your best to track it down. The story may never be complete, but you will very likely find enough to make the search worthwhile. Stories are also good material for writing up in narrative form as part of your family history book or records, something we'll be looking at in Chapter Nine.

A runaway heiress

My Uncle Roy's notes on his family history, from which I quoted earlier (see p. 43), contain an allusion to Margaret Richards, the wife of my 2 x great-grandfather Edward Owen. (He was the son of the Edward Owens who fought in the Napoleonic Wars, but chose to drop the 's' from his name, which makes it easier to distinguish him; see Appendix I, p. 244.) He was a Baptist minister, and also the maker of the furniture that I was able to see at the home of my cousin Harold (see p. 27).

Edward's marriage to Margaret in 1836, according to my family tradition, 'followed his elopement with the daughter of a disapproving landed family'. This had tickled Roy's interest, and he asked my father to try and track down the family involved. My father was no stranger to *Burke's Peerage*, the standard tome for noble pedigrees, as he'd fathomed part of his own ancestry that way, but he didn't turn up anything that was likely to relate to Margaret Richards, let alone to support Roy's further claim that, 'I heard that they – the Richardses – were related to the Townsend family', the well-known aristocratic British family into which Princess Margaret nearly married.

I too was keen to find a 2 x great-grandmother who might have missed out on her inheritance in the cause of love. After all, what possibilities might arise from that? I nourished my slender hopes. Early on, the trail led me to a beautiful and ancient black and white timbered mansion in Wales, and I asked my husband to take a photo of me standing outside it. Could this be her lost estate – and perhaps mine? No, as it turned out – definitely not. One can always dream, but this was not to be. The reality eventually turned out to be the shabby little farm known as The Gate (see p. 153); this was her place of origin.

The way I discovered this was through help from Alison M. – not the Alison cited from the survey respondents, but a fourth cousin who I met through the internet, and who lives in New Zealand. David Richards, Margaret's father, is our joint direct-line ancestor, and one of my 3 x great-grandfathers. Alison has done superb research on the Richards family, finding the document of administration which was used to wind up the estate of The Gate after David died in 1836, very shortly after his daughter's apparently scandalous marriage. By the time I visited that part of Wales to see for myself, I had learned from Alison's researches and my own that Margaret was educated well enough to write her name, but that the family had not been well off. One of her brothers did slightly better for himself, taking on a bigger farm, and another was most probably a grocer. She could certainly not have come from 'a squire's family', as my father put it.

However, Alison recognised something about my story, and thought it might apply to one of her own direct-line great-grandmothers, who appears on one of the lateral branches of my tree. She wrote to me that 'the family tale could refer to her, as she eloped with someone who was not considered equal'. So here we had two different versions of the same family story, which had been passed down through two different lines. According to my own mother, the young woman in question was Margaret Richards, my 2 x great-grandmother, and she was thrown out of the house after she married Baptist minister Edward Owen. According to Alison, it was about a different member of the family altogether. But if so, who was it, and how did it happen?

Finally, we came up with the likely answer to this conundrum. It lies in a grand confusion of identical names. As mentioned, Alison and I are both directly descended from David Richards of The Gate, but whereas I am descended from his daughter Margaret, Alison's line is through her brother, also called David Richards. This David became a wealthier tenant farmer than his father, so when his daughter (who was also called Margaret Richards like her aunt – my 2 x great-grandmother) announced in 1859 that she was about to marry a man who her parents thought was beneath her status, they banned her from the family home. Although this was a cruel act, their concern did have some basis, since the census recorded two years later shows her husband's occupation as 'workhouse porter'. They lived in the workhouse, where Margaret was the cook. Even though they were not inmates as such, life there must have been hard. But despite her parents' disapproval, the story ended well, for this couple emigrated to New Zealand, starting a new life for their own family, and one which her great-granddaughter Alison is able to enjoy today.

How did the confusion with this story come about, and what part did my own family line play in it? As I wrote later in my own narrative:

> Would my direct-line ancestors have known about this event? Probably, since the excluded Margaret was the first cousin of David Richards Owen, my great-grandfather. And, in 1859, as a lad of sixteen, he was still living with his family in Sarn, near Newtown, which was only about eleven miles from Hill Farm at Bwlch-y-Fridd, where his Uncle David farmed. Edward had taken up a minister's post at Sarn in 1854, moving there from Painscastle with the family, and thus bringing his wife Margaret Owens, née Richards, much closer to her own family roots. So there was probably quite frequent contact between minister's wife Margaret and her brother David, the prosperous farmer. It's likely that family news spread fast. It must have been a difficult year for both families, since Edward and Margaret's son Stephen died in September 1859. So the chances are that the tale about the runaway bride lodged itself firmly into the collective family memory, but with misunderstandings and mistaken identity as it was passed down through two more generations.

Although the lineage has become tangled in the tale, the final solution is actually a simple one – a case of the mistaken identities of two women who shared exactly the same name. But where does that leave the question of a noble family, a cherished notion that my family had clung to? Alison again provides a likely answer. Her 2 x great-grandfather, David Richards (father of the Margaret Richards in the wedding story), himself married a woman called Mary Hudson, who is thought to have been from a very well-connected and wealthy Shropshire family. So Margaret, the bride, would be making a match that her well-bred mother objected to, and since her parents now had reasonably prosperous status – a move up in the world for David, perhaps with the help of his wife's money – they may have resisted the idea that their daughter was taking a downward path.

Although I have no particular desire to find aristocracy in my family, I've nevertheless relished the story of an ancestress who abandoned this for love, and I'm now happy to credit my distant cousin Margaret Richards with that honour, rather than my own 2 x great-grandmother of the same name.

TIPS FOR DIGGING OUT A STORY

- Keep your parameters wide, and be ready to recognise information from a slightly different quarter than you expected.
- Look very carefully at the kernel of the story: what does it tell you? What elements might it have mixed up?
- Ask 'new' cousins on the same ancestry trail, and other family members, whether they can shed any further light on it.
- Note that information may have been telescoped, names switched or other details mixed up as part of the oral-history process.
- Try searching in an older or younger generation if the

story doesn't seem to relate to the person identified. People can accidentally 'lose' a generation, especially when harking back to an ancestor they never knew personally.

- Keep an open mind about the outcome of the story – it may be quite different from what you originally thought, but equally fascinating in its own way.
- Write up your story if you can, and enjoy it for what it is.

The Role of Story-telling

To pass on your findings, and fully enjoy them yourself, they need to come to life, thus fulfilling the age-old human desire for stories, and plenty of them. This book, for instance, would be drab without stories; a dinner party would be dull without them, a child's life impoverished and our evenings sometimes hard to get through without recourse to film, television, novels or radio. There is no shame in liking stories. Indeed, some of the best teaching is done in this way – think of religion and science, for instance – through stories, anecdotes and parables. A good historian or researcher is always careful to try and make it clear what is evidence and what is speculation, but interpretation and story-telling are actually an intrinsic part of discovering and relating the material that we find. There is no such thing as a completely objective presentation of the facts in a historical context.

So allow yourself the pleasure of savouring the stories that you find, and of passing them on to others. If you are writing an academic dissertation, you may need to chart every step of the way, including dead ends in your research, and how you arrived at this or that hypothesis, backed up by official evidence. But to enjoy your own family history fully, and to communicate it, you need the power of narrative and plenty of human interest, as well as the facts. Add footnotes if need be, to explain or qualify, but keep the story intact.

I'd like now to let two of the stories from the survey shine out in their own way. The first is not in a completely polished form, but shows us the ingredients of the narrative, and how it might be developed further as a written or oral account. The second is already written up, giving a good idea of how a story from family history can be lively and engaging on the page – an important consideration, if you want other people to share in your discoveries.

Two drowned sisters

A terribly sad fatality occurred in the fog last night near Redhill, on the northern boundary of Bournemouth, involving the deaths of two young ladies who, mistaking their path, walked into the river and were drowned.

Bournemouth Daily Echo, 25 January 1908

Karen sent me the outline of a story that had been passed down in her family, and which she was able to research and fill out both for herself, and for other living relatives:

When my dad was growing up, there was a story in the family that his great-aunts drowned in the River Stour in Dorset in a tragic accident, as they made their way home from church in the fog in 1908. They were both very young, still in their teens. Anyway, when his mother passed away several years ago, among the photos we found a picture of the grave of the two girls, along with the grave of their mother, but had no info on where they actually were. He also had a photo of the schoolhouse where they lived and taught, but we had no idea where that was either.

After some intense Googling, I found the graveyard where the girls were buried and made contact with the churchwarden there. So in May this year, we spent a few days in the area doing some more local research and came home with so much info – it was quite an emotional time!

We found the grave of the two girls, and spent two afternoons at the local library, looking at over eighteen pages of newspaper articles regarding the story of the events surrounding the two girls falling in the river. We found descriptions of the rescue attempts and inquests, as well as detailed descriptions of the funeral. As they were school-teachers, some reports mentioned up to a thousand people attending, including lots of the schoolchildren they used to teach.

To top off our trip, we spent an afternoon driving around the area to see if we could locate the schoolhouse. Just when we were at the point of surrendering, I saw a building that looked familiar, so we parked up – and yes, we had found the house!

Dad and I went and knocked on the door, and after telling the current occupants our story, ended up with a guided tour around the outside of their property (we felt too embarrassed to ask about seeing inside too).

The newspaper reports were incredibly detailed, and a few passages quoted below illuminate the story further, and reveal just how poignant it was:

The two girls had been to Bournemouth shopping, as was manifest from the name on a paper parcel, namely, 'Bernard Knight'. They left home at East Parley (where they resided with their father and mother, Mr. and Mrs. Wm. Green) during the forenoon, and after walking some two miles across the fields, reached the ferry at Redhill, known as Marshall's Ferry. They returned early in the evening, and it was as near as possible half-past six when they re-crossed the river, a young man named Charles Corbin ferrying them over. They were then carrying a couple of parcels, and appeared to be in the best of spirits.

The fog at this time was so dense that it was impossible to see many yards ahead, and progress by the path at the side of the river leading to the lane by which the main road to Parley is reached was particularly risky for anyone not knowing the road well. But the two unfortunate girls had walked that way scores of times, and when asked if they could find their way, replied, 'O yes, we shall be all right.'

... They started off, and were soon lost to sight in the dense fog, and that was the last time they were seen alive. Whether they lost their way and turned unintentionally towards the river in the fog, or whether they decided to retrace their steps and follow the well-marked path by the side of the river will never be known.

... Search was shortly afterwards made by the river bank with lanterns, but no trace of the poor girls could be found. Close to the place where they must have gone into the water was the imprint on the bank of a small heel, and a yard or so lower down the imprint of another small heel, showing where the girls stepped or fell into the swiftly flow-ing river. These marks were not apparent last night, but they were easily discernible when our representative visited the scene of the sad occurrence this morning.

... A search along the bank last night by lantern light revealed near the spot where the footprints were a small millinery bill, bearing the name 'Bernard Knight, Bournemouth' on it, and a little lower down, close into the bank, was a white muff, and a portion of a piece of paper in which other articles had been wrapped, and bearing on it the name of Mr. Knight. The latter was recovered from the water by a Mr. T. Legg.

Bournemouth Daily Echo, 25 January 1908

The inquest, after the recovery of the first body, recorded details of the conversations the girls had had on that last, fateful night:

The first witness called was William Green, father of the deceased, who was greatly affected, and had to be assisted to the witness stand. He said the deceased was 16 years of age on 25th December last, and she was an assistant-teacher at the East Parley School.

... Witness: My wife and two ladies – Mrs. Joliffe and Mrs. Harvey – were in front of me with lamps. I had a bicycle lamp. Thirty or forty yards before I got to the ferry I heard a splash, and heard a woman's voice cry out. I took the lamp and ran to the spot, and saw the girls distinctly in the water. I am satisfied in my own mind the young girl drowned the first. I distinctly saw two persons in the water. I saw something like two handkerchiefs. The younger one was behind. I saw the elder one drifting near a tree, and thought she would catch hold of it.

The Coroner: Were you able to do anything for them?

Witness: From the time I threw down the lamp and took off my clothes and picked up the lamp I could not see the younger one. The younger one was drowned first. I could tell her by her hair. I went into the water, and I clasped hold of something, but it was not one of the girls. I called for help, and my wife and a man came.

Bournemouth Daily Echo, 28 January 1908

THE UNVEILING OF THE STORY

Karen's account is revealing, not just for the tragic story it describes, but for the steps she took which brought out the truth and full picture of these events. These steps were not only essential for reclaiming the story, but are also the kind of multi-faceted activities that enrich the experience of family history for the individual who is doing the research. This combination of approaches is what makes the quest so fulfilling.

Here are the elements of the research process that Karen followed:

1. The story had been passed down through the family, but, as is often the way, was inaccurate. We know now that the girls weren't coming back from church, as family lore related, but from a shopping trip. The information had probably been telescoped, to encompass the fact that they

were pious girls, who were pupil-teachers at a church school. Commendably, Karen didn't take this all as fact, but treated it as a basis from which to research.

2. She began with only a little evidence – the photos of the grave and the schoolhouse where they lived – but was able, eventually, to use those to good effect in tracing their physical whereabouts.

3. Googling the internet produced results, but it needed time and patience in this case. It's sometimes tempting to think that the internet will always give us instant hits, but working through different leads and sites may be essential.

4. Karen had previously enlisted local help, in the form of the churchwardens, and although they actually didn't seem to be able to pinpoint the grave she was looking for, nevertheless it's a good policy to consult local experts and officials where you can.

5. She took time to search in the local library there, another valuable resource to use when you're in an area relating to your ancestors. Most regional newspaper archives are housed at local libraries, and if you know the dates of the relevant events, you can often find reports of them quite quickly. Asking the librarian for assistance can speed this up, and make sure that you cover all the likely newspapers of the period.

6. The newspaper reports, typically for those of the time, were amazingly long and detailed. Readers then seem to have had an appetite for the minutiae of tragedies and court cases, so you can reasonably expect to see conversations reported verbatim. You may, therefore, often discover what your ancestors actually said – a precious opportunity that rarely comes any other way, unless you have letters that they've written.

7. Karen was able to drive round the area to see the lie of the land, and search for the house in which the girls lived. Taking the photo with her meant that she was able to spot

it on sight. Having all the evidence with you is essential – I failed to find my great-grandfather's grave in a cemetery recently because I had forgotten to bring the photo of it, taken by my brother, and there was no one around to show me a burial plan.

8. Karen was able to talk to the occupant of the house and, by creating a rapport, to have a tour around the outside, even if she didn't quite dare to ask to see inside. There is no right or wrong here, since often you have to go on instinct as to whether to request such a viewing or not. What does usually pay, though, is to talk to the owner or occupier, to explain why you are there, and to see what might be possible.

All in all, Karen's account is an excellent example of how we might go about piecing a family story together, and the kind of approaches that can be taken. She now has a wealth of information which she could use to write up the whole story about her 2 x great-aunts, if she wishes.

A curious tale of a severed head

Steve has not only uncovered some very strange tales about a long-ago 4 x great-uncle, but has written them up in story form, with the title 'To the End of the World: the story of William Gaze – Pioneer Settler'. This gives us a chance to appreciate how raw research data can be fashioned into a narrative, as well as enjoying the incidents he recounts. (Or perhaps 'enjoying' is not quite the right word, as you will very shortly see ...) Below is an extract, preceded by an account of Steve's research and the family connections, which are also written up in a lively and engaging fashion, and the tale of how William arrived in Australia and was granted land there.

The story of William now moves on to 1832. There had always been some friction between the white settlers and the native Aborigines, but this had been mainly petty theft and pilfering. Violence had always been a minor problem. On the 14th June William, and a young friend John Thomas, were clearing his land in readiness for seeding. A group of about 20 Aborigines approached and took up a threatening position near the men's hut ... They speared William's dog through the head, and the men were in no position to get to their hut where they kept their weapons, as the Aborigines had taken up a position blocking the path. William and his friend decided that their best course of action was to cross the Canning River, and make to the nearby Garrison for assistance.

The Aborigines began to advance as the men fled, spears whistling around their ears. John Thomas managed to cross the river, but William slipped and fell. He received a spear in his back, but managed to stagger forward for a while until further spears brought him down. On looking back, John saw his friend surrounded by Aborigines and being repeatedly speared. He fled to the Garrison to raise the alarm, and returned later with two soldiers. There they discovered William, still alive, but fatally wounded with five spears still in him and many other wounds. The spears were cut off near the skin and William was then carried back to the Garrison by his friend. We can only imagine what pain he must have been in as these spears were up to 15 foot long with 3-inch barbs!

A surgeon was called, but William died of his wounds on the 17th June. Before he died, he managed to dictate his Last Will and Testament, signing it with a cross, not because he could not write but because he was so incapacitated. The State Record Office sent me a copy of his Will, and this showed that he was clearly a carpenter, like his father, as most of his possessions were carpenter's tools and equipment. William dictated that his possessions be auctioned, and that after settlement of any bills, the remainder of his Estate should be sent to 'Emanuel Gaze of Hucclecote near Gloucester England'. Hucclecote was within the Parish of Churchdown at that time. Probate of the Will was granted on the 14th August 1832, and this was the first Probate granted in the Colony, being recorded as Number 1 Page 1. We will never know, I suppose, if Emanuel ever received this.

William was able to identify his attacker as one Yagan (sometimes written as Agan or Egan), the son of a local tribal elder. Yagan had been responsible for many thefts up until now, but the death of William moved him into a new league. Yagan was eventually shot some months later, and the British removed his head, pickled it and sent it to England! Here the head remained in the Liverpool University Museum for over 100 years.

The story of William Gaze and my family now takes an even stranger twist. My Uncle (James Edwards) trained as a vet at the Liverpool University. On qualifying, he worked in the Gloucestershire area before opening a practice in Churchdown. As he once said to me, he must have walked past the head of Yagan many times without giving it a second thought, and he must have walked the same roads and lanes in Churchdown as William and his father did all those years ago. From a young age, I have always championed the rights of the Aborigines and when, during the 1970s and onwards, there was a demand from Aborigines around the world for the British Government to return various 'body parts' taken during the 19th Century, I totally agreed with this. There was a particular demand for the return of an aboriginal head in Liverpool Museum, and in 1997 a tribal elder arrived in England to take receipt of the head. There was much press coverage of this, and the head was retuned to Australia with much ceremony. It is only now that I have come to realise that this head belonged to Yagan, the murderer of my ancestor. In fact, there are many statues of Yagan in the Western Australian area and he is held up as an Aboriginal Freedom Fighter in the face of Colonial invasion.

However, had it not been for the murder of my ancestor, who is to say if Yagan would have achieved his fame?

WRITING UP A STORY

I've made no attempt to edit or shorten Steve's story, so it's a genuinely excellent example of how to write a narrative from family history. Here are some comments which may help you with a similar endeavour, based on the way that Steve has worked:

1. Set the context, as Steve has done in this case, by describing the problem of violence between the white settlers and the Aborigines.

2. Give plenty of detail, probably as much as you have, about the actual incidents you're describing. If your reader can picture the scene, and follow the action as it unfolds, so much the better.

3. Weave in details of any documentation or records, if you can do so without interfering with the flow of the narrative. Steve has done this successfully in the passage relating to William's will. Put other necessary 'hard' references as footnotes if they would weigh down the text too much.

4. Break up your paragraphs so that they are not too visually indigestible on the page – I have, as editor here, divided up some of Steve's lengthy paragraphs into two or three separate ones.

5. Tell us what you are going to tell us. Steve does this when he opens the penultimate paragraph: 'The story of William Gaze and my family now takes an even stranger twist.' This helps to focus the mind of the reader so that they can take in the information, as well as creating a pleasurable sense of anticipation.

6. Bring in any connections with the present time that enhance the story – in this case the way Steve's uncle had been walking past the head of the man who murdered his ancestor for years without realising it.

7. Don't be afraid to edit the story after you've written it, but leave a little time before you come back to it again.

You will find many more tips for writing memoirs and family history stories in my book, *Your Life, Your Story: Writing Your Life Story for Family and Friends* (see Resources, p. 254).

A spectrum of stories

As it happens, both Karen's and Steve's stories have a touch of the gruesome about them; they just happened to be two of the most quotable stories that came my way, and have illustrated many useful points. But among the many stories the survey respondents mentioned, there is a wide range of moods, so it's a pleasure now to be able to share some of these with you in brief.

THE HUMOROUS TALE

Ann, the Lancashire lass from a mining family, describes what her great-grandfather got up to in the back yard:

> He had known that the entire area was one big coal field, and decided to dig in the communal yard. He dug down and was lucky. He found a seam that went under the houses, so he followed it, shoring up as he went. He stockpiled this in the yard and began to sell it to the neighbours, subsidising his income. Using shot to blast the coal out, he was rattling the windows of the houses opposite and was reported to the local squire, the landowner, who confiscated his 'stash'. So much for local enterprise!

EXTRAORDINARY BEGINNINGS

Naomi, living in New Zealand, recounts the unusual circumstances surrounding her grandmother's birth, following her great-grandparents' emigration to Australia to take part in the gold rush:

> 'Were you born in a tent?' How many of us, living in New Zealand, heard that call from a warm living room in winter as we went out of the room, leaving the door open? But that

couldn't have been said to my grandmother, because she would probably have answered 'Almost.' She was Annie ... a new addition to her family who had not long arrived at Beechworth, Victoria, Australia, still living in their travelling 'coach', a covered wagon.

FAMOUS AND ILLUSTRIOUS ANCESTORS

Some people start the family history trail because they've heard talk about famous ancestors in the family tree. My cousin Irene (who is quoted elsewhere, from the survey) and I think we may have our own famous ancestor to discover, but as yet there is no proof: 'In my mother's family, as you know, I believe there is some connection to Sir Joshua Reynolds, reinforced by the fact that my mother was quite a skilled artist,' Irene wrote to me. A story for the future, perhaps.

Margaret is directly descended from the Priestley family, whose most famous member was Joseph Priestley, the eighteenth-century sage credited with the discovery of oxygen. Elizabeth can cite a line of circus performers in her ancestry – acrobats and equestrian stars – along with a famous commercial artist who designed posters for some of the best-known films of the twentieth century. Mick, as we've seen, is related to the artist Thomas Webster RA (see p. 141), and Jeanette to William Penn. Sheila M.'s ancestor consorted with royalty, serving as a state coachman for thirty-six years, and Brenda uncovered an archbishop in Jamaica. William has a family of sporting ancestors, in whose memory the Goldthorp Cup (the family name) was awarded, and also a professional ice-hockey player in the USA.

If you do have a famous ancestor, or one who is in the public eye, you are in a fortunate position, as you can almost certainly find much more about their doings and personality through existing research and records. You will have rich pickings for your stories, even though collating these may lack some of the excitement that comes with venturing into unexplored territory.

COLOURFUL ANCESTORS

We've come across quite a number of colourful ancestors and lovable rogues already, so I'll just cite one more here, from Tam's research into his wife's family:

> One George Fear, whose tale crosses five continents as well as the Boer War and two world wars, told lies continually to authority about his background and life and led the search a merry dance. He was a wild type with one eye who would – and did – fight anyone.

RASCALLY AND RACY ANCESTORS

There are plenty of these too, and to continue with a quote from Tam: 'It is the grand tapestry of life, and the "bad 'uns" are the interesting ones.' He quotes the second of his three 'Fear' stories:

> One Jacques Fear, who was divorced in the late 1800s after committing incest with his sister-in-law. They ran away and returned covertly to England and hid from authority by telling lies on official documents. One of his children was a well-known journalist who did much the same thing with another man's wife.

Ann's stories, too, reveal an 'interesting' great-grandmother:

> Great-grandmother's 'carrying-ons' were infamous, and she was questioned about her relationship with the under-manager at the local pit. His body was exhumed after his other 'fancy woman' had been charged with the murder of her two husbands.

Sheila S.'s 2 x great-grandfather George was convicted for forgery, and later took up residence in Bath, where he gambled away the rest of the family money. Virginia also has a criminal ancestor: 'One of the Cockman sons became an innkeeper, and was convicted of receiving stolen goods (a side of lamb) from a gang of thieves. He spent six and a half years on a prison hulk in the Thames.'

William discovered family records from a convict prison in Western Australia: 'I found George Goldthorp, a semi-literate silver-smith from York, who was transported for theft. I was able to upset a very respectable businessman ... by informing him that his Goldthorp grandmother was one of George's descendants.'

Rob made his own dramatic discovery in Salt Lake City, in the main library of the Church of Jesus Christ of Latter-day Saints, who run the major genealogical project Family Search. He was looking into the divorce of his great-grandparents at the time:

> The stunning revelation in the more than fifty pages of legalese wording, however, provided one paragraph which stated: '... that in or about the month of December 1899, the said Lewis William Davis and Annie Scanlan were arrested in the State of Oklahoma, one of the United States of America, charged with making and passing counterfeit money and brought back to Boston, where said Davis was tried and sentenced to four years imprisonment and said Davis is now confined in the jail at Charlestown in Suffolk County, in the State of Massachusetts, one of the United States of America.' I'm sure the whole of the Salt Lake Library must have heard my gasp!

DRAMATIC EVENTS

From Rob's family research too comes a dramatic story of his grand-parents' involvement with the explosion in Halifax Harbour, Nova Scotia, in Canada:

> My maternal grandparents, Joseph and Nellie, and their extended family resided only 300 metres from the blast site of the *Imo* and *Mont-Blanc*. These two ships, germane to the war effort, had collided in Halifax Harbour on 6 December 1917. The *Mont-Blanc*'s formidable cargo consisted of tons of picric acid, gun cotton, TNT and benzol [related to the

chemical benzene]. She was literally a floating bomb. The collision set the benzol on fire which, in turn, ignited the remaining cargo. The ship exploded, levelling sixteen hundred buildings immediately, including that of my grandparents, and damaging a further twelve thousand. Nineteen hundred people died instantly and a further nine thousand were injured. Miraculously, though they suffered injuries, my grandparents survived. Pension claim records filmed by the LDS church have revealed the family's plight in the following months.

There are many war tales and stories of dramatic and horrifying accidents too, like that of Sandra's 3 x great-grandmother, who lost a leg when it was crushed in a steam threshing machine (an early and dangerous form of mechanised harvesting). Geraldine's ancestor was press-ganged away to sea and Joy discovered that two of her ancestors were knocked down and killed in the same street, in completely separate incidents. And Ruth is still wondering how her grandfather got his wooden leg!

COURAGE AND BRAVERY

My 3 x great-grandmother, Maria (see Appendix I, p. 244), accompanied her husband Edward Owens on at least part of his active service during the Napoleonic Wars. I know little about the details of her own travels on the Continent with the regiment (except that she gave birth to a daughter in Sicily), but it's inspired me to read about the women who were camp followers in Wellington's army, and the way they had to survive on meagre rations, caring for their children as best they could in harsh conditions, and sometimes even giving birth on the march itself. Although war heroes often take pride of place in ancestral stories of bravery, we should spare a thought for the women too, either on the home front or, occasionally, at war themselves.

MAKING THE MOST OF YOUR ANCESTORS

Don't be afraid to bring out your ancestors' more colourful side! Milk the material that you have for the kind of features and detail that help to build a lively story. Do stick as closely to the truth as you can, and don't exaggerate too much, but be sure to make the very best of whatever you've discovered.

Other Lives, Other Stories

I am always curious about other people's lives, especially those from earlier times. While other people buy vintage postcards for their pictures, I buy them to read what's on the back. Not long ago, I bought several boxes of old postcards at auction, and have spent many happy hours sifting through them, speculating about the brief and often enigmatic messages that they contain: hints of love affairs ignited or abandoned, holidays enjoyable or tedious, families united or separated.

If you have the time and inclination, you can apply the same research techniques as you use for your family history research to looking into the lives of other individuals. My own searches of this type have, so far, been related to objects in my possession, including several china christening mugs, inscribed with names and dating from the nineteenth century. One, it turns out, was given to a baby who later became a successful brewer and benefactor of his municipality. I like to think of this small, squalling and naked infant in contrast to the wealthy and probably self-satisfied and corpulent entrepreneur that he became. I have also put together brief histories of the owners of wills bought as antique documents at flea markets, and started to look into people named on the deeds of the old cottage we live in. The main stories that I've uncovered, relating to two embroidered samplers in my possession, will follow shortly.

There are many other ways you can use these techniques, and in so doing you may unearth amazing stories and bring old objects to life. A project in our local village churchyard, using the same kind of archive resources as for family history, has found a kaleido-scope of life stories relating to the people who are buried there. Here's one:

> Edward Fyffe inherited his father's tea business and during a visit back to his birth place he met Ida Stanton Brown, born in Nailsworth in 1860. Ida was the granddaughter of Isaac Hillier, who owned the bacon-curing factory in the town. He married Ida in Hackney in 1884 and they quickly had two daughters, Martha and Ida. His wife fell ill with tuberculosis and in 1887 Edward took his family to the Canary Islands to help her recuperate.
>
> While there, he discovered the delights of bananas and Edward decided that England was ripe for the exotic fruit. He began commercial imports of bananas in 1888 through his company, E. W. Fyffe, Son and Co., one of the first commercial shipments of bananas to the United Kingdom. The business expanded quickly and, at the age of forty-four, Edward (and his partner James Hudson) sold up and he retired to Trullwell House in Box. There, they enjoyed the local life and he was the first in Box to own a motor car. Edward, Ida and the girls travelled widely, Jamaica being a popular destination. Ida Stanton died in 1911, aged fifty-one, but Edward lived for many more years before his death in 1935 aged eighty-two. Edward had amassed a considerable fortune and £38,493 was the sum distributed after his death.
>
> The Churchyard Books, Amberley, Gloucestershire

Fyffe's bananas have been an everyday fact of life in much of Britain for many decades, but whoever has previously thought about the story behind them – except, perhaps, to wonder at the slightly strange name that they bear. Now I know that the banana king is buried directly opposite where we live!

A tale of two samplers

My mother passed on two samplers to me, made by little girls of eight and nine years old. Until recently, I had simply admired their neat stitching – the letters of the alphabet, flowers, birds and trees set out in tidy symmetry. Samplers were a way for girls to learn embroidery skills; I have always loved them, with their quaint, old-fashioned look, and find them intensely evocative of a bygone era. After researching my family history for a few years, I realised that I could do the same for my samplers. Who were the little girls? What kind of a background did they come from? I suddenly wanted to know, and realised that with the powerful search facilities of the internet at my disposal, it might be possible to discover their story.

SETTING BOUNDARIES

For any research task, you need to decide roughly what your aims are, and to have an idea of approximately how far you are prepared to go to accomplish them. Where the research concerns your own family lineage, it pays to be meticulous, checking and cross-checking as you go. However, for an object about which you are curious, but which has no family significance, you are unlikely to want to make this too strenuous a task. This will also probably mean that you'll choose not to be too exacting in finding proof of the results. That may sound like heresy, but it works well, providing you do not falsely claim certainty of the facts, and point out where there is only probability, or even just possibility. In the examples which follow, I'll show how I set about finding the stories behind my two samplers in this way, and how the discoveries unfolded.

SAMPLERS

From the seventeenth to the nineteenth centuries, young girls, often as young as eight, created decorative samplers as a way of practising their stitching and embroidery. These were usually cloth panels sewn in silks or wools, often with a mixture of flowers and birds, letters and numbers, and even houses and human figures. Sometimes poems and prayers were embroidered, and the girl's name and age may also have appeared, along with a date and place. Occasionally, details of her whole family were included too. Although samplers were worked in both Europe and America, it is mainly the British and American examples that include these personal details. They were often sewn by girls at school, as part of the curriculum. Most are colourful, but those stitched in orphanages, or by Quaker girls, for instance, are more restrained and sober in appearance.

REBECCA WENSOR

My first sampler states that it was stitched by Rebecca Wensor, aged eight years, in 1828. Rebecca was born before the start of official registration of births in 1837, but as she would only have been twenty-one at the time of the first census records available (1841), I thought that there would be a good chance that she could still have been unmarried then, and that I might catch her under the same surname. Wensor is an unusual name, which could have given me a head start. But I quickly realised that it could be an alternate spelling of Winsor, a more common name, found particularly in the West Country.

Intuition, common sense and circumstantial facts count for a lot in this kind of research, rather than the dogged, no-stone-unturned kind of approach we might follow to prove a blood line. For a start, I reckoned that the chances were high that the little girl would have spelled her name in the sampler in the way that the family usually did. Unlike the census enumerator, who might jot down a surname according to how he heard it, a child who spent months labouring over a sampler would have wanted it to be her best work, and would have taken care to get her name right. Even though families may themselves have spelled their names differently at different times, I was prepared to give her the benefit of the doubt.

I tried two major websites, Ancestry and Find Your Past, to search and cross-check entries in the census. There were no Rebecca Wensor entries that I could discover for the 1841 England census, and only one Rebecca Winsor, but since she was married this was almost certainly not her maiden name.

But on checking the name Wensor on its own, I found a few entries for Lincolnshire, including the Bourne area. I remembered then that my parents had lived for a while in the little town of Bourne after they got married, and that my mother had told me that this was where she had bought the sampler. So, with an exciting sense of the path opening up in front of me, I pursued the Wensors of Lincolnshire. One couple, Samuel and Mary Wensor, farmers of Deeping Fen, looked about the right age to be Rebecca's parents. Although farmers were not necessarily wealthy in those days, it did strike me that a farmer's daughter might be sent to a modest kind of school, where she would have to learn her letters and embroider a sampler; the family would be a little higher on the social ladder than agricultural labourers. In New Sleaford in 1841, a pupil called Eliza Wensor was boarding at a little school run by one Mary Smith; at age twelve, she could perhaps have been a younger sister or cousin of Rebecca, and also following the path of learning.

Then came an unwelcome discovery. I couldn't find any records in the official registry for the marriage or a death of a Rebecca Wensor or even Winsor, born around 1820. But in a collection of parish records posted on the internet, I did find the death of a Rebecca Winsor, aged 11 in 1831. She was buried at Deeping St James in Lincolnshire.

The age and the location fitted, and judging by the scarcity of anyone else bearing the same name, I think my little embroiderer probably died three years after sewing her sampler. So although the trail hasn't taken me very far, I can now surmise that Rebecca was most probably the daughter of a Lincolnshire farming family, living in the flat fenland country, receiving some sort of basic education, as well as carrying out her household tasks. I have also found a Wensor Farm on the map, close to Deeping St James, which could well be that of her family or relatives. This is a poignant conclusion to the story that I have for her, but one that helps me to appreciate the work that she put into the sampler, still treasured nearly two hundred years later.

AMEY ROSS

My second sampler proudly announces that it was stitched by Amey Ross, Boston, aged nine years, in 1833. Amey made her sampler square and bold, with two handsome trees flanking flowers and baskets of fruit, setting out her letters and numbers at the top, and her name carefully stitched in a slightly wobbly octagonal frame at the bottom. It's fortunate for my search that she left such a valuable clue by including the name of the place in which she lived. Boston, Lincolnshire, is also within the area where my mother bought some of her first antiques, so probably both samplers found their way on to the local market stalls after house clearances.

Amey was born a little later than Rebecca, in 1824, and the closer that any dates creep to 1837 for the first official BMD records, and to 1841 for the first full census, the more likely we are to find results easily. Again, it might have seemed at first that she didn't know how to spell the name Amy correctly but, for the same reasons that I researched Wensor rather than Winsor, I decided once more to give her the benefit of the doubt, at least to start with. And although neither the 1841 nor the 1851 census gave any sign of an Amey or Amy Ross of the right age, both showed an Amey Ross who was born in about 1801. Obviously, this was not Amey herself, but the unusual spelling suggested that it could be a family name, so that this woman could well have been Amey's mother or aunt. Amey senior, a widow, is recorded as living in Skirbeck with her daughter Hannah in the Boston area of Lincolnshire, the right location for 'my' Amey. In 1851, she is described as a laundress, and her birthplace as Ely in Cambridgeshire. Later, I discovered that her maiden name was Woods.

As for young Amey in 1841, the most likely entry I found was for an Anne or Anna Ross, working as a servant in the rectory at Wyberton, close to Boston. At age seventeen, the dates are right, and I think that the enumerator probably wrote down young Amey's name inaccurately, which commonly happened. But then there was a fully accurate name in the marriage record of 1848 for an Amey Ross in Boston. I sent off for it and waited eagerly to see what it would say.

The search was at a crossroads; if I had found no more census entries for Amey Ross the younger, and no marriage registration, then I would have left it there. I had made a fruitless general search on the internet under her name, something which can often throw up surprising results, however, now that so many records and odds and ends of family history have been put online. Without travelling to Lincolnshire to look at old parish registers for myself though, it would have been difficult to go further.

But the certificate arrived, and launched my little embroiderer into the next stage of her life. On 9 November 1848, Amey Ross had married Allen Reynolds in the parish church of Skirbeck, Lincolnshire. Witnesses were Hannah Ross and Daniel Lote, thus making it even more likely that the Hannah from the census is Amey's sister. Amey's father was cited as William Ross, a gardener. Allen's father was named as Charles Reynolds, farmer.

Now, this is where family history can get a little spooky: Charles Reynolds was also the name of one of my paternal 2 x great-grandfathers, who came from Yorkshire. I experienced a strange sense of connection, though logically I knew it was very unlikely that they were one and the same. My Reynolds family came from north Yorkshire, and from a different social background, and although it's possible that the Reynolds 'clan' did spread from Yorkshire to Lincolnshire, it would be a mighty project to look into, and one which probably wouldn't deliver a new blood relative in the end, only a fascinating, but coincidental connection to my own line. I decided not to get too sidetracked by the Reynolds issue.

Allen was born about 1820 in Frithville, Lincolnshire, and his occupation was that of a miller. He and Amey, now Amey Reynolds, set up home in Spalding, where they lived for the whole of their married life. I traced them through the census from 1851 to 1881, moving only from Deeping Road to Holbeach Road. Over time, Allen became a master baker too, and took on apprentices. In 1871, Amey's mother, the older Amey Ross, came to live with them, but had almost certainly died by 1881, by which time there was a niece called Amy Rogers living with them as 'servant to uncle'! (Note the more conventional spelling of Amy.) What is significant is that there are no signs on any of the census records of children born to Amey and Allen.

Then came one of those extraordinary moments when the view shifts from official listings to a first-hand, eye-witness account of the Reynolds couple. Using another general internet search (something like 'Reynolds miller Spalding'), I found extracts taken from a nineteenth-century memoir called *The Jottings of Isaac Elsom*, which says:

> On July, 1856, death first entered the family of the Elsoms of Spalding, for on that day, Eliza, the eldest child, who was eighteen days short of eight years of age, passed into the Spirit World like a ripe old Christian! Her body was carried in its coffin to the cemetery in the spring cart of Mr. Allen Reynolds, miller and baker of Holbeach Road, Spalding, a dear friend of the family; in whose cart, one time or another, all the members of the Elsom family had many a happy ride! Mr. & Mrs. Reynolds had no children of their own, but seemed to find pleasure in numerous and various acts to members of our family, as long as they lived. The writer has much satisfaction in recording this fact.

This caused my heart to leap! Here is a picture of Amey Reynolds as a real person, as a neighbourly woman, friendly to children, and happy to offer them rides in her husband's delivery cart. Perhaps she loved children all the more, having none of her own. Then we can imagine her grief at seeing the cart take away the sad little coffin holding the almost eight-year-old Eliza, whom she may have known since birth.

Allen's death came in 1886, aged sixty-six, and Amey's in 1890, at the same age. I wonder if she had kept her childhood sampler, or if it had already strayed into someone else's possession? But this will probably remain as speculation; I've now rounded out her story to my own satisfaction, and am unlikely to find out much more, since, as a childless woman, Amey is far less likely to turn up in a family tree posted on the internet.

At this point, I felt that the balance of energy and time expended in this quest – about four hours in all, over a three-week period – matched its importance. I have been moved by the story, and feel a personal connection with Amey's life that enhances my enjoyment of her sampler, now hanging in our living room. I also owe it to whoever will inherit the sampler to make sure that this record of her life is preserved alongside it. By revealing Amey's story in this way, I have added value to the sampler, not so much in terms of money (though provenance always helps, with an antique) as in terms of its meaning to whoever owns it next. It has also been a way of honouring Amey's life, and all her efforts to stitch so neatly, in that long-ago year of 1833.

TOP TIPS FOR RESEARCHING NAMED OBJECTS

- Decide whether the person concerned is likely to be easy to trace – e.g. if they were born earlier than the nineteenth century records may be thin on the internet and you may have to spend much longer – or travel – to find them.
- If you feel a search will be worthwhile, define the type and length of research that you want to do; set yourself flexible limits.
- Be prepared for probabilities rather than certainties.
- Use at least one, preferably two, major research websites for census records, BMD registers and any parish records available.
- Do a general Google or internet search, and try an image search for the places associated with the person (e.g. old postcards may turn up with a view relevant to the place and time).

- Check out any locations cited using an internet map search; www.bing.com/maps is very good in that you can switch to an Ordnance Survey view for the UK, which may show names of individual farms and country dwellings, and features of the landscape.
- If the surname is unusual enough, check for living descendants on sites such as Ancestry and Genes Reunited, but be cautious about accepting any posted family trees as reliable. You could also try the Guild of One-Name Studies at http://www.one-name.org.
- Accept that not all searches of this kind will yield satisfying results.
- Use books, museums and the internet to fill in social history, information about the objects, events, occupations and environments that are associated with your individual.
- Write up your findings and keep them, so that you can pass on the information with the object. If it will be inherited, make sure the legatee can find or be given the written account.

The common life

Investigating other lives can be a gentle and entertaining pastime, which contrasts with the often intense and obsessive research put in while discovering one's own family history. And yet it has purpose, and enriches our understanding of the past and the people who made the world that we now live in. We are all connected to each other; extend the family branches far enough, and we are all related. It is good, now and again, to drop the fierce distinctions of family members and unrelated individuals, and to remember that we are all part of the common life, and that it includes each and every one of us.

BECOMING AWARE OF OUR COMMON LIFE

With eyes gently closed, visualise, in whatever way you like, your family standing around you. Begin with close members, then expand the frame to include everyone, past and present, who forms a part of the family. Don't dwell on individuals, or try to picture every single person, but just get a general impression. Let there be chatter and movement, if you can.

Next, open the boundaries wider, to include all the multitude of unnamed people who are distantly connected to your family, then wider still, so that the network extends like finely branching filaments, encompassing all those alive, and all those who have lived on this earth. Keep this gentle and light; just gathering a fleeting impression is fine.

After a couple of minutes, bring your attention back to your own body and let the other connections melt away. Breathe deeply, sense the connection between your feet and the ground and open your eyes.

I suppose I feel part of a stream of sentient lives, ideas, feelings, actions, as though I come from somewhere, and am not just a 'new start' from birth.

We heard this quote from Bernard earlier, but I am repeating it here, because it chimes in so well with the kind of awareness of the 'common life' that family history can generate.

From here, we move to looking at the strands of family life that weave their way through the generations. What have we inherited from our ancestors, and what do we learn from them? Stories and reflections will illuminate this theme, along with visions of ancestry from other cultures.

CHAPTER EIGHT

Family Wisdom

Discovering the part that ancestors can play in human life may come about in unexpected ways. When I visited one of the remotest islands in the world, I had no idea that it would lead me into an intense experience of this kind. Here's how it happened.

The Mother at the Centre of the World

It's 2 March 2008. Mother's Day in the UK, but we are spending it in the South Pacific, far away from gifts of flowers and chocolates, and restaurants packed with families taking Mum out to lunch. In fact, we are in a completely different civilisation altogether, visiting Rapa Nui, otherwise known as Easter Island. Robert and I have been transported here as lecturers on board a cruise ship, and today is our second and final day in this extraordinary place. We catch the tender boat from our ship and ride the fierce waves to the shore. The captain has warned us all that we might not even be able to land, after six days of sailing from the Chilean port of Valparaiso. All in the lap of the gods, he says.

And gods are what they have here. Yesterday, we watched the island emerge from the haze with growing excitement – a rounded volcanic scoop of land dressed in soft greens and greys. We began to make out cliffs and swathes of grassland, then, finally, the first of the giant statues for which the island is famous: the Moai. Nearly a thousand of these stone statues, with their huge heads and staring gaze, are placed around the island, many at the edge of the land, facing inwards towards the people they protect and command. Each face has its own character. When we landed, I made straight for the first Moai I could see, standing on the rim of the harbour, and was seized with a spine-tingling sense of awe as I gazed up at him. In fact, I felt overwhelmed. This was a place I had known of since I was a child, but had never dreamed I might be able to visit. Now we were stepping into its mythical world.

There are still many questions and mysteries surrounding the old culture of Easter Island, but it's known that the statues were carved between five and eight hundred years ago, and it is thought that they represent the deified male ancestors. Certainly, today's inhabitants treat them as such, and asked us to respect the Moai by never treading upon the ahu, the sacred stone platforms upon which they are set. On the first day, then, we became acquainted with these ancestors, along with the herds of bright bay horses that roam the island freely, the green-sided volcano with its extraordinary internal lake and the exqui-site beaches fringed with palm trees. The island, once stripped of its trees, is back to a better natural balance again, planted also with stately groves of eucalyptus. All through the centuries of change, the Moai have presided as immortals over the landscape.

Now it's day two of our visit, and we have barely a morning to see whatever else we can of this magical island. Something has tickled my imagination in a guidebook that I browsed on board the ship: a men-tion of an ancient round stone representing 'the navel of the world'. Te Pito Te Henua is one of the other names for Easter Island and that in itself means the navel and uterus of the world, so this stone would therefore be the navel of the navel. Robert agrees: we should try to find it.

Friends on board recommended that we seek out the woman taxi driver on the quayside, probably the island's one and only female cabbie among the ranks of beaming and burly male drivers. We spot her easily, and though they'd mentioned her simply because of her general helpfulness, hiring her cab for the morning turns out to be crucial to what we discover.

'Ah, so you want to go to the place that we visit for energy,' she says, when we ask her about the site, for which we have only rough directions. She takes us over to the north coast of the island, veering away from a well-frequented beach (though that, in Easter Island terms, may mean only a handful of people) to turn down an unpaved road which emerges by another small and completely empty beach. Among the rocks above the sea line, a round wall of stones and boulders has been created, about three feet high and eight feet in diameter. Within the circle it encloses, a huge and beautifully smooth ovoid stone has been placed, like a giant egg. Four similar but smaller stones are set around it at regular intervals, forming a square. It has a Celtic feel about it – we could almost be on the west coast of Ireland or in the Hebrides – but here we are, over two thousand miles from any mainland and over eight thousand miles from home.

It is first and foremost a place for women, our driver tells us. She invites me alone to accompany her into the circle, and seats me on one of the smaller stones, encouraging me to place my hands on the great stone egg in front of me. She sits opposite and does likewise. 'Put your hands on it gently,' she says. 'Relax.'

Women of the island have been coming here for hundreds of years, she explains. They come to pray for help, for safe childbirth and even for the delivery of their babies. The stone is the mother, their mother, and the island's mother. 'What do you feel?' she asks me.

I feel as though the stone is not a stone at all, but an egg with the shell stripped away, and the delicate but all-powerful pulse of life moving within its membrane. I sense the women who have laid their hands here, and the ancestral mothers whose spirit is contained within the stone itself. Currents of energy seem to be running up my arms.

I tell her some of this, and she is satisfied. She then steps outside the circle and invites Robert to come and join me. Now I can suggest to him how to sit and place his hands and, rather to his surprise, he too experiences waves of energy.

We leave the enclosure. It's time to get back to the harbour and board our ship for another six-day voyage, back to the coast of South America. Both of us are reflective after the experience, and feel privileged that one of the islanders trusted us enough to teach us about her sacred site. We first met the father of the island in the myriad forms of male ancestors, but now we have also met its mother – the one stone representing all the female ancestors.

This is a Mother's Day that I won't forget.

Finding the Source

Such a sense of direct connection with the ancestors, the line of mothers and of fathers who brought us into being, seems far removed from modern society. But perhaps family history may be one of the ways in which we can re-establish that kind of link. As your family tree grows, you may find that you feel in touch with your ancestry as a source of support. Something is distilled; the wisdom of your family is there in essence for you to tap.

It's become apparent to me, both from my own experience and from that of those family historians who took part in my survey, that this is possible. The process of researching and growing your tree will begin to generate this connection. And it can be developed still further, by both active and more contemplative practices, as I shall explain in this chapter. In fact, we've already covered a fair amount of this ground through the reflective exercises suggested in previous chapters. This could be a good time to review them, and try them out again (see pp. 41 and 149).

It's my belief that in previous generations, genealogy was a respectable pursuit, but one that was constrained by a dry and scholarly approach. This could be admirable in terms of its research techniques, but was short on meaning, colour and variety. Today, a new way forward is opening up: we want to know not only the names and dates relating to our ancestors, but their personal significance to us. What light does it shed on our own lives? What can we learn from our ancestors? Understanding them may even change the way we live, and the way that we view ourselves. It can be daunting or unsettling for that reason, but it is also inspiring, and may give us a new source of strength and knowledge.

The old research methods, solid and reliable, need not be

abandoned, but can be infused with more exciting pursuits, such as visiting old family haunts, collecting family stories and handling and investigating objects from your heritage, as already discussed. All this helps to put us in touch with our family ancestry. Just as current academic studies are now much more open to the principle of 'reflexivity', or personal involvement with the subject, and recognise that this has its own validity, so we can adopt the more personal approach in family history. The earlier methods undoubtedly did fire up enthusiasm in genealogists – I know how my father loved his research trips to Ireland, for instance – but somehow, it wasn't quite acceptable to make much of that, or to include much apart from bare facts in accounts of one's ancestry. Now we have the opportunity to adopt a more rounded approach, and to acknowledge the effects that this may have on us.

From this interaction between you and your ancestry, wisdom can be generated. Try it, and see.

Different times, different lives

Do you think about the differences between your life today, and those of your ancestors? If so, you are in good company, since I have had an incredibly strong response from other family historians in this respect. Time and time again, they write about how much they appreciate the quality of modern life, compared with the hardships that their forebears have suffered.

Researching former lives can shock us: losing children to disease, falling on hard times and resorting to the workhouse, seeing family members for the last time as they emigrated, overcrowding, early death through overwork or occupational hazards, lack of education and being severely restricted through class and birth, are all factors of life in the past which can upset and trouble us even today when we read about them. My informants mention all of these problems, and more. And suffering wasn't just restricted to the poor. Being wealthy was not automatically a passport to an easier life, since illness could strike anywhere, and infant death was common.

APPRECIATING WHAT WE HAVE TODAY

I asked the question in my survey: 'Do you feel that you have learned anything from your ancestors, or from their lives?' This proved to be something that struck a chord with many respondents. As Jim said, 'A great deal, particularly about their abilities, skills and their courage and ingenuity to survive while so many of their contemporaries and neighbours perished in wars, purges, genocides, etc.'

The respondents recognised and admired, too, the skills and endurance needed simply to keep going, when compared with the advantages we have today. Ken D. noted, 'Times were hard – how could a family of eighteen live in a small cottage?' while Teresa affirmed, 'I appreciate the hardships they must have endured just to survive. I feel proud to know that I exist because of them and that I am part of their family. And Josie pointed out, 'I admire the migrants who left the UK without any hope of returning to see family. How lucky we are to catch a plane, use email and phone.'

Many commented on how fortunate they felt compared to their ancestors: 'Genealogy has given me a better understanding of the journey my ancestors made, the deprivations they endured and the sacrifices that they must have made to bring me to this point in time,' wrote Ian. 'Now I know what my ancestors have been through, and it gives me a better appreciation of what I have today.' And, 'How lucky we are in today's society given the deprivation and loss suffered by many,' said Ruth. 'My granny lost siblings to whooping cough in a Gorbals tenement. We don't suffer that any more.'

Do these comments resonate with you as well? Does it put you in mind of other benefits that we enjoy today, as compared to the hardships and limitations of your ancestors?

LUCK, GUILT AND GRATITUDE

I was born into the post-war generation, and grew up with a strong resistance to acknowledging how lucky I was – something I should have been doing, according to my parents. The country's men and women had fought and sacrificed so that I could now enjoy my delicious blancmange (no – please take it away!). Did I think there was food to waste? Rationing would have taught me the error of my ways, they said. And did I think there was money to burn? I had no idea of how to make money go far because I hadn't experienced the depression of the thirties, followed by wartime thrift. And so it went on.

Each generation probably tells the next that they are very fortunate, and, of course, to some extent they are. There was, though, an exceptionally big jump forward in the second half of the twentieth century, and my generation truly felt we were far removed from our parents' ways, and that the Second World War really had nothing to do with us any more. We were ready to move on, enjoy what came our way and celebrate life with a freedom that our parents had never had. (Think 1960s.)

Perhaps this was only natural. But it left me with a faint trace of guilt, and, as the years have rolled on, an unsatisfied curiosity about the war years, and the lives of my family before I came on the scene. What I'd blocked out in my youth now became something of pressing interest. Taking up family history therefore meant not only examining my ancestors' lives, but my own too, and uprooting any obstructive attitudes that might prevent me from knowing my forebears properly. My earlier defences and resistance had to go.

The generosity of my survey respondents in acknowledging their own good fortune, and the gratitude they express towards their ancestors, is heart-warming. Of course the past isn't all bad, just as it's also inaccurate to bathe it in a romantic golden light. But having the grace to acknowledge our comparative fortune today – in terms of modern medicine, adequate food supplies and longer life expectancy – is a major step in the process of opening up our connection to our ancestry. Expressing feelings of gratitude for what we have, or sorrow for what our family members went through, is liberating. It goes along with discarding what we were told to think about our family's earlier life and times, and seeing for ourselves, as best we can, what those times and lives were like.

It also blends with the efforts that we make to tread the ground, and dig out the evidence in pursuing family history. Jim and Gayl (see p. 158) asked themselves why they were making such a lengthy and costly trip from the USA to research Gayl's ancestry in Great Britain. The answer came loud and clear once they had done the legwork. Understanding the past can bless the present. As Jim put it:

> Why such devotion? Having lifted Gayl's ancestral veil and had a glimpse, we have some understanding. Gayl's ancestors struggled to achieve high levels of education and expertise. They understood the concept of freedom. They worked, sacrificed and fought for generations to weave the fabric of modern civilised conduct. They acted on their own volition. By desire rather than coercion or conscription, they sacrificed to create the freedom and opportunity that we have been graced with for our entire lives.

And Rob feels that what he is doing in this regard will influence the next generation in a positive way: 'I know that I will be able to pass on to my descendants stories that will evoke many different emotions.'

Are Our Ancestors 'Out There' Somewhere?

If we feel a connection with our ancestors, does this mean that they still live on, in some sense? This is a tricky question. Every faith has its own version of what happens to us when we die, from reincarnation to going to heaven; even the belief that an individual becomes completely extinct after death is just that, a belief. Each person's outlook is almost bound to be influenced by their upbringing. But personal experience also plays a part in shaping our views. I was brought up in a Christian church, and can still attend its services with an easy conscience because I was baptised into it, although I have since participated in other practices, including Buddhist meditation and Sufi ceremonies. At the heart of all this is a 'way to knowledge' which does not entirely depend on one specific outward form.

My own 'take' on this is that at the core of every religion is a 'way' to spiritual knowledge, and that such a 'way' is also found in other traditions of a more mystical or esoteric nature. As for God, he, she or 'it' can be defined in many ways, but in the end, there can only be one god, spirit or truth, though religions may contain a plurality of approaches, revealing faces and aspects of the unity. Each way or religion has a partial understanding of this because the ultimate is – ultimately – beyond our knowing. We are limited in our understanding both by the nature of our individuality and the context that we live in. But we do also have the capacity to extend our spiritual knowledge and to develop our own being through religious practice of one kind or another. We also have the capacity to enter what might be called different states of consciousness, and perceive a larger scale of existence. We may at times 'transcend' our normal state of mind and experience something of a different order, even if we find it hard to talk about it afterwards or indeed to remember it in detail.

Where does this leave the question of the soul, of migration to another life after death, or an ascent to heaven? These are questions to which I have no firm answer, nor even a comprehensive working hypothesis. And I would warn you to be suspicious of me if I did! It's one thing to follow the particular viewpoint of a religious faith, developed through centuries of ritual, prayer and debate, but the fixed view of an individual could at best be a crankiness, and at worst a dangerous cult. (I once met a man who belonged to the 'eternalist' school of belief. No one should die, he maintained. It was possible to live for ever – we just hadn't perfected the art yet.)

But I have had experiences that have become the touchstones of my spiritual outlook, as I am sure many other individuals have, even if they don't cohere into consistent 'beliefs'. As a small child, I saw an angel, a figure of golden light, and even through my teenage atheistic years I could not reject the truth of the experience. In adult years, I have 'remembered' what it is like to die in 'another life', so powerfully and spontaneously, and in a way that I could never have dreamed up out of my ordinary imagination, that I cannot dismiss the experience. Whether 'I' experienced it in a former life, or whether I tapped into some kind of collective memory is another question. And, to take another example, around the time of certain people's deaths, I have had amazing experiences connected with their passing, which provoked awe and wonder, and the realisation that the spirit does 'move on' in some form or other.

So I cannot say that I maintain a single belief system about what happens to us after death, even though the question has gripped me since I was quite small, and sometimes caused me fear and anguish, as well as occasional joy and relief. But I uphold the view that there are indeed mysteries in the universe, and that there is a spiritual dimension to life that we can explore, respect and understand in some measure.

I have laid my cards on the table because, once you begin to consider the real implications of ancestry as a kind of living presence, awkward questions arise as to how this operates. Practically every culture and civilisation has had some belief in the ongoing significance of the ancestors – as members of the household, as oracles and guides or just as a watching presence. But in most contemporary societies there is no unified belief about this outside the walls of a church, mosque or synagogue. Spiritualism, which peaked in popularity in the late nineteenth century, partly addresses this; its practice is to call on the spirits of the departed and to invite them to speak to us, and so in some ways is akin to the ancient tradition of operating ancestor oracles. It is not necessarily the way that many people wish to go today, however, in terms of spooky séances and pronouncements by mediums.

In a gentler vein, many contemporary clairvoyants, who perhaps read Tarot cards and ask for guidance from the spirit realm, will also pick up on ancestors and relatives who have passed away and transmit their concerns and advice. I visited one for a reading some years ago (I told myself it was for research purposes, but I was, of course, keen to hear what she would say!) and rather to my surprise she described a couple of deceased relatives with some accuracy. She told me I had a great-grandmother called Mary, which I later discovered to be true, but also that she died of painful stomach cancer – not true: I checked her death certificate. Mary urged me to wear dark green; I've no idea why, but I do actually now wear more green than I used to. And just recently, I came across her obituary: one of the tributes paid to her on a wreath sent a small but distinct shiver up my spine: 'In every good work, she being dead yet speaketh.'

But although such readings can be fascinating, and may contain much of value, it's a good idea to keep a sense of discrimination. If ancestors are mentioned, there is still no consistent sense as to how and why the psychic is able to make a link to them. Often psychics talk about reincarnation as well, which is an inherent contradiction: if Uncle Joe is out there and willing to chat with you, how come he has also passed into another life and is even now learning to walk and talk as a child in India?

There may be a lack of well-defined spiritual theory about the nature of the ancestors in contemporary life, but I do invite you to open up your own thoughts on the matter. It will cross your mind anyway, if you dig into family history. Where have all those people gone? Are they in any sense still present? Maybe we all leave traces of ourselves as energy and spirit in the world, which can still be accessed. Maybe the family itself has a kind of life and it's possible to tap into this. We have new views thrusting up in science, such as the theory of 'morphic resonance' proposed by biologist Rupert Sheldrake, according to which every individual forms part of the species mind, and from there this can be extended both through to a wider sphere of creation and also, possibly, backwards in time to include those who are dead and gone. Though debated fiercely, this idea does seem to have resonance for a modern world, and goes a long way in helping to explain how we may sense a contact with our ancestors. As Norma says:

> My ancestors have really come alive for me ... I often wake up in the night thinking about them and I often count my blessings, for my life has been so easy compared to theirs.

Tapping into Ancestral Activities

If you wish to further the connection with your ancestors, then I can suggest a very safe and delightful way to do so, which does not require any particular view of your ancestors as living entities, or otherwise. It involves becoming aware of simple, everyday activities that you undertake and in which your ancestors would also have participated. Here's an example.

It's a warm, sunny day in early September. I take a basket and set off down the lane, looking for blackberries. I enjoy the sense of being off on a gentle hunt, then of handling the rich dark berries, plucking the best, adding to the growing mound in the basket. I taste some berries for sweetness, relishing some and spitting out the odd sharp one. My hand and eye grow quicker and more confident.

I also now remember picking blackberries as a child. One after-noon in late summer, my mother allowed me out with friends to see what we could find. We walked and walked, and I returned – proud, but tired – with a decent heap of berries for her. She too must have picked them as a child; growing up as she did, in East Anglia, perhaps the hedgerows weren't quite so prolific, but she would have gone out with her sister Maisie. Did they wear little white pinafores or smocks over their dresses, as I've seen in some of their early photographs? No trousers then, of course. And what about my earlier 3 x great-grandmother in Wales? Blackberries must have been a good source of food in autumn. I've seen the lane where her cottage stood. Did she teach her children the skill of seeking them out, and sometimes go with them, laughing at their enthusiasm, and consoling them when a finger was pricked?

As I pick, I sense the continuity of several generations of women for whom blackberry picking was a seasonal activity – something they would have known from childhood and passed on to their own chil-dren. I am at the end of a long chain of blackberry pickers. Not quite at the end though – I've taught my own daughter to do the same, and soon she will take my little granddaughter out through the Somerset fields to find the berries herself, and to wonder at their bloom and sweetness.

You'll see from this that there are three elements present:

- observations and sensations of the current experience
- reminiscence
- speculation to link up the generations.

I have tried this out with a variety of activities, such as pegging out the washing, making pastry and wrapping Christmas presents. It works well for everyday activities – those that might get overlooked in terms of any significance, but in which my ancestors would have participated. Their ways might have been somewhat different, but there is a core to the activity which we share. And lest it might be thought that these are very – well, housewifely – activities, I should add that it strikes me sometimes when I'm writing too. I think of my uncle writing his books on medieval French literature, of my grandfather furrowing his brow as he wrote the week's sermon and, indeed, of his father and grandfather too, also knocking up yet another homily for their Baptist congregation. We must all have sweated over our task!

Here's how you tap into ancestral activities yourself. Be aware of your daily activities, and from them choose a task which you think your ancestor might also have carried out. Examples are:

- chopping wood
- lighting a fire
- knitting
- dressmaking
- counting the takings from a stall or shop
- shaving
- comforting a child
- going to church
- baking a cake
- sharpening a knife
- shopping in the market
- digging up potatoes
- writing a letter.

As you perform your chosen task be mindful of the following:

- Relax into it, and allow yourself to experience fully the sensations that it involves.
- Remember previous occasions of doing the same activity, especially ones from childhood.
- Recall any memories of other relatives of an older generation doing the same thing.
- Speculate about earlier ancestors that you know of who would also have done this. Allow yourself to dream a little about how they went about the task, the setting, their character and their mood.

Teasing Out the Threads

Just as remembering your ancestors through daily activities can create threads linking you to the past, so you can pull out and identify some of the threads that run through your family history from past to present. This too will help to strengthen your sense of connection with your ancestry. It may also highlight some of the attributes passed down through the family, and the wisdom and skills which are a part of its identity.

When I wrote up my mother's family history as a book in 2009, I decided to open it by describing the three main threads that I had picked out on her side of the family. I had been fascinated right from the start of my research with the idea of family heritage, and the kind of characteristics and drives that are passed down through generations.

This proved a good starting point for my book, hooking the reader in with the promise of more stories to follow. But finding the threads has turned out to be highly relevant to my own life too. They have answered questions about my direction and motivation. Why have I always had an urge to write? Why have I also had a desire to trade? And where does my interest in psychic subjects stem from? Much to my astonishment, these and other aspects began to feature in the general family tendencies. I had no idea previously, for instance, that my mother had a strong line of traders and shopkeepers in her ancestry. This has made me feel more a part of my family, and that I can claim my heritage with pride.

The threads of the family story

Here then, is the gist of what I wrote (I've edited and shortened the accounts somewhat, to make them easier to grasp out of context). There are three main threads in the family history of my mother, Kathleen Owen (see also Appendix I, p. 244):

THE OWENS FAMILY OF ABBEYCWMHIR

The Owens family came from the Abbeycwmhir area of mid-Wales, then in the county of Radnorshire. They had lived there from at least as early as the eighteenth century, and remained until the younger generation began to disperse in the mid-nineteenth century. Their moves took them down south to Blaenavon and Pontypool to find work in the mines and iron industries, to America to begin new lives, to other parts of Wales such as Newtown and, in the case of Kathleen's family, to England. Her line produced three generations of Baptist ministers, and when the second of the three, David Richards Owen, was sent to Hemyock in Devon for his first posting, the family grew new roots in English soil. (The name by then had become Owen, without the 's', in this branch of the family.) Along the way, other local families linked in, especially the Kinsey and Richards families of Montgomeryshire.

The Owen family line seems to have strong interests in music, foreign languages and – dare I say it – preaching and its associated activities, since many have become teachers! Writing, too, has played a part. There is also a tendency to have red hair and psychic abilities.

MASEY AND WALKER FAMILIES FROM HEMYOCK, DEVON

When David Richards Owen took up his new ministry, he soon met and married a local girl named Mary Masey Walker. Her background, consisting of the Masey and Walker families, forms the second thread of the story.

These families had lived in the Hemyock area for generations, at least as early as the seventeenth century in the case of the Maseys, and the eighteenth for the Walkers. Hemyock is a small village in Devon, divided from the town of Wellington both by the Blackdown Hills and the county boundary for Somerset. Between them, the Maseys and the Walkers worked as shopkeepers, tailors, innkeepers and butchers, so they played key positions in the trading life of the village. Eventually, the Masey–Walker union led to the establishment of a big dairy enterprise in Wellington, which grew to become the major industry and landmark of the town. It was finally sold on to a national company, and closed in the 1980s. Trading has remained a strong drive in the family.

LEE AND BROWN FAMILIES OF BEDWORTH, WARWICKSHIRE

David and Mary Owen, my great-grandparents, had a large family; there were thirteen children in all, of whom Bernard Walker Owen, Kathleen's father, was the fourth. The family had settled in Northamptonshire on returning from a few years spent living in Ohio, USA. Bernard's chosen wife was Hannah Eliza Brown, whose family had also settled in the county. Their origins, however, were in Warwickshire. Hannah's mother was Sarah Ann Lee, her father Henry Brown, and the Lee and Brown families had lived mainly in the crowded industrial town of Bedworth, where almost everyone was employed either as a ribbon weaver or a miner. Before that, the Browns were in nearby Coventry, where the earliest member of the family discovered so far was practising as a watchmaker, a local Coventry trade.

Conditions were harsh and times became very hard in Bedworth in the mid-nineteenth century. When the ribbon-weaving industry fell into sharp decline, real famine set in and money was raised to ship some of the poorest families off to Canada and Australia, to give them a chance of a new life. Henry Brown, Hannah's father, took his own initiative to move the family away, by joining the railways. This gave him mobility, and they finally settled in Northamptonshire. Perhaps this family line is that of the survivors – those who worked hard to keep going, and found ways to cope with tough times.

APPLYING THE KNOWLEDGE

These threads reflect three basic characteristics: the preacher–teachers, the shopkeepers and the hard-working survivors. They are my interpretations, but I believe they lie at the core of these families. My evidence is based on a mass of research, on photographs and family recollections, which I've distilled over the course of several years until I feel I can almost touch and taste the essence of each line.

Embodied there also are the lessons that family members can teach me – the family wisdom that has been generated by experience and circumstances, as well as character. From the preaching line, I learn that writing is not a self-indulgence for me: it's what I do, it's a trait I've inherited, and one I should make the best use of. I should also take care not to preach – it's fine for a minister to do that, but not for a writer! I now know that my drive to discover and research new areas of interest is also probably from this line of the family, and that I'm carrying on a tradition in so doing. (As if to emphasise this, just this morning, a day after I'd written those words, a scanned copy of the obituary of my great-grandfather David Owen arrived by email. Charting his last phase of life, it reads: 'Compelled to relinquish all active work he remained a keen student to the end, studying the times in every phase – whether political, scientific or religious.' I may not have his breadth of knowledge, but the urge to attain it is still there.)

From the trading line, I've seen too that it's natural for me to wish to buy and sell. But, just because it's in my blood, it doesn't mean that I have to do it the whole time. I've learned a lot through running my own trading businesses (vintage clothes, then Russian crafts), but that phase is probably over now. Along the way, I've thought a lot about the rules of fair trading, and have taught myself (painfully) to do accounts, check stock and so on. And indeed, I have made reasonable money out of my trading activities; though I can also see that this is never guaranteed – several of my ancestors on the trading side of the family went bankrupt, even though others succeeded beyond their wildest dreams.

From the line of survivors, I hope I have inherited a bit of grit and determination. I would not want to get too caught up in any anxieties they might have suffered on account of the harsh conditions, nor follow the inclination that occasionally arises to take work simply because it will pay something. Sarah Lee put her daughters out to service because it was safe, and I suspect she thought it was better to be safe than sorry through being overambitious. But they were determined girls with initiative: two ran a post office, as we've seen, and one of these later became a cabin steward.

In a simple and perhaps even homespun way, this is some of the wisdom that I have gathered from my ancestors. I am a part of my ancestry, but I am not my ancestors. They come bearing gifts, but they also come with a few health warnings: lessons which have been learned along the way need not necessarily be repeated, and different times call for different measures.

Survey respondents also found qualities to admire, and to inspire them. Miriam feels that:

My ancestors give me a sense of pride, in that they could overcome difficult times in their lives, and they inspire me to do the same. Their faith was very real and it helps me keep my belief. They followed their dreams and succeeded in life, so it has helped me follow in their footsteps.

And Jane says of her ancestors: 'They've taught me they were brave, tough people, usually going off to find a better life for themselves and their families. I am very proud of what they have achieved.'

Among the characteristics mentioned several times over that the respondents especially respect are perseverance and resilience, along with the capacity to hold true to one's faith, and to be guided by it.

Teresa's thoughtful response shows that there is a range of different ways in which we can connect with our ancestors, both by putting them on the map and being put on the map ourselves:

> I feel very happy finding out about my ancestors. I have been able to find out where they lived and what they did for a living. Some of them ended up in workhouses even though they had children around. It is sad to think that at the end of their life they were not cared for. To me, it is important that I know their history.
>
> I also feel very proud and at the same time very sad for my two grand-uncles who gave their lives in the First World War, along with countless others. If I had not started my family history quest, their existence would have been left to the history books, but I feel I have brought their memory back to life, and now I think of them every armistice day.
>
> I also feel happy to know that where we lived in England my ancestors were all around us and that gives me a sense of knowing where my roots lay.
>
> I have learned a lot from my ancestors; many were poor and had hard lives. Some lost not one but several children and others lost wives and husbands at an early age. That must have made life very difficult, especially for the women who were often left with many children to raise. Despite difficulties, they managed to carry on. I guess I have learned that life can be hard and that we really have nothing to complain about when we look back into the lives of our ancestors.

Tracing the storylines

Can you tease out the threads of the storylines in your family ancestry? As before, it may be easier to look at one side of the family at a time –

mother's or father's. How many threads you pull out can vary, but aim to find between two and six. Three is a particularly good number – three strands can be woven into a braid, for instance.

You might like to write up these threads following a similar approach to the example quoted from my family history (see above). Don't try to explain all the family relationships within the account: it tends to deaden the narrative and can cause confusion. If others are going to read it, you can always supplement it with a family tree if needed. Keep your account reasonably brief, around 150–250 words; this will help you to see the story more clearly, and to pick out the essential ingredients. Then it becomes a tool which you can use to orientate yourself within your own family background.

After you have done this, contemplate the ways in which the threads may still be passing through your own life:

- How have these storylines affected you?
- Does this understanding of your family lines have an emotional impact on you?
- Can you draw new strength or inspiration from them?
- Do they offer opportunities that you haven't yet grasped?
- And are there activities or attitudes which you feel you can now drop?
- What lessons have been learned along the way?

Making a Special Place for Your Ancestors

You are now at the stage where you are familiar with your ancestors in a general sense, and probably feel you know many of them well as individuals, and I hope that your life is much richer for it. As human beings, though, they were undoubtedly not perfect, and we needn't treat them as saints. As Pat says:

I do recall at one of the Welsh Family History courses one of the lecturers saying, 'If we could go back and meet our ancestors we wouldn't necessarily like them.' That was because in the past people had different attitudes and outlooks on life that don't always coincide with our own views.

With that in mind, I'd like to introduce the idea of making a special place in which to honour your ancestors. If I use the word 'shrine' for this, I hope you will bear with me. The original meaning of the word 'shrine' is that of chest, or cabinet. So far, so good; there should be no objections here. It is also, according to Chambers Dictionary, 'A place hallowed by its associations'. Even better – this is a rather poetic and appealing concept. Or it can be 'a casket for relics'. Now this third meaning might sound too much like a place for storing holy bones or shreds of the True Cross – a religious structure rather than something with a family orientation. But it could also mean, could it not, a memory box, where items of a cherished personal nature are kept, including photos and artefacts associated with your ancestors? A shrine does not have to be in a place of worship, nor does it have to have religious overtones or connections with tribal customs. It could be any of those things, but in this case, let's take it in its more general sense and think of it as a special place or container that is associated with your family history.

Making a shrine for your family ancestry may not be something that you would wish to make a flamboyant exhibition of, but bear in mind that it is something that many of us do anyway, by filling a wall with photographs, or creating a display of Granny's best china along with Grandad's war medals. In any case, it means keeping a sense of proportion: houses whose walls are filled from top to bottom with gloomy oil paintings of deceased relatives can be oppressive, and even sinister, as their gazes follow your every move. There is certainly no suggestion that you should 'deify' your ances-tors, nor supplant your life with theirs, but just have a way and a place in which you can honour their existence and enjoy their company.

Here are some ways you might consider for setting up a special place for your ancestors:

- Choose a wall or surface, such as the top of a sideboard, on which to arrange a selection of photographs of your ancestors and relatives.
- Make a family history memory box, with some of the key pictures and small artefacts; pick a special box, chest or casket for this.
- Create an archive for your research material which is more than just storage, and which can be beautifully organised, housed and labelled.
- Form a collection of objects associated with your family and find a place where they can be displayed together.
- Create a 'treasure trail' for children or grandchildren – a written guide to the special photos and objects in your home which they can follow round the house, learning about the family history as they go.
- Take a dedicated corner to be your family shrine and choose a few prime photos and objects associated with the family history to place there.
- Use additional decoration where appropriate: flowers, cloths, candles, dried grasses or leaves, drawings and so on.
- Place a comfortable chair near the main spot where your ancestral collection is set up, and use it to take quiet moments, to reflect on your life, to ask questions about the past and – perhaps – to listen for answers.
- Let your shrine be part of the household, where life goes on around it. It need not be too secluded.

What Difference Does It All Make?

This is a question that any of us may ask from time to time, as we plough through yet another series of census returns, or realise, as we open the post, that we've ordered the wrong birth certificate again. Sometimes the data can seem overwhelming, and it passes through your mind that building the Taj Mahal out of matchsticks might be quicker, and more fun. I hope that such a mood will never linger for long, however, and that the following testimonies will encourage you to identify what has value to you, which may then act as a light to keep you going. These family historians, treading the same kind of path as you, have discovered the thrill of the journey, the sense of belonging to a family network, and a surer recognition of their own identity. They take delight in their affinity to a particular ancestor, in the spectrum of family experience they have uncovered and they recognise the bond with those who lived many years ago.

> This is an absolutely fascinating journey to be on. It really puts into perspective the fact that we are only tiny particles in this world.
>
> David Sm.

> I like the thought of being part of a huge network of interconnecting families, some members of which I feel more drawn to than others.
>
> Maggi

> I feel closer to my living relations and realise how important it is not to lose contact. I have cousins living all over the world and must stay in contact with them.
>
> Norma

> Family history has helped me to find some roots and a sense of belonging – this chiefly through meeting and communicating with relatives. My parents were not interested in their families, so it has been a revelation to find, for instance, that 'we' all go grey quite young – often with quite an elegant white streak! Or that other people can see my grandmother in my face.
>
> Fran

> I'm a more complete person.
>
> Vicky

I feel myself to be something of a maverick, both in my working life, my home life and in the conformist world of the
small English village where I now live. My instincts are to
rebel, as my ancestor did [the Revd A. J. Tancred, who we met
in earlier chapters], against the dead weight of this conform-
ity. The 1960s are still my spiritual home.

Bernard

My son once said I was multicoloured, a rainbow. Wasn't
that a nice compliment? I realised that I was multicoloured
because of my family and their jewelled stories passed down
through the ages. My family history has made me what I am
today. It gave me my features, habits, likes and dislikes, and
a window to look through, to see into the different world of
yesterday.

Ann

I have found it quite an emotional journey, discovering these
past lives and, yes, I definitely feel more in touch with them.
Even the simple fact of reading gravestone inscriptions of
young children who had died when only a few days old has
reduced me to tears. Reading the dates of when these people
lived and died, trying to understand their lives, gives me the
feeling of a shared bond. Visiting an old church where several generations of my father's family were christened,
married and buried, made me feel close to them. I could
imagine the joy of the young brides passing underneath the
leafy archway over the gate at the end of the path leading
from the church.

Irene

A Prayer to the Ancestors

This was used by a friend recently at her wedding service, and I was
struck by how simple but yet how powerful it is. It is one version of a
Druidic prayer, also known as the Gorsedd Prayer, originally composed

by an eighteenth-century Welsh poet, Iolo Morganwg. Perhaps it helps to show that acknowledging our ancestors can be a way of bringing blessings into our lives, and connecting us to a greater universe.

> Ancestors, grant us your protection,
> And in Protection, Strength,
> And in Strength, Understanding,
> And in Understanding, Knowledge,
> And in Knowledge, the Knowledge of Justice,
> And in the Knowledge of Justice, the Love of it,
> And in the Love of it, the Love of all existences,
> And in the Love of all existences, the love of the Ancestors
>   and all things good.
> So may it be.

CHAPTER NINE

Passing on the Legacy

As the story of your family history emerges, you will probably find yourself wondering what to do with it next. Very few of us are content simply to say, 'Ah, yes, so this is where I come from,' and leave it at that. It would be little short of a crime simply to let it slip back into obscurity; if it is precious to you, then so will it be to others, especially those who come after you. So acting as a link between past and future generations, you as the researcher are now in a unique position to become the messenger or story-teller, and to pass it on.

Writing up the family history is the most obvious choice for passing on your knowledge, but there are alternatives, such as live story-telling or creative representations of the family line, as we'll see later on.

Telling the Story

We'll start with the task of writing it up, which can seem very daunting at first. Gathering your family history data is 'always work in progress', as David Sw. says, so where do you stop, and how do you include it all in what you write? In a recent survey, a leading genealogy magazine found that while many of their respondents had made a start, none had finished writing up everything that they knew. But the reason for this apparent lack of success soon becomes clear when we look at how this particular question-and-answer pair was phrased.

Q: 'Have you written up your family's story?'
A: 'Yes – everything I've discovered' – 0%

Your Family Tree, December 2009

This casts a different light on it. No one could manage to write up everything that they'd found, but answers to other questions in the survey reveal that everyone was either writing something, or hoped to do so at some point.

There is a 'double whammy' of two factors conspiring here to act as a deterrent. The first is the difficulty of choosing the right moment to write it up, since the story never seems to be complete; the second is that of knowing what, if anything, to leave out from your carefully gathered research material. But if you can see them as two separate challenges, this will help you to deal with the issues involved, and not allow them to defeat you.

Adopting realistic goals is key here. For two of my own survey respondents the task is threatening to get the better of them. As Susan says, 'I keep meaning to put it all in order, and write extra information up, but it's a "to-do" thing. Much of it is handwritten in pencil so that I can alter it as I find new information.' And Bernard laments, 'I have done so in a rudimentary way; I am forever working on a definitive version which is always just out of reach!'

I have a great deal of sympathy with both Susan and Bernard in this respect, but getting the job done inevitably means abandoning ideas of completion and perfection, and doing a good job within the limits of what you have. With this in mind, I'd like to suggest two guiding principles for writing up your family history:

1. Be prepared to select from among the material that you gather. You may be concerned that every snippet of information is too precious to leave out, but including absolutely everything is impractical, and you will put yourself under unbearable pressure if you try. Writing any kind of book, memoir or article always entails gathering more information than you can possibly use. The selection process is part of turning it into a good

       narrative, making it workable for you as the writer, and
readable for others.

2.   Family history research is never-ending, and lasts as long as
your own interest in digging out more of the story. So this
means that you have to choose, quite deliberately, a point at
which you have a 'good enough' amount of material to
write about, and the time to give to the venture. Although
family history is a more open-ended project than most
other research assignments that are written up, there are
definite parallels: with scientific papers, for instance, that
have to be composed at a certain stage of knowledge even
though future research may displace some of the findings.

What to write?

You may choose to write a full-length book, but bear in mind that this
is very hard work – as an author, believe me, I know! Some of our
family historians have done this; Ken Z.'s story of rediscovering his
ancestral landscape in the Ukraine runs to four hundred pages, and
Miriam has compiled a book on her family line and given copies to her
close relatives. Others are planning to do the same. Sheila M. is collab-
orating with a second cousin:

> Margaret and I are planning a 150-year family history using
> all these writings, with introductory chapters to each set of
> diary entries or writings, placing the person and their work
> in the context of the family and the times when it was writ-
> ten. It is a mammoth task, but well on the way.

Sheila is lucky in having a large collection of diaries and letters written by different members of her family, and both Ken's and Sheila's
projects illustrate the fact that it's more straightforward to write a
lengthy text when there is either a narrative element or ready-made
material that can slip straight into context. Even so, these are major
undertakings which require a great deal of time and effort.

Other options are to:

- write up short narratives relating to different stories within the family history
- create memoirs about particular family members
- make bulletins which become a kind of running story that you can circulate around the family
- write articles for family history journals (as several of the survey respondents have done)
- create a website on which you can upload stories and new research findings as they become available.

Each option is a genre in its own right, and brings particular opportunities and limitations. The style involved may be informal or serious, entertaining or factual, depending on the form you choose to write in and your readership.

Your readership

If you have children or grandchildren, you will almost certainly think of them as your primary target audience. Even though they may not yet be interested, as a number of my respondents mention wistfully, the day will probably come when they become intrigued by their origins. Other family members, such as nieces and nephews, siblings and cousins scattered far and wide across the globe, are also on the list of potential readers. And although the main flow of information is passing from one generation to the next, nevertheless for some family historians it's appropriate to write it up for parents, aunts or uncles who are still alive. Even those of us who no longer have that opportunity may privately dedicate our research to those who have already passed away, as a tribute to their lives.

Where the family is not the readership – perhaps there are no other surviving members, or no relatives who have any interest in the family history – then there are worthwhile opportunities to leave both a written record and your research data to a library or archive.

Joan considers herself at too advanced a stage of life to tackle a writing project, but she is making sure that her work will not be lost:

> All my family archives, letters, trees, diaries, etc. are left to the Lancashire Record Office; all boxes are labelled, and they have told me they have a van which they use to collect every-thing when the solicitors tell them.

How I Wrote My Family History

In the autumn of 2009, I had a gap in my writing schedule. I'd planned to take a break from putting words on paper, give my brain a rest for a few months. It was not to be. A little imp began dancing around that brain. 'Why not write the family history now?' it asked me jauntily. 'It's a lovely opportunity. You've got what you need – and think what fun it will be!' It kicked up its heels and clapped its hands in glee. I succumbed.

It was, actually, a brilliant opportunity and one that I enjoyed, but it was hard work and resulted in a far longer narrative than I had planned: over 40,000 words, which is just about enough for a full-length book. I chose to do it via 'My Canvas', which offers the chance to design your own page layout and include text of any length, and as many illustrations and photographs as you like. 'My Canvas' is the pub-lishing branch of the Ancestry website; you upload your material in page format as you go along, and when your project is complete, you can choose to order bound copies, as well as emailing a link to the online version to selected potential readers. It remains your book and copyright, and there is no charge unless you order a printed copy – which you will almost certainly want to do.

This is just one example of the way that internet publishing and print-on-demand books are going, and you can read more about the process and companies who offer it in the Resources section (see p. 254). I was attracted by the idea of creating my own page design and including both colour and black-and-white pictures. Skipping to the end result, the quality of the printed edition was superb, and I was relieved to see that none of my text had somehow slipped outside the page boundaries and that the photographs and illustrations had come out clearly. It was worth ordering one sample copy so that I could tweak and correct minor details before ordering a number for my family, who were either given copies (my children, in this case) or who bought them off me at cost price. Here's the rub: such a book is expensive, and my 128-page version cost me approximately £70 a copy. But about twenty have been eagerly purchased by family members, and the investment overall for my own copies has been relatively modest, at under £300.

Choosing the material

When I embarked on writing up my research, I had reached the stage of collecting enough material to write a comprehensive family history of my mother's side, concentrating mainly on her father's line, with its different branches. Sometimes, it's only when you come to write up the family history that you realise where the fat and lean areas are: I had planned to write up her mother's line too, but discovered that I only had enough to define the essential storylines there. This isn't due to a lack of interest on my part, but stems most probably from the fact that I haven't found many new relatives on this Brown and Lee line, whereas in my grandfather's Owen line, cousins have popped up all over the world and between us we have filled out the story. It probably comes back to the old issue of a family name being passed down the male line, and the way in which this makes research progress much faster in general. However, I was able to include a summary of the material about my grandmother's family story at the end, and have earmarked it for further development.

I created a plan for the structure of the book. This was to set the scene first of all, with some details about my mother and her life, then take the story back to my earliest-known ancestors on the Owen line, dating from the eighteenth century. From there, I would work forward in time. Where another branch joined the family, such as the Richards family, I would relate how this happened, and describe their earlier history too. Eventually, I reached the point where my grandmother met my grandfather, and all that was needed then was to give a brief account of their lives, and of the children they produced, including my mother. I could then round off the narrative with a little more about her and a summary of the Owen legacy in terms of family characteristics.

Along the way, I did a little extra research as I wrote, filling in some of the gaps. For instance, I wanted to chart as many members of my grandfather's family as I could – his own mother had eleven siblings, and she herself had thirteen children, including my grandfather. Once I started to try and fill in these generations systematically for the book, however, I realised that I didn't know all their stories, and I couldn't resist digging further, uncovering new tales of emigration, bankruptcy, heroism and seduction. But, fascinating though these were, I had to keep them within bounds, and use them mainly to round out the contours I'd already decided on for the narrative.

LIMITING THE TEXT

I made a decision to write very little about my mother's generation. The focus was to be on the past generations who I hadn't known personally, and I felt that to put the spotlight on my own parents, and aunts and uncles with whom I had been very familiar, would bring in a different kind of emphasis, and in a way would be too personal. It's ironic that when researching earlier generations, we can't get enough intimate detail and are forever hungering for more, but when it comes to writing about relatives that we've known, a kind of natural restraint usually creeps in. The older generation marks the borderline between your own life story and that of your family history – two separate projects when it comes to writing. Although they can certainly overlap, each involves a different process with different degrees of personal revelation.

Although I surprised myself by writing as much as I did, I at least had a framework to guide me – the chronology just mentioned, plus a self-imposed ban on writing about earlier generations of great-aunts and uncles, unless there was a particular reason to mention them. And in a very pragmatic way, 'My Canvas' also allowed me to see precisely how much I'd clocked up in money terms for a printed version each time I saved my most recent update. This helped to curtail some of my more expansive sections.

Stories and illustrations

Over the previous few years, I'd regularly written bulletins and emailed them to other members of the family, including news of my latest discoveries, and cameo portraits of some of our mutual ancestors who were beginning to emerge from the mists. Many of these findings opened up more questions, and the bulletins I wrote had a sense of questing and of suspense as we waited for more answers to appear. Now, in the family history book, I could use extracts from some of them, which helped to liven up the text and vary the texture of narrative style. I was also able to infuse something of their tone into my writing, to enhance the atmosphere of story-telling and create a sense of direct communication with the reader. Right from the start, I was aware that very few of my contacts would wade diligently through lists of data or dull reports of how I came to find my 3 x great-grandmother's marriage record. We all crave stories, and they are the lifeblood of family history.

Illustrations proved important too. When these bulletins had been sent out as emails, I noticed that cousins abroad were particularly glad to have visual descriptions and photographs to accompany them, since they couldn't easily visit the locations themselves. So it became a priority to select pictures, not only of the ancestors, but of where they lived and of historical events and activities relevant to their lives. This often meant searching in a more general way for illustrations from social history.

The hard data was also in my book, mostly in the form of sections of the family tree; 'My Canvas' has the added bonus of creating these charts directly from a family tree that you have uploaded to the Ancestry website. You can make minor alterations where necessary, but the bulk of the work is done for you.

Care in saving Work

It is vital to keep a back-up of your writing as you go, and this is especially important if you are working online, with something like 'My Canvas'. Sometimes I struggled with the page layout and lost portions of my text. This wasn't too disastrous, however, as I always wrote the original in the normal way – in this case as a Word document on my PC. I would always recommend writing your text offline and uploading from your own file on to the website or internet file, both for security and ease of editing.

I first saved each new topic in the text as a separate file, and later, when the book was complete, I also made a file combining these as a full text version. Both have their uses: the former if I want to pull out a particular story, perhaps to email to someone, and the latter if I want to search the whole text for a particular reference or name.

Sources

How many of your sources should you list in your written family history? A conscientious genealogist would say 'all of them', but I found this was too onerous and would have increased the time spent by about 50 per cent, as well as the length of the book. Given how widely available and easily accessible census and BMD records are now, I considered that listing all of these would weigh the book down, and so I only included general references to them (e.g. Wales census 1861) and more specific pointers to the less usual records. My own archive will, I hope, contain enough well-documented material for any seriously interested family member to find what they need, if I'm not around to show them.

Finishing off

Once the project was complete, I ordered a proof copy of the book to check the finished result. Inevitably there were typos, and a few wonky page layouts, and it went through two more versions before I got to what I considered the final edition. It was important to acknowledge it as such, and to say, 'Yes, I've done my best. If there are still minor flaws, so be it. Now I've decided that it's ready and I want people to read it.' This gives you the satisfaction of completion, and avoids falling prey to nagging doubts or – even worse – the temptation to include new material as you find it. And of course, you will find new material. I keep a file now, referencing everything that I've discovered since writing the book, so that I can make an appendix or separate bulletin when I'm ready. At least, that's the theory!

Although I am an established author and delight in seeing the first copies of a book that I write, complete with publisher's logo, beautiful cover design and so on, my delight in producing this family history was equally intense. From a professional standpoint, I knew that there would never be any chance of publishing it commercially, but in terms of a sense of achievement, and of it meaning something special to family members, the level of satisfaction was very high. I do recommend you to take the same view. Individual family histories are very, very rarely of interest to a publisher, and to aim at that market could turn a joyful project into a hard slog that might easily end in failure. Writing for your own family is a win–win situation, since your readers are already out there, and there is no question of your work being rejected for publication. You will surely be thrilled by their appreciation when they see and read what you've produced.

TOP TIPS FOR WRITING YOUR FAMILY HISTORY

Here are my top tips to take you through the whole writing process.

Setting it up

- Decide who your main readership will be. You may need to accept that the younger generation will take an interest in it later, rather than sooner.

- Consider what type of narrative you'd like to write – a book, memoirs of different ancestors or a short resumé, and so on. Take into account how much time and energy you have available. Even if you have done all the necessary research, a book of modest length, such as the one I wrote, will probably take you the equivalent of at least three months' full-time work.
- Figure out a work plan, in broad terms. When can you set aside time for it? Will you compile it continuously, or maybe at intervals?

The writing process

- For writing tips, plus ideas for creating a narrative from your stories, see my book *Your Life, Your Story: Writing Your Life Story for Family and Friends* (see Resources, p. 254). Many of the techniques suggested for life-story writing can be applied to family history as well. Also recommended is *Writing Up Your Family History* by John Titford (see Resources, p. 254).
- Use boxes and sections, etc. to help you with the narrative. If you're uncertain how to do this, look at magazines and browse books, especially large-format, illustrated ones, to give you ideas. These devices can help to break up a continuous story and they look appealing on the page to the reader.
- Try to pull out the threads you can describe as storylines, in the way that we worked on in the last chapter.
- Anything with a narrative element will be easier to write and easier to read, so include plenty of short anecdotes and episodes from the lives of your ancestors.

What to include; what to leave out

- Include illustrations if you can. As well as family photos and historical documents, search for relevant pictures on the internet – for instance, old postcards such as are found on the eBay website can give just the local view you're looking for. (If you are considering publication of your family history, either on the internet or in printed form, be very careful over copyright issues, and seek permission where necessary.)
- Consider future generations, and make sure there is enough information and references for them to understand what you're talking about.
- Don't expect to include everything, and keep entries for individual ancestors in proportion to their significance and place within the family story.
- Accept that other information will come along later. Fill in whatever gaps you can, but you'll be waiting for ever to fill them all.
- Don't recount all the steps you have taken in the research process. It can dull a good story and make it hard to follow. Only do this if there was a real quest involved in your research, or if you are writing genealogical teaching material.
- Weave in some social history if you can. Expand themes which have especially interested you and that you've researched (in my case, this was that of women in the Napoleonic Wars and the lives of Victorian shopkeepers).

Saving your work

- If working online, write and save every section of text in a normal word-processing file first.

Applying good genealogical practice

- Decide how thoroughly you will list your sources for documents, certificates, etc.
- Including an index could be helpful.
- Distinguish between researched or documented information, and material which comes from anecdote, family stories, memories or speculation. Let the reader know which is which.
- Where there are mysteries or questions, bring them in, and define them as such. Readers love a puzzle, and may like to take up the challenge to try and discover more.

Relating to your ancestors

- If you feel strongly about your ancestors, allow yourself some emotion when writing, but do guard against sentimentality. Not everyone will have the same investment in their ancestry as you may have. If, on the other hand, you tend to be more detached in your outlook, aim to engage with your ancestors with empathy. Don't just stick to names and dates.
- Be aware of the gap between historical ancestors and those within living memory. Decide how you're going to handle that, perhaps by just giving brief details of the lives of more recent relatives. Be careful of including living relatives, and ask their permission if need be.

Feedback

- Consider inviting your relatives to read your work before completion. Listen to their views, and even their criticisms, but both they and you should accept that it won't be perfect. They're lucky to have someone to do it for them!

The Family Reaction

By the time you're ready to pass on your findings in full, perhaps in the form of a book or pamphlet, you'll probably already have shared elements of these with other family members. What do they make of it all? If you write it up now, will they applaud your efforts, or think you deluded? And will their response affect how you go about it, or even deter you completely?

If you haven't yet told your relatives what you're up to, be prepared for mixed reactions when you do. Judging by the reports I received from the survey, most family historians have not received universal support for their work. Ron lists the range of responses he has encountered:

> Polite or enthusiastic interest.
> Crazy man!
> Keeps him off the street!
> While he's doing that it keeps him off my back.
> Why doesn't he cut the grass again, or get on with the compost heap where he belongs?

It's true that a few people taking part in the survey had met with unequivocal praise, like Margaret: 'The general consensus of my family is very complimentary. They remarked on my patience, perseverance and the time and effort I put into it.' But many encountered a varied response: 'Both indifference and interest' (Melanie); 'Some interest, but mild amusement in others' (Lorna); or even, 'They think I am quite mad, but are interested in how far back I have got' (Sheila M. G.). William's close family are not so polite, and make plain their view that it's 'something daft that Dad messes about with now that he has retired'. David Sm.'s comment, echoed by several others, that 'Most of my family are pleased I am doing this research,' is a polite way of saying that there is a significant minority who are not.

The message here seems to be that you may need to become a little thick-skinned in order to weather indifference or even ridicule from certain quarters. Children are often the worst offenders, but we still love them and make allowances for it. Aren't they interested really, deep down? 'Not a lot, but they are young and will change their minds as the years go by,' Keith assures. Ah well, perhaps they will come to it in their own good time. 'My family are not impressed with my research, but in fairness, I was not very interested either until I was older and had some time to work on it,' says Geraldine.

It can hurt too when certain relatives deride what we do. 'Some think I'm "sad",' Ken D. admits, but he also confirms that 'it is really appreciated by most'. It can also be a blow when someone very close to you refuses to acknowledge your research. Teresa only receives mild acknowledgement from her relatives, and rejection from her brother: 'My family are not particularly interested in my research; they do listen when I tell them what I have discovered, but the interest stops there. My sibling is not at all interested for reasons only known to him.'

It's a fact that your research may not please everyone. At intervals during this book, I've mentioned the question of older relatives, or sometimes even those of the same generation, who consider family history a dangerous and undesirable pursuit. However carefully we handle our contact with them, this reaction may be unavoidable. Lizzy encountered this problem, though warm support from elsewhere has eased the situation:

> It is interesting how some of the family have reacted to my research. My brother thinks I am unnecessarily stirring up the past and doesn't see the point of it. My step-aunts on my father's side think it is very interesting though.

And Janet's experience has been similar:

> Some are not at all interested in the past, and their attitude is that maybe we shouldn't go raking it up. Others are horrified by what I have found. Luckily, my immediate family are very interested, and listen to all my stories without looking too bored.

Brenda found resistance even closer to home, and her account of this reveals how someone can resent having their existing beliefs undermined:

> My mum has been a bit upset by some of the things I have told her. Only little things like where her father was born and where her grandparents were married. My research doesn't match with the things she thought she 'knew'. It has made her question what she thinks she remembers her mother told her and made her realise that there was a lot of information she had never been told and many family members she was unaware of.

In my own family, I've likewise found a mixed reaction, ranging from indifference to great enthusiasm. Writing up my mother's history was a major milestone, however, and some members who hadn't stirred to give me a nod of acknowledgement before were delighted to see the book either online or in printed form (it helped that I was able to give them the choice, as the online version is free to view, so they were not under pressure to buy a bound copy). From a couple of cousins, stony silence has prevailed, and probably I will never know if they have looked into the pages of the book, or what they thought of it. But I'm glad I wasn't put off the project by an earlier lack of appreciation in certain quarters. It was worth committing myself to write it.

Taking a view

If you wish to survive the gamut of family reactions, it pays to develop a philosophy, as Irene shows:

> My four offspring aren't particularly interested in our family tree, although I think my elder daughter may develop an interest as she gets older. I hope that eventually one of them will acquire an interest in their heritage – or maybe one of my grandchildren or even great-grandchildren may

oblige – and then my research will not have been in vain. Perhaps due to the fact that the younger generation tends to live life in the 'fast lane', researching family history is too tedious and painstaking? I hope, in later years, it will give my children a sense of identity, as it has for me.

A little healthy selfishness is a good thing here. Have faith in the work you're doing, enjoy it for its own sake and cherish the belief that it will probably hit the mark somewhere, some day, as Ian affirms:

As for why I do it – well that is entirely selfish – it suits my investigative tendencies without having to revert to poking my nose into my neighbours' lives! I don't watch a great deal of television, it's easily accessible, it doesn't matter how long it takes – after all, they [the ancestors] are not going any-where – and it's something I can pass on to my nephews and cousins because of the shared links. Above all though, it gives me a better understanding of who I am – a humbling thought now I know what my ancestors have been through – and a better appreciation of what I have today.

Creating a Heritage

Whatever the current response from your family circle, take heart in the fact that by gathering together the stories of your ancestors, you are creating a heritage both for your existing relatives and for the generations to come. Whether you pass it on through writing it up or by compiling an archive, the work you are doing is of huge value. Even family historians without close family can, as we've seen, make a contribution towards the general sphere of genealogical research. Imagine your joy if you were to discover a cache of papers, narratives and family trees deposited in a library which you could connect to your own ancestry. How exciting this would be, and how grateful you would feel to the person who had worked so diligently to compile this archive.

VALUING YOUR WORK

The most important thing is to value your own work, whatever the immediate feedback; doing this work for its own sake has meaning and worth, and may bear fruit in the future in ways that you cannot imagine now. With this in mind, here are a few points to remember:

- Think of the ancestors who you are honouring and paying tribute to.
- Be patient with your children and the younger generation, who will probably take an interest in the end.
- Refrain from forcing your findings upon those who simply don't want to know about them, possibly for deep and personal reasons of their own. Their appreciation isn't necessary to validate your work.
- Take time out to enjoy what you have created – read what you've written, sift through the data, relax with a family album.
- Accept praise where it's offered; don't measure it against a lack of interest or rejection from other quarters.

The Teller of Tales

Janet's mention above of telling stories is a reminder that writing down your family history is only one way of passing it on. The oral tradition, with its telling of tales, is also an important means of handing on the knowledge, and is something we can work with today. In traditional African societies, the role of the story-teller in transmitting genealogy is considered vital, and such a person is known as a griot (male) or griotte (female). The concept of the griot has now become popular in a much wider sphere, and the term has been adopted into contemporary global culture to denote a person who gathers and shares histories of a personal, family or community nature. Any one of us can become a griot or griotte, if we so choose.

In Western societies, although tales of noble lineage were once passed on through the songs and recitations of bards and minstrels, more humble pedigrees did not have professional performers to recount them. Instead, they were handed down through the stories told by older relatives in domestic contexts: around the fire on a winter's night, at a family celebration or on walks with grandchildren.

If we think back to the days before television or radio, and to a time when families were poorer and lived closer together, we realise just how favourable such a culture was towards the passing on of family lore. Even though not everyone was literate, telling stories would have been both a natural and powerful form of transmitting the family history. Such habits persisted in certain families, and there are family historians today who can date their own interest to early childhood, when they listened to the stories told by their older relatives; it seemed a natural progression later to start following their own lines of enquiry. Perhaps those who are exposed to the family history in childhood are more likely to accept this as their heritage, and to develop and pass it on themselves.

At any rate, when we've reclaimed our family stories through our research, let's tell them to our children and grandchildren. This is very much in tune with the times, since school projects often now involve drawing up a family tree, or asking grandparents about their early lives. We need to put the stories back into circulation. Sure, they will get edited and added to, and perhaps they will end up as family folklore, rather than the strict truth. But, as family historians, we can have the best of both worlds; simply make sure that your research data is accessible in some form, so that future generations can check out the facts for themselves.

Creative Activities with the Ancestors

You can also use your imagination and your talents to create beautiful and evocative things from the material of family history. Take the example of Sue Hiley Harris, an Australian-born weaver descended from British emigrants, who has created a stunning collection of 'ancestor bags' relating directly to her forebears. The initial inspiration for these came from Aboriginal string bags, which were sometimes used for storing ancestral bones. Sue knew very little about her own ancestry until she started researching for this project, and discovered to her amazement that many of her relatives also worked as weavers in the textile industry in the Bradford area of England. (She herself reversed the emigration trail, and moved back to the UK as a young woman.) Her 'bags' are made from long, narrow woven strips; each one represents a specific ancestor and is composed of different sections, loops and colours denoting, among other things, a chronology of that person's life, the children they had and their relationship to Sue's line of the family. The code is precise, but yet the overall effect is that of artistry and, when the bags are hung in the configuration of her family tree, they create an eerie presence which has profoundly moved visitors to her exhibitions. 'I feel I have now got to know my ancestors,' she says. (You can visit her website at www.suehileyharris.co.uk.)

Don't be restricted, therefore, just by the meticulous and factual research that you carry out, or even by the effort to write up your family history in a methodical way. You'll find a number of contemporary book titles in the Resources section (see pp. 252–3) in which authors have chosen either to write up their quest on the trail of their ancestry as an exciting narrative, or have used themes from family history in a fictional context. Perhaps one of the most evocative is Julie Myerson's *The Lost Child* (see Resources, p. 253), a factual account in which she traces the life story and family history of an obscure eighteenth-century child artist and recounts this in parallel with the unfolding drama she experiences with her own teenage son, who is almost 'lost' to her through drug abuse.

At the moment, including the theme of ancestry in creative endeavour is a growth area, and you may be able to find inspiration in the work of others and make a contribution yourself, either for your family or for a wider audience. Here are some ideas, just to get the ball rolling:

- Stitch a sampler or tapestry with a family history theme.
- Write imaginative stories that could have happened to certain of your ancestors (making it clear that this is fiction).
- Paint a landscape that your ancestors inhabited.
- Make a model of a house that they lived in.
- Create a beautiful or unusual family tree – this could involve fine calligraphy, quirky drawings, pepped-up photos or any other interesting visual elements.
- Keep a journal of your quest to find your ancestors, with the possibility in mind of writing it up as a narrative. (In this case, the story of your quest predominates, rather than the history that you discover, so it is a different activity from that of writing the family history.)
- Make a collage of family photos, either digitally or by hand. If you are using prints, don't forget to make copies to use, rather than experimenting with the originals.
- Write an imaginary diary for a year in the life of one of your ancestors, using material gleaned from your research as the backbone, and fleshing it out through your general knowledge of their life and times.
- Draw cartoon portraits of your ancestors, bringing in as much of their character as you can.
- Create a hanging with an abstract design that somehow captures the colours and spirit of your ancestry.

Your Onward Journey

This is now as far as I can travel with you on the journey through the different stages of searching for your family history. It's been thoroughly gratifying to share suggestions with you for making this a lively and rewarding process – suggestions taken from both my own experience and from those of other researchers who have kindly contributed to this book.

However, this is not the end of your quest, of course, which I hope will continue to involve you wholeheartedly – a path marked with exciting discoveries which will bring you many benefits and pleasures. Keep it inventive, creative and enjoyable. And remember that your family history is a connection to the history of the world itself. Your ancestry links you to the story of the whole of humanity, both its past and its future. Even though you may research only a fraction of this span of human existence, your family story plays a vital part in it, and the knowledge that you gain from it is sure to enrich your life immeasurably.

Family Tree of Kathleen Owen (Mother of the Author)

**Pedigree Chart for
Kathleen Florence Owen**

Bernard Walker Owen
b: 24 Jun 1882 in
Wellington, Somerset
m: 04 Jul 1907 in Baptist
Chapel, Brington,
Northants
d: 23 Sep 1972 in
Nottingham

David Richards Owen
b: 10 Feb 1843 in Builth,
Brecon & Radnor
m: Jul 1873 in Wesleyan
Chapel, Hemyock, Devon
d: 16 Dec 1920 in Gt
Bowden, Northants

Mary Masey Walker
b: 15 Nov 1853 in
Hemyock, Devon,
England
d: 15 Feb 1936 in
Finchley, Middx

Edward Owens
b: Abt. 1803 in Llandinam,
Montgomeryshire
m: 12 Aug 1836 in
Llanwnog,
Montgomeryshire, Wales
d: 23 Jun 1877 in Kerry,
Newtown

Margaret Richards
b: 1807 in Llanwnog,
Montgomeryshire
d: 17 Sep 1884 in
Newtown,
Montgomeryshire, Wales

Thomas Walker
b: Abt. 1818 in Hemyock,
Devon, England
m: 24 Oct 1844 in Prescot
Chapel, Wellington
d: 1902 in Wellington

Catherine Masey
b: 1825 in Hemyock,
Devon, England
d: 1909 in Wellington

Edward Owens
b: 1776 in Abbeycwmhir,
Radnorshire (prob)

Maria Kinsey
b: 1782 in Wotton-under-
Edge, Glos

David Richards
b: 1779 in Llanwnog,
Montgomeryshire

Margaret Brees
b: 1779 in Llanwnog,
Montgomeryshire

John Walker
b: Abt. 1789 in
Hemyock, Devon

Margaret Manfield
b: 1796

James Masey
b: 1792 in Hemyock,
Devon

Elizabeth (Betty) Masey
b: 1796 in Hemyock,

Kathleen Florence Owen
b: 10 Jan 1912 in Barton Fabis, Leics
m: 07 Sep 1939
d: 09 Mar 2000 in Church Stretton, Shropshire

Hannah Eliza Brown
b: 21 Feb 1882 in Great Brington, Northants
d: 22 Oct 1971 in Nottingham

Henry Brown
b: 20 Jun 1849 in Bedworth, Warwickshire, England
m: 22 Feb 1875 in Bedworth Church
d: 22 Feb 1922 in Great Brington, Northants

Sarah Ann Lee
b: 18 Dec 1850 in Back of Collycroft, Bedworth, Warwickshire
d: 09 Mar 1934 in Chiefswood, Coleshill Road, Atherstone, Warwickshire

James Brown
b: Abt. 1811 in Coventry, Warwickshire, England
m: 21 May 1848 in Parish Church, Bedworth
d: 24 Apr 1872 in Bedworth, Warwicks

Sophia Pickard
b: 1820 in Bedworth, Warwickshire
d: Bef. 1881

Thomas Lee
b: Abt. 1812 in Bedworth, Warwickshire, England
m: 12 Mar 1844 in Independent Chapel, Bedworth, Warwickshire
d:

Jane Adie
b: 1810 in Bedworth, Warwickshire
d: Abt. 13 Jun 1885 in Bedworth, Warwickshire

Daniel Brown
b: Abt. 1768 in Warwickshire, England

Ann Fulford
b: Abt. 1763
d: Bef. 1843

Samuel Pickard
b: Abt. 1791 in Warwickshire

Ann Goodger
b: Abt. 1791 in Warwickshire

William Lee
b: Abt. 1791

Elizabeth Crutchlow
b: Abt. 1791

James Adie
b: 1790 in Warwickshire

Maria Adie
b: 1790 in Warwickshire

Appendix II

A Note on DNA Testing

The advance of genetics in recent years means that some elements of a person's ancestry can be traced through analysing a sample of their DNA. It is still a somewhat controversial and chaotic field in terms of family history, in terms of how specific it can be and whether it is likely to be misleading. David Sm., for instance, undertook a DNA test which first classified him in a broad way, and then reclassified him as more sophisticated techniques became available. As the analyst said to him in an email, 'We always have to practise "throwing out" of theories to keep moving on with this genetic detective stuff.' Now, it appears, he is likely to be the descendent of a black Roman soldier or slave who lived in the north of England. Neither I nor David has the expertise to know how accurate this may be.

However, I did ask an expert on the archaeology of Roman Britain about David's case, and he confirmed that this is indeed possible. Roman Emperor Septimius Severus (AD145–211) came from North Africa himself; he was certainly dark-skinned, if not black, and during his reign brought many North African soldiers with him to the Scottish borders, who, putting it politely, interbred with local women. So such a line of descent from African stock may be more common than previously thought in Britain.

What can be told from a DNA sample depends upon whether you are male or female, as well as the kind of test applied and the current state of knowledge. An article on the reliable Genuki website (http://www.genuki.org.uk/big/bigmisc/DNA.html, updated May 2010) sets out the role of DNA testing in ancestry, and I would recommend that you source this or another up-to-date appraisal of the situation before parting with what can be a considerable sum of money to trace your roots. I signed up to a National Geographic DNA project in about

2006, hoping to discover exciting elements of my ancestry (preferably romantic and Celtic), and was disappointed to learn that I was simply one of the majority in the British Isles who had originally migrated out of Africa via Western Europe. I had not looked into it thoroughly enough beforehand to know what kind of information it would reveal. Claims by sites that you can 'fill in missing branches of your family tree' using their DNA test should be taken with a pinch of salt. Where specific family names have been tested and compared, you may have better luck, but otherwise you are fishing in a very large sea of genetic information.

Be aware, too, of privacy concerns, as some testing organisations may wish to store your DNA and match it up with other samples on their database. Obviously, this is one way in which the knowledge can progress, in terms of the role DNA can play both in health issues and matters of ancestry, but at the same time, you need to be clear about what you are signing up to. Remember too, that the further back you go, the more direct-line ancestors you have, so that a line which can be identified by DNA may be one of thousands which has contributed to your make-up.

In the future, perhaps DNA testing will be an essential tool for family history research, and an article in the *Who Do You Think You Are?* family history magazine (November 2010) promises a 'third-generation' form of testing will give us far more information about our recent ancestry. But in its current state, it's little more than a sideline, and one which can be confusing. Keep an eye on developments, however, and get ready to jump in if and when it offers something that will really shed light on your history.

Resources

Recommended Reading

The books listed below are all recommended as being of value to the family history researcher, but I've given them discriminating reviews to highlight both their strengths and weaknesses, so that you can make an informed choice before buying. Do pick out the latest edition if possible, rather than buying an earlier version; many good, standard works on family history are revised at regular intervals. You may find that you need to order books, rather than buy them off the shelf, since very few bookshops have a comprehensive section on family history, and many really good books are sold by small, specialist publishing companies. It therefore helps to have prior guidance, and not just to order on title alone. Checking descriptions and reviews on the internet is also very useful, and the online bookseller Amazon supplies most of the books cited here (www.amazon.co.uk or www.amazon.com).

Specialist publishers

You may find it worthwhile browsing the catalogues of some of the smaller, specialist publishers who focus on family history and related areas. Here are some of the leaders in the UK:

Amberley Publishing: www.amberleybooks.com (local history)
Countryside Books: www.countrysidebooks.co.uk (family history and genealogy)
Halsgrove: www.halsgrove.com (social and local history)
The History Press: www.thehistorypress.co.uk (genealogy and local history)
How To Books: www.howtobooks.co.uk (small but worthwhile section on family history)
Old House Books & Maps: www.OldHouseBooks.co.uk (exploring and explaining the past)
Pen and Sword: www.pen-and-sword.co.uk (military)
Shire Books: www.shirebooks.co.uk (also websites for other countries: social and family history)
Society of Genealogists: www.sog.org.uk (family history)

Standard research guides

Each of these books covers the chief aspects of researching family history, and it's useful to have at least one of these as a key resource.

Adolph, Anthony, *Tracing Your Family History* (Collins, new edition, 2008)
> This has received good reviews from family history journals, but the typeface and layout are poorly designed, making it hard to read in places. The research content is useful.

Barratt, Nick, *Guide to your Ancestors' Lives* (Pen and Sword Books, 2010)
> Nick Barratt is a well-known writer who frequently appears on family history television programmes in the UK. He is also an expert on house history and social history, and weaves the three elements together in this practical guide to finding out more about who your ancestors were, and how they lived.

Barratt, Nick, *Who Do You Think You Are? Encyclopedia of Genealogy* (Harper, 2008)
> Associated with the popular television series of the same name, this attractively presented book sets out to make the first and intermediate steps in family history research clear and enjoyable.

Chambers, Margaret, *Finding Families: The Guide to the National Archives of Australia for Genealogists* (Hale and Iremonger, 1998)
> A guide to the records held by the National Archives of Australia.

Herber, Mark D., *Ancestral Trails: The Complete Guide to British Genealogy and Family History* (reprinted The History Press, 2008)
> A substantial tome, probably more for reference than for reading straight through. Although it is respected as a classic guide in its field, the 2008 reprint is sadly lacking in essential updates; the Family Records Centre in London referred to in great detail, for instance, had already closed by then.

Hey, David (ed.), *The Oxford Companion to Family and Local History* (Oxford University Press, 2010)
> A densely written volume, partly a collection of essays, and partly a useful A–Z of family and local history. Although this might be offputting for the novice, it could be a useful reference book for the committed researcher.

Rogers, Colin D., *The Family Tree Detective: A Manual for Tracing Your Ancestors in England and Wales* (Manchester University Press, 4th revised edition 2008)
> A useful and comprehensive guide to research which has become a standard reference book.

Ideas for working on your family history

Blake, Paul and Loughran, Maggie, *Discover Your Roots: 52 Brilliant Ideas for Exploring Your Family and Local History* (Infinite Ideas Limited, 2006)

A jaunty look at how to persuade your relatives to tell their stories, make a creative scrapbook and approach archives without fear. It's a stimulating book that doesn't quite take each idea far enough, but is a good trigger for your own research activities.

Hart, Cynthia, with Samson, Lisa, *The Oral History Workshop* (also listed as *Tell Me Your Story*) (Workman Publishing, 2009)

How to 'collect and celebrate the life stories of your family and friends'. Practical advice for making audio and video recordings, suggestions for questions to ask, etc.

Shrimpton, Jayne, *Family Photographs and How to Date Them* (Countryside Books, 2008)

Enjoyable to browse through and rewarding to study in detail, this book could prove invaluable in helping to date and identify those mystery photographs which every collection of family memorabilia seems to contain. Aspects of dress, hairstyles and photography are the chief focus, taken chronologically from 1850 to 1950.

Symes, Ruth A., *Stories From Your Family Tree* (The History Press, 2008)

Historian Ruth Symes pieces together various stories from her own family tree to show how diligent research into existing family legends, memories and objects can restore these accounts to their full glory. Although Ruth's experiences may differ widely from your own family context, it's instructive to read how she goes about it, and she includes specific search tips which may help your individual enquiries.

Ward, Margaret, *The Female Line: Researching Your Female Ancestors* (Countryside Books, 2003)

Many of us are particularly interested in tracing the mother's line of the family, and in societies where the father's name is perpetuated this can be tricky. This book can't solve all the problems likely to be encountered, but offers some advice, and is especially interesting on the status, legal position and occupations of women in history – knowledge which in itself may help to trace female ancestors.

Specific regional or ethnic ancestry

There are specific guides to researching various nationalities and lineages. It's only possible to list some examples here, but if you have a particular ethnic or national origin, try an online search to see what might be available (e.g. 'Malta + family history') or ask an archivist at your local record office to check for you.

Crooks, Paul, *A Tree Without Roots* (Blackamber Books, 2008)

How to trace British, African and Asian Caribbean ancestry.

Maxwell, Ian, *How to Trace Your Irish Ancestors* (How To Books Ltd, 2009)
>A clear and practical guide to researching Irish family history.

Rowlands, John & Sheila (eds), *Second Stages in Researching Welsh Ancestry* (Federation of Family History Societies, 1999)
>Specialist help for those who need to tease out their Welsh roots, as opposed to following a general approach to British ancestry.

Specific occupations, periods and religions

Drummond, Di, *Tracing Your Railway Ancestors* (Pen and Sword Books, 2010)
>Many of us will have at least one ancestor who worked on the railways, so this is a welcome guide to tracking down possible sources for records of their work, and to resources which fill in the background to life on the railways.

Fowler, Simon, *Tracing Your First World War Ancestors* (Countryside Books, 2008)
>Help with finding your way through the complexity of First World War records, which requires more than a simple online search. A good, detailed resources section.

Gandy, Michael, *Tracing Nonconformist Ancestors* (Public Record Office (PRO) Publications, 2001)
>A guide to researching ancestors who were Methodists, Baptists, Quakers or of another nonconformist persuasion.

Society of Genealogists, *My Ancestor Was ...*
>A popular and expansive series, covering many things that your ancestor might have been, including 'Bastard', Baptist, Jewish, Merchant Seaman, Coalminer and Policeman.

Social history, topography and general background

This is obviously a very wide subject area, but here are some suggestions which may serve to help you track down the type of books that you'll find useful:

Clist, Brian and Draycott, Chris, *The Book of Hemyock* (Halsgrove, 2001)
>Part of the Halsgrove series of parish and community histories, some of which may be out of print, but are invaluable if you are researching that particular locality. Try an internet search or a library request if you cannot find the title in the current catalogue. The Hemyock one has proved enormously helpful for researching the branch of my family that comes from Hemyock in Devon, and contains many details of local names and occupations. The authors are themselves experienced local family historians living in the neighbourhood.

Miles, David, *The Tribes of Britain: Who are we? And where do we come from?* (Phoenix, 2006)

The big picture of Britain's settlers, from earliest to contemporary times.

Murray, Venetia, *Where Have All the Cowslips Gone?* (Bishopsgate Press, 1993)

Memories of local life in Wessex, collected by the author and illustrated with old photographs. If you keep an eye out for books such as this one, which covers a location relevant to your relatives or ancestors, you will almost certainly find it useful background to your research, covering life in earlier times, with details of shopkeeping, farming, celebrations and village scandals.

Scott, Rebecca, *Samplers* (Shire Publications, 2009)

A beautifully illustrated guide to the origins and types of embroidered samplers, focusing chiefly on Britain, but with references to European and American samplers too. See Chapter Seven for examples of how samplers can be linked to an ancestor or provide a family history in their own right.

Seymour, John, *Forgotten Household Crafts* (various editions, including Dorling Kindersley 2007 and National Trust)

Delightful and meticulously illustrated account of household crafts, equipment and tasks, by a respected chronicler of British country life.

Yesterday's Town (series, with various authors and locations; Barracuda Books)

This valuable series covers a number of specific English towns, from Dover to Pershore, Brackley to Wellington. They contain many useful historic photographs and details of each locality, its shops, businesses and inhabitants. You may have to find second-hand copies, or request them from a library, as they are now out of print.

Creative writing and family history

Some authors are now choosing to write about their ancestors and families in the style of a memoir, or even including dramatised accounts of their lives. There are also novels in which family history is a prominent theme. Examples of these are:

Forster, Margaret, *Isa and May* (Vintage, 2011)

A novel about a young woman who starts to look into her family history and discovers secrets and cover-ups. This goes hand in hand with her scholarly research into the nature of grandmothers. Beautifully crafted, with a strong storyline. The same author also wrote *Hidden Lives: A Family Memoir* (Penguin, 2001) – a quest to discover hidden aspects of her grandmother's life, and to link her own life with that of her mother and grandmother.

Goodwin, Daisy, *Silver River* (Harper Perennial, 2008)

Journalist and TV presenter Daisy Goodwin explores her heritage by travelling to Argentina, meeting relatives, and piecing together the surprising and sometimes shocking history of her family as colonial emigrants.

Kay, Jackie, *Red Dust Road: An Autobiographical Journey* (Picador, 2010)
Jackie, who was adopted as a baby, seeks out her birth parents: a white Scottish former nurse, and a black Nigerian expert on trees. She describes her meetings with them and other relatives, and travels to her ancestral village in Nigeria along a 'red dust road'. A thoughtful and stimulating narrative from this leading poet and novelist.

Myerson, Julie, *The Lost Child* (Bloomsbury Publishing, 2009)
An interweaving of two true life stories: one, the author's own son going through a teenage crisis involving heavy drug use, and the other, tracing the family history of Mary Yelloly, a child who painted an extraordinary album of sketches of her life and family home in the eighteenth century.

Hardy, Jeremy, *My Family and Other Strangers: Adventures in Family History* (Ebury Press, 2010)
Jeremy is a well-known comedian, who decided to research his family history and write a book about it. Not surprisingly, it's very funny in places, but also wistful, political and sometimes infuriating! His experiences with archives, graves and visiting old family haunts will resonate with many of us, and some of the philosophy he distils is brilliantly expressed.

There are also novels which take on the theme of ancestry and weave powerful dramas around it:

Torday, Paul, *The Girl on the Landing* (Phoenix, 2009)
A somewhat surreal story by one of the most original new writers, which questions the power of genes, the true origins of the British, and the spirit of ancestry which can overwhelm the rules of so-called civilised society.

Walker, Alice, *Now is the Time to Open your Heart* (Phoenix, 2005)
A couple decide to follow their own separate paths to discover who they are – Kate travels to South America and follows a shaman's bidding, while Yolo goes to Hawii and experiences the harder realities of kinship. An intriguing and unusual novel by a highly acclaimed author.

Writing up your family history
Gilchrist, Cherry, *Your Life, Your Story: Writing Your Life Story for Family and Friends* (Piatkus, 2010)

An acclaimed guide, by the author of this book, to the practicalities of writing your own life story. It contains a chapter about family history, and shows ways of integrating this into a written life story. Many of the techniques and exercises suggested throughout this book can also be applied to writing your family history.

Titford, John, *Writing Up Your Family History* (Countryside Books 1996; new edition 2009)

Friendly and encouraging advice on how to plan and write up your family history. At least half the book is devoted to the question of publishing your book, and the new edition does not entirely get up to speed with computing and the internet; nevertheless the guide to writing is worthwhile in its own right.

Creating Your Own Family History Book

'My Canvas' is the publishing arm of the Ancestry website, and offers a free facility to create your own family history book via their website. It has an enticing range of design features, including decorative backgrounds and photo frames. You can insert as many photos, maps and illustrations as you like. Only a basic grasp of word-processing and handling digital photos is needed, and the results can be superb. If you are a subscriber to Ancestry, and have uploaded your family tree to its website, 'My Canvas' will automatically generate charts in your book for your selected direct-line ancestors. You can invite others to view your work online, again for free, and order bound copies priced according to length. My 120-page family history, including postage from the USA, was not cheap, but well worth the cost in terms of quality and creating a family legacy. You can sometimes find 'My Canvas' discounts on offer, either in family history magazines or on the website itself, which can make a real difference to the overall cost, especially if you're ordering several volumes at once (visit www.ancestry.mycanvas.com).

'Blurb' has easy-to-use software which you can download from the internet, and then design your own family history album at leisure. It's more suited to predominantly visual projects, mainly with photos and illustrations, rather than long sections of text. You can print out and proof your book, then upload the finished result and order bound copies directly from the company. Production quality is excellent. The finished costs, including postage from the USA, put it on a par with an expensive specialist illustrated book, but worthwhile if you only need a few special copies (visit http://www.blurb.com).

Print on demand

If you wish to write a book with more text than photographs, you may find that 'print on demand' publishers suit your needs best. You will need to give them the complete book in its final layout and in an electronic version; you can order as few or as many copies as you like, but producing a small print run of 50–100 copies is probably the most economic option. Look for local or online printers who offer this service. Here are two of the leaders in the field:

Anthony Rowe

A well-established and reliable company, known for producing good-quality volumes and offering transparent quotes for the costs.
Head Office: Bumper's Farm, Chippenham, Wilts SN14 6LH; tel. 01249 659705; http://www.antonyrowe.co.uk.

Lulu

An online company which is a popular choice for all kinds of self-publishing, including hardbacks and paperbacks and various other types of format. Visit their website for the latest details at http://www.lulu.com/uk.

Computer Software

Do check family history magazines for the latest releases. The leading genealogy software programmes are generally considered to be: Family Historian, Family Tree Maker and Roots Magic. Also worth a look is *The British 19th Century Surname Atlas* from Archer Software.

Websites for Family History

Here is a selection of useful websites which are completely or closely associated with family history. All the sites listed here were functioning at the time of going to press. Some are free to view, some have limited free searches with pay-to-view facilities and some are subscription only; most centre on UK records, unless otherwise specified.

General genealogy websites

www.findmypast.co.uk: a reliable, leading UK site, with censuses for England and Wales and a variety of other data.
www.ancestry.co.uk and www.ancestry.com: a world leader in commercial genealogy websites; vast collection of data, more uploaded frequently.
www.familyrelatives.com: a broad-based genealogy website with some unique databases.

www.rootsuk.com: includes more unusual records, but limited in scope.

www.familysearch.org: a free worldwide database of genealogy run by the Church of Jesus Christ of Latter-day Saints; a key resource for family historians.

www.bbc.co.uk/familyhistory: provides general information and advice.

www.worldvitalrecords.com: has various databases, mostly from the USA, and including records of UK marriage witnesses.

www.sog.org.uk (Society of Genealogists): has some online data, but mostly for checking resources available at their London library.

www.thegenealogist.co.uk: broad but not comprehensive for the UK; very little for Wales.

www.freebmd.org.uk: includes transcripts of GRO records 1837–1983.

www.britishorigins.com (Origins Network): provides general family history for UK and Ireland.

www.coraweb.com.au: an Australian gateway site for tracing your family history.

http://freepages.genealogy.rootsweb.ancestry.com/~billingh/: homepage of the mailing list and digest list for the discussion of genealogy and family history of people in Australia and New Zealand.

Umbrella or hub sites

www.pricegen.com/english_genealogy.html: links to other for English genealogy sites.

www.cyndislist.com: an impressive, ever-growing site, listing worldwide genealogy online resources.

www.ukgdl.org.uk: genealogy sites for British links and beyond.

www.genuki.org.uk: genealogy and topography for Britain, with links to other sites.

www.affho.org: the website for the Australian Federation of Family History Organisation

Family history forums

www.rootschat.com: a leading forum for family history topics.

www.british-genealogy.com: for posting general queries; good reputation for generating responses.

www.genforum.genealogy.com: a Q & A forum, and website also offers free genealogy lessons.

http://www.bbcwhodoyouthinkyouaremagazine.com/forum/: a family history forum for the well-known genealogy magazine.

http://forum.yourfamilytreemag.co.uk: hosted by *Your Family Tree* magazine.

National and regional databases
British National Archives
www.nationalarchives.gov.uk: a search facility which also links into catalogues for local British archives; some digitised records available online.
Scotland
www.scotlandspeople.gov.uk: a comprehensive, official website for Scottish family records.

Wales
http://cat.llgc.org.uk: the National Library of Wales; treasure house of records, with wills fully digitised and free to read online.

Northern Ireland
www.proni.gov.uk: Public Record Office for Northern Ireland.

www.ulsterancestry.com: offers research services for Northern Irish ancestors.

www.emeraldancestors.com: specialises in Northern Irish ancestors.

www.ancestryireland.com: specialises in Northern Irish ancestors.

Ireland
www.census.nationalarchives.ie: free-to-view transcripts of 1901 and 1911 Ireland census.

www.nationalarchives.ie: general listings and advice for family history research in Ireland.

www.groireland.ie: General Register Office of Ireland; for reference only, no records available to view.

www.irishgenealogy.ie: church records from Dublin and Kerry.

www.irishnewsarchive.com: search facilities to locate names, etc. in digital newspaper archive.

USA
www.footnote.com: has a huge number of historical documents, censuses, etc.

www.genealogybank.com: a large database of genealogy records.

Australia
www.archives.tas.gov.au: Archives Office of Tasmania.

www.prov.vic.gov.au: Public Record Office Victoria.

www.archives.qld.gov.au: Queensland State Archives.

www.records.nsw.gov.au: State Records NSW.

www.archives.sa.gov.au: State Records of South Australia.

India
www.indiaman.com: online genealogical magazine relating exclusively to the British in India and south Asia from 1600 to the twentieth century.

South Africa
http://ancestry24.com: general South African family history website.
www.national.archives.gov.za: National Archives of South Africa.

BMD certificates
These are the official General Register Office sites for BMD records. Each has its own mode of operation, so please check the individual websites for details.
www.gro.gov.uk: General Register Office for England and Wales – the official site for ordering English and Welsh BMD certificates online. (Note: you may be able to obtain these certificates via other genealogical websites, but are likely to be charged extra for the service.)
www.gro-scotland.gov.uk: General Register Office for Scotland.
www.nidirect.gov.uk/gro: General Register Office for Northern Ireland.
http://groireland.ie: General Register Office for Ireland.

Censuses
http://censusfinder.com: lists a variety of UK census transcripts, with references to the sites where the records are found.

Wills
www.hmcourts-service.gov.uk/cms/1226.htm: a guide on how to obtain copies of British probate records.
http://cat.llgc.org.uk (the National Library of Wales): navigate to Wills section for fully digitised transcripts.

Burial records
www.deceasedonline.com: a small but growing database of burial, cremation and memorial records.
www.ancestry.co.uk: England and Wales National Probate Calendar (1861–1941).

Military
www.roll-of-honour.com: memorials, etc. to war dead; not comprehensive.
www.military-genealogy.com: various registers and medal rolls from the First and Second World Wars, Waterloo, etc.
www.britishwargraves.co.uk: lists cemeteries and memorials photographed.

www.1914–1918.net ('The Long, Long Trail'): the British Army in the First World War.

http://1914–1918.invisionzone.com/forums: forums for the above site.

www.cwgc.org: search for memorials to Commonwealth soldiers on this highly respected site.

www.napoleon-series.org: Napoleonic Wars site with busy forum.

www.awm.gov.au: Australian War Memorial, Canberra.

Immigration/emigration

www.ellisisland.org: records of passengers and ships arriving at Ellis Island from 1892 to1924.

www.childmigrantstrust.com: site relating to children sent abroad.

www.theshipslist.com: associated with the Ancestry website, but with many passenger lists and ship records free to search.

www.movinghere.org.uk: guidance and resources for tracing the origins of immigrant families into the UK.

Criminals

www.blacksheepindex.co.uk: lists of criminal names taken from newspapers and journals.

www.oldbaileyonline.org: full transcripts of Old Bailey court cases (1674–1913), free to view.

Occupations (examples)

www.thepotteries.org: history of the potteries, Stoke-on-Trent.

www.railwayancestors.org.uk: Railway Ancestors Family History Society.

www.welshcoalmines.co.uk/forum: Welsh mining ancestors.

Nonconformist ancestors

www.bmdregisters.co.uk: specialist resource for tracing British noncon-formists, but not comprehensive.

Jewish genealogy

www.jewishgen.org: a free genealogy website with databases and other resources for researching Jewish ancestry and finding family members.

Early genealogy

www.medievalgenealogy.org.uk: for medieval genealogy, with various avenues to explore, including uploaded or linked family data.

Genealogy and family history societies

www.ffhs.org.uk: for locating regional UK family history societies.

www.sog.org.uk: the Society of Genealogists, established 1911.

www.safhs.org.uk: the Scottish Association of Family History Societies.

Finding your relatives

www.lostcousins.com: matches you with your relatives, through entering census data.

www.genesreunited.co.uk: make contact with other members whose trees match yours.

See also www.jewishgen.org, p. 259.

Names

http://genealogy.about.com/od/naming_patterns: very useful on naming patterns; links to information on other sites.

www.britishsurnames.co.uk: statistics about name frequencies.

www.one-name.org (The Guild of One-Name Studies): check to see if the name you're researching is covered.

www.nationaltrustnames.org.uk/default: a free site where you can look up the geographical distribution frequency of a surname.

Maps and topography

www.bing.com/maps (formerly 'multimap'): find places, see Ordnance Survey maps, check distances between locations.

www.curiousfox.com: 'The village by village contact site for anybody researching family history, genealogy and local history in the UK and Ireland.'

www.genuki.org.uk: an invaluable UK site, giving details of topography, gazetteers and records for individual localities.

www.old-maps.co.uk: easy to access old UK maps of village or area of interest.

www.english-heritage.org.uk: a lucky dip of historical and contemporary English local photographs and records, with an excellent search facility by location.

www.mapseeker.co.uk: search and order historic maps.

www.ancestralatlas.com: a relatively new website for comparing family data by map location; should work well as more people join.

Historical directories

www.historicaldirectories.org: a highly useful free site containing a digital library of local and trade directories for England and Wales (1750–1919), hosted by the University of Leicester.

Newspapers

http://newspapers.bl.uk/blcs: a selection of national and regional British newspapers (1800 –1900), fully searchable. Access is free through some local libraries, otherwise pay-to-view.

www.gazettes-online.co.uk: search the London/Edinburgh/Belfast Gazettes (especially useful for notices of bankruptcy); excellent-quality PDF page views, fully printable.

http://archive.timesonline.co.uk: search for reports of your ancestors in the *Times* archive (1785–1985).

http://newspapers.nla.gov.au: search digitised Australian newspapers for free.

Photographs

www.earlyphotographers.org.uk: trace the photographer on your family portrait.

Currency converter

www.nationalarchives.gov.uk/currency: find out how yesterday's price or sum of money compares to today's value.

Writing and archiving your family history

www.arcalife.com: principally for creating a family history narrative, tree or archive.

http://ancestry.mycanvas.com: the publishing branch of Ancestry; excellent facilities for creating a family history book (free online, charges for hard copies).

www.blurb.com: particularly good for more visual or photographic productions; excellent print quality.

Genealogy products

www.parishchest.com: a friendly and useful site for buying CDs and books; also offers monthly email updates.

www.genfair.co.uk/index.php: describes itself as a 'one-stop shop for family historians'.

www.familytreeexpert.com: quirky quotes about family history ('When I grow up, I want to be an ancestor'), plus genealogy products.

Index